THE Word IN Motion
OLD TESTAMENT

Rachael Carman
Illustrated by Anderson Carman

Contributing Authors:
Davis Carman, MS
Jerry McCaghren, MDiv
Bonnie Newell, PhD Religious Studies
Doug Powell, MA Apologetics
David Webb

apologia

The Word in Motion
Volume 1: Old Testament

Published by
Apologia Educational Ministries, Inc.
P.O. Box 896844
Charlotte, NC, 28289-6844
www.apologia.com

Published in partnership with
Walk Thru the Bible Ministries

ISBN: 978-1-946506-62-7

Cover and Book Design: Doug Powell
Illustrations: Anderson Carman

Printed by Asia Printing Co., Ltd, Seoul, South Korea
April 2021

10 9 8 7 6 5 4 3 2 1

To the glory of God and His Kingdom.

To the families who seek to know and serve the Lord.

To my grandchildren and those yet to be born.

Table of Contents

Acknowledgments

There's nothing like a great story. And although this curriculum is about the best story of all time, the backstory of how this curriculum came to be is pretty good in its own right. From the first time I attended a Walk Thru the Bible live seminar to when this textbook arrived in the Apologia warehouse was a total of twenty-five years. I know, right? That's a long time from concept to publication by any industry standard.

During this lengthy incubation period, God was at work teaching me perseverance, patience, diligence, and faith. The Word in Motion was always God's project, for God's people, based on God's Word. And it finally came together in His perfect timing, which was much later than I'd originally hoped but which I can now say, without hesitation, was indeed the right time. Through twenty-five years of writing, wrestling, and waiting, nothing has been wasted. Nothing. I'm as grateful for everything that was left on the editing room floor as I am for what made it to print in these two volumes.

It was my mom, Nancy McCaghren, who first suggested that our young family attend a Walk Thru the Bible live seminar. The event was held at Calvary Church in Charlotte, North Carolina. Phil Tuttle was the presenter that weekend, and his enthusiasm for God and His Word was inspiring.

Then an idea flickered in my mom brain. Although we were still new to homeschooling at that time, it occurred to me that the Walk Thru the Bible motions and outline might be adapted into a wonderful curriculum that parents could use at home with their children. I successfully arranged a meeting with Phil at the Walk Thru the Bible offices in the Atlanta area. I walked in full of energy and passion and with a baby on my hip. Phil listened to my idea and then kindly advised me to fan the flame and keep him posted. I really appreciated how encouraging you were that day, Phil. Thanks for not laughing out loud and for sincerely listening. I felt heard.

Fast-forward to 2011, and I was back in Phil's office. This time I had a speaking ministry and publishing platform in Apologia Educational Ministries. We actually signed a contract and got to work. My team put in a great many hours of writing, development, discussions, and meetings. Unfortunately, it proved to be the wrong time yet again, as the project ran into a series of speed bumps, detours, and roadblocks. Phil did leave the door open for future discussions, though it seemed to me that this project was on life support and flatlining, if not already dead and buried.

Fast-forward again, this time to 2017. That year, I kept crossing paths with Phil Tuttle and Walk Thru the Bible. To be honest, this irritated me. I didn't want to be reminded of my failure, my dead dream, the never-finished project. Yet I could sense the Holy Spirit was moving. So Davis called Phil—again—and to say their discussion went well would be an understatement. Phil moved The Word in Motion from his list of "woulda-coulda-shoulda" projects to Walk Thru's "ongoing partnerships" file, and it seemed this might finally be the right time. We met with Walk Thru's Genny Baxley, who clearly believed in my dream. Thank you, Genny, for trusting me with this project and supporting us through its development. And thank you, Maggie Eldridge, who helped me register for Walk Thru training and consistently prayed for me. I love your heart!

The motions for the Bible story lines were provided by Walk Thru the Bible. I want to thank Jane O'Conner for helping me put together hand signs to go with the key words for each book.

Thanks to Lisa Nance and the moms at the HELP co-op who field-tested some of the curriculum content. You and your children provided me excellent feedback and reminded me each week of the many families I was working to help. I miss you all and think of you often.

David Webb, my editor, you and I have worked together on several writing projects. Thank you for staying true to my voice and yet editing it all in a way that others can read and enjoy! Thank you, Doug Powell, for the beautiful layout of the book and for your apologetic and doctrinal expertise. You both advised me and contributed to the development of each lesson, helping me to avoid errors along the way.

Thank you, Anderson Carman, for the spot-on illustrations, especially those of the real and raw characters and events of the Bible. It's been a particular pleasure to work with you on this project from the time you were only three years old and learning the original Walk Thru the Bible outline.

Thank you, Matt Barclay, for the multiple roles you played on this project. You were video master, audio recording expert and editor, and general apologetic and doctrine fact-checker. Thank you for your patience and honesty with me in the studio and for our various discussions of Scripture and God. Kamilah Peebles, you were the perfect onsite assistant for the video shoot, organizing the props, the scripts, and me—no small task. I also appreciate your work in the marketing of this curriculum. Thanks for your passion for the families and for all of the ways you challenge me to get the message out there. Thanks for your professionalism as well as your friendship.

Thank you, Michelle Moody, for leading the marketing team at Apologia. Ladd Lesh, thanks for steering the ship so ably and for shouldering the day-to-day operations. I am also grateful for the proofreading team of Lori Jaworski and Gerri Smith. It's good to know you have such keen eyes. The team at Apologia is the best!

Thanks to the women who hold up my weary arms—my prayer team: Jane Blythe, Jan Critz, Nita Erlien, and Kamilah Peebles. Each of you provided me words of encouragement at just the right time. You challenged and inspired me by your own spiritual diligence and perseverance. You faithfully and boldly took me, this project, and the families who would use this curriculum before the throne of grace. I'm so grateful.

Davis, you walked with me through all of this—a project that has occupied my thoughts during almost three-fourths of our thirty-four years of marriage. You're my man. You listened to my dream, my drafts, and my discouragement. Even when I thought the project was dead, you held on to hope. And you dared to call Phil and knock on the door one more time. Thanks for heading up this project and making it a priority at Apologia.

And thanks to my children—my original focus group—Charles, Anderson, Savannah Anne, Molly, Lilly, Joseph, and Benjamin. Thanks also to my daughters-in law, Tessa and Laura, and my three grandchildren (so far)—Cosette, Atticus, and Vincent. Thank you all for your encouragement and support as I've worked to complete this curriculum. You inspire me as you seek to honor God in word and deed. May God and His Word guard your hearts and guide your steps.

Introduction to the OLD TESTAMENT

Welcome to The Word in Motion! Whether you were raised going to church, you're new to the Christian faith, or you're just curious about the Bible, you're in for an amazing adventure. The Bible is the story of God's love for mankind and all of creation. But it's not just any story. It's the most important story ever told.

So we gathered a team of award-winning scholars, teachers, authors, and artists to develop an engaging and colorful resource that makes the Bible clear, understandable, and meaningful for the whole family. The Word in Motion is published by Apologia in partnership with Walk Thru the Bible Ministries. The curriculum is based on Walk Thru the Bible's updated forty-point Old Testament and New Testament outlines with accompanying motions and Bible book key word flash cards.

Just like the Bible, the Word in Motion curriculum is divided into two volumes: the Old Testament and the New Testament. In this first volume, we will study the Old Testament. We'll actually begin at the beginning. We'll discover who God is and what He's done. We'll learn about the men and women He spoke to and the promises He made to them. We'll see how those people responded and how God kept His word.

It's true that the Bible can be intimidating no matter what your background, and the thirty-nine books that make up the Old Testament loom especially large. All the history, laws, prophecies, songs, and genealogies can be overwhelming and confusing. It can also be hard to remember the names of all the people and places and when and where these events took place and in what order. And so many Christian parents simply skip over reading and teaching the Old Testament, reasoning that it's okay because we no longer live "under the law."

But we conveniently forget that the Old Testament is the Scripture that Jesus learned as a boy. In fact, it was the only Scripture available to the first-century church until the Gospels and letters of Peter and Paul began circulating. Indeed, Paul spoke primarily of the Old Testament when he wrote to Timothy, "All Scripture is breathed out by God and profitable for teaching, for reproof, for correction, and for training in righteousness, that the man of God may be complete, equipped for every good work" (2 Timothy 3:16–17). Why then would we ever want to shy away from studying the first two-thirds of God's Word and teaching it to our children?

The Old Testament is also important because it sets the stage for the rest of the story. Said another way, the Old Testament helps to illuminate the events, themes, and teachings of the New Testament. If you skip the Old Testament, you'll miss the backstory of the Bible, and your family's understanding of the gospel will lack the richness and fullness that a study of both Old and New Testaments can provide.

A Perfect Book Full of Imperfect People

Earlier, I welcomed you to an adventure. Maybe you've never thought of Bible study as an adventure. But why not approach it that way as a family? Adventures take us to unknown places where we meet new people, gain new perspectives, and learn new things about ourselves and the world we live in. The pages of Scripture offer all this and more.

Through this study, we'll visit some ancient locations and learn about cultures and practices that are foreign to us today. There we will meet some ordinary people who found themselves in extraordinary circumstances—people who were just living their lives when the Creator of the universe spoke to them. Imagine that: God's voice speaking to you. We'll look at what He said, to whom, and how they responded. We'll see what different people did after He gave them clear instructions. We'll also take a look at some things God is making clear to you and me today, how we are responding, and the choices we are making.

Here's something you need to know about the people we'll be meeting: Not one of them is perfect. I know, right? It's easy to think that if your name and story made it into the biblical narrative, then you must be a paragon of virtue. But it's just not so. We'll meet kings and shepherds, soldiers and slaves, wealthy landowners and poverty-stricken widows. There will be gardeners and architects, poets and priests, construction workers and prophets. We will meet brothers and sisters, husbands and wives, friends and neighbors. We will find them to be sick and healthy, weak and strong, rich and poor, happy and sad, blessed and oppressed. In other words, they are people just like you and me. Some obey God, but many disobey. There will be examples of good and bad, right and wrong. All the people are real and on a faith journey of their own, and all of their stories are raw and unfiltered.

Why is this important? Because the Old Testament vividly reveals a cycle that still spins today: the sin cycle. We need to understand what sin is and what it means for us. Simply put, sin is disobedience to God. God created us and loves us and has set boundaries for us because of His love. When we choose to go against His love and miss the mark, we sin. Some people want to believe that sin doesn't exist, or at the very least that it doesn't matter. But the Bible clearly illustrates that not only is sin real, but the consequences of sin are also real. Sin leads to death and separation from God. We reap what we sow, and when we choose sin over God, we sow the seeds of our own destruction (Galatians 6:7–8).

And yet there is a solution for sin, but a price must be paid. In the Old Testament, God establishes a payment system for the forgiveness of sin through animal sacrifices. This is a foreshadowing of what's to come in the New Testament, as it points to Jesus as the ultimate, once-and-for-all sacrifice as the perfect Lamb of God. By studying the Old Testament, we learn just how much we need a Savior. Seeing God's people struggle against their sinful nature builds anticipation for God's gift of a Messiah—His one Son, Jesus Christ. So you see, there is hope, even in the Old Testament.

What Makes This Curriculum Unique?

There are plenty of Bible studies and curricula out there, as well as books and resources designed as guides to the people, places, and books of Scripture. So what sets The Word in Motion apart, making it the right choice for you and your family?

It's Engaging

The Word in Motion will engage a student's head, heart, and hands. During this study, you and your children will be encouraged to listen, see, talk, and move. Isn't that awesome? What's more, integrating auditory, visual, verbal, and kinesthetic learning styles reinforces fundamental biblical truths. That is, we're supposed to use our ears to hear, eyes to see, mouths to speak, and our hands and feet to serve while loving God with all our strength and living worthy of the light to which we've been called. The Christian faith isn't meant to be a passive, sit-still faith but, rather, an active, growing, and thriving faith. Hence the title, The Word in Motion.

Auditory learners will benefit from the video and narrative components (especially with a parent reading to them). Visual learners will engage with the videos and the beautiful illustrations. Verbal learners will thrive during discussions and, if they're ready, when reading to younger siblings. Kinesthetic learners will love the whole-body motions designed to help them remember the forty-point Old Testament outline and the hand signs that help them remember the key word for each book of the Old Testament.

In other words, this curriculum is designed to meet each of your students right where they are and in the way they learn best. The companion notebooking journal also includes a variety of activities for children to express themselves and build their understanding through writing, memorizing, presenting, analyzing, and creating. Your whole family will love it!

It's Foundational

The study of God's Word is essential for all of God's people, and as parents, we're charged with the discipleship of our children (Deuteronomy 6:7; Ephesians 6:4). It is important, therefore, that we know and teach what the Bible teaches. The Word in Motion provides the whole family with tools for learning and remembering the people, places, and events of the Old Testament and how they are connected to the bigger picture of God's story. Thus, you and your family will be equipped with an outline of the Old Testament that enhances your understanding of Scripture while offering opportunities for more in-depth study.

In addition, your family will also learn the major theme, a key word, and a hand sign for each book of the Old Testament. There are thirty-nine books, which might sound like too many to study in detail, but it is actually possible for you and your students to know and quickly recall the messages contained in every one of them. If someone were to ask, would you be able to tell them what the book of Obadiah or Haggai or Zephaniah is all about? By the end of this course, you'll be able to answer with a confident "Yes!"

Knowing the key people, places, and events of the Old Testament narrative and the theme of all thirty-nine Old Testament books will build a solid foundation for a clearer understanding of the events recorded in the Gospels and the teachings of the New Testament.

It's Timely

We know that a smaller percentage of people now attend church than in times past. And research has revealed that among those who claim to believe, biblical knowledge is marginal, as more and more Christians are being conformed to the world's belief system. Now is the time for families of faith to take a stand and become more biblically literate. As the people of God, we need to know what the Bible says and what it doesn't say. We need to know who the God of the Bible is, so that we can worship Him alone and not the gods of this world. We need to know how to pursue a right relationship with God and how to live as His children. And we need to place our hope in Jesus, not the world, for He is the One who will never fail us.

As parents raising the next generation, we need to know these truths ourselves and teach them diligently to our children. We are charged with the responsibility of training our children in the fear and admonition of the Lord. This means that we must intentionally instruct them in the ways of the Lord, His love, His commandments, His grace, and His truth. We cannot give what we do not have, but we can lead our families on a journey to learn these important truths together.

This curriculum has been developed with specific tools to help you and your family remember God's story, respond to His invitation, and rejoice in the hope of heaven that we have through Jesus Christ.

Preparing for Adventure

So what can you do to prepare yourself and your family for this adventure?

First, pray. Thank God for the revelation of His Word, the Bible, and the opportunity to learn from its truth. Ask Him to open your eyes and ears and heart—and those of your family—for all that He wants to teach you through this study. Ask Him to bless you as you lead your family in this study of the Old Testament, and thank Him in advance for all He is going to show you.

Second, prioritize this study. The truths you and your kids will learn in this study hold the potential for significant life change. Together, you will discover that the time you spend seeking God in His Word is never wasted time. He always blesses it.

Third, prepare your mind. Know that like any other worthwhile endeavor, this is going to be challenging. Determine now that you will stay the course and see it through. When you come to a topic that is difficult or unclear, instead of giving up, dare to dig deeper. Dare to exercise faith and persevere, and encourage your family to do the same.

And finally, enjoy! This is an adventure, remember? Most adventures include risk, unforeseen roadblocks, imposing trails, and dangerous crossings. But they also come with awesome views, lifelong memories, and exhilarating discoveries! Lean into the journey. Whether or not this road is familiar to you, breathe it all in and enjoy a new perspective as you learn to stand on the rock-solid truth of the Bible.

Once again, welcome to The Word in Motion curriculum!

Rachael Carman

How to Use This Curriculum

The best way to work through The Word in Motion: Old Testament curriculum is as a family—specifically, read by Mom and/or Dad with their children gathered around them, perhaps even snuggled together on the sofa. Just as seeking God through prayer and studying the Bible is a great way to begin the day, starting each school day with Bible class sets a positive tone for the rest of the day while cultivating a high view of God by making His Word a priority in your family.

Over the next few pages, we will walk you through how to use this curriculum. We will also introduce you to its primary components and then break down the parts of a lesson and show you how they reinforce the teaching. We will also suggest a general weekly rhythm for doing The Word in Motion, one that will allow you to complete a full lesson each week, for a total course time of thirty weeks. For more detailed course scheduling recommendations, we have included a lesson plan in the notebooking journal that suggests specific pages to read each day and identifies the corresponding activities to complete in the notebooking journal.

Before we get started, it is important that you remember to embrace and encourage the joy of learning, especially when it comes to studying the Bible. You are helping your children to establish healthy spiritual habits that will serve them well throughout their lives. To that end, The Word in Motion is not a curriculum to grit your teeth and grind through just to get it done. No, this is an adventure to enjoy together as you explore the magnificent wonders of God's story and the eternal truths of His Word.

Now, without further ado, here's what you need to know to get the most out of this curriculum.

Your Guide on This Journey

Meet Wyatt. He will be your tour guide as you take this journey through the Bible. Wyatt wears a blue hat and white T-shirt with the Word in Motion logo. You'll see him at the start of each video and textbook lesson, and he found his way into several pages of the notebooking journal. Wyatt will help you learn the motions, and you'll see him in most of the video lessons and Bible book key word flash cards.

The Tools You Will Use

The Word in Motion curriculum comes with three primary tools you will use to guide your family through this Bible study. These tools are the teaching videos, textbook, and the companion notebooking journal.

In addition, you will want to keep your Bible close at hand. You will be encouraged throughout this course to read directly from God's holy Word. Your children need to see and understand that it's important to always go to the original source and seek out what Scripture says directly instead of just taking someone else's word for it. Please note that this curriculum uses the ESV as the default translation. However, be assured that this curriculum will work just as well with your family's preferred translation.

Now let's take a look at each of the tools you will use to teach from The Word in Motion.

Videos

Each lesson begins with a four- or five-minute video you will stream online through Apologia's Book Extras site. Your family should watch the video together. In it, I'll teach the first half of the lesson. (In other words, the combination of the video and the textbook narrative comprise the entire lesson.) I will present some background, context, and a related Bible story. I will then teach you one or more motions or hand signs that go with that week's lesson.

In Lessons 1–15, you will learn forty motions that will help you remember the people, places, and events of the Old Testament. Developed by Apologia's publishing partners Walk Thru the Bible, these motions are key to learning and remembering the story line of the Scriptures. The motions incrementally build on one another as you progress through the course. During the week, there will be several opportunities to review the motions so that by the end of the course, your family will be able to master a complete forty-point outline of the entire Old Testament.

Similarly, in Lessons 16–30, I will teach you a hand sign to remember a key word and theme for each of the thirty-nine books of the Old Testament.

Textbook

In addition to the Bible, your textbook for this course is *The Word in Motion: Old Testament*. Beginning at the literal beginning, the textbook will enable you and your family to explore the key people, places, and events of the Old Testament. Along the journey, you will gain a deeper understanding of how all the parts of the Bible fit together to form the glorious story of God's love for humanity and His plan for our redemption.

The textbook contains a total of thirty lessons, each of which is designed to be completed in a week. Thus the course may be completed in thirty weeks. The textbook is divided into two parts. Part 1 includes Lessons 1–15 and covers the history revealed in the Old Testament. Here you will find biblical narratives that tell the storyline of God and His people, along with discussion questions. Part 2 includes Lessons 16–30 and provides an overview and summary of all thirty-nine books of the Old Testament with full-color visual aids.

Other teaching components in the textbook include biblical narratives that tell the story of God and His people in chronological order, discussion questions about the narrative, character profiles, essential doctrines of the Bible, assigned Scripture readings, memory verses, and insightful sidebar articles that bring to life many different facets of biblical history and culture.

Mom or Dad can read aloud the textbook to the family, or you may choose to have your kids take turns reading aloud. Either way, study questions and answers are best discussed as a family. Using this model, every family member will learn from each other. This approach initiates an ongoing conversation about God and His Word that can be continued, cultivated, and processed in the car, at the playground, during meals, and at bedtime. Look for Deuteronomy 6 moments to teach your children diligently as you rise up, sit down, walk along the way, and lie down.

Notebooking Journal

Notebooking is a creative way for kids to personalize and capture what they have learned in an artful keepsake. As kids do the activities in *The Word in Motion: Old Testament Notebooking Journal* and think about their lives in light of each lesson, spiritual truths will come alive for them and make real-life application engaging. Everything they learn in this course will be processed and documented somewhere in the notebooking journal pages. Therefore, each student will need to have his or her own notebooking journal. Please keep in mind that the pages may not be reproduced.

Audiobook and Book Extras

Two other resources are available to help you on your journey through the Old Testament and The Word in Motion. The first is the free Book Extras website. Here you will find not only the course videos but also useful links to sites and materials for supplementing your studies. The Book Extras have been selected to help you take this study deeper and are most appropriate for, though not limited to, parents and older students.

The other resource, *The Word in Motion: Old Testament Audiobook* is available for purchase as an MP3 download exclusively through Apologia. I recorded the audiobook as a teaching supplement. It is best utilized as a repeat of the textbook lessons, not as a substitute for the family reading the textbook together. Listening to the audiobook while running errands in the car or at bedtime would be an excellent use of this resource.

What's in a Lesson? – Part 1, Lessons 1–15

As I mentioned, the Old Testament course is divided into two parts. Part 1 includes Lessons 1–15 and covers the historical events revealed in the Old Testament narrative. Each of these lessons contains the following elements.

Video

Begin each lesson by watching the online video teaching together. Each video opens with a brief teaching to introduce the lesson's content. This is followed by a demonstration of one or more motions that correspond to the forty-point outline. These motions will help you remember key people and events from the lesson.

Motions

Each week, you will learn one or more new motions and practice the motions you've already learned. The motions for the week's lesson are sequentially numbered and listed on the first page of the lesson. You will want to review these motions often. If you need to refresh your memory about the motions you've already learned, turn to the "Quick Reference to the Old Testament 40-Point Outline" provided in the textbook. You can also review the motions by watching the summary video on the Book Extras website.

Passage

This is a reference to the Bible passage you can read for more details of the story covered in the lesson. Again, it's important to stress that the primary source for this curriculum is God's Word, the Bible.

Take It to Heart

This is a memory verse that goes with the key theme of the lesson. There is a page in the notebooking journal where students will be able to practice the memory verse by copying it in their best handwriting. Memorizing God's words and hiding them in our hearts is a great way for us to guard our hearts.

Narrative

This is a three- to four-page illustrated narrative of the biblical story line, including key people, places, and events of the Old Testament. This is not a repeat of the video, so make sure you watch the video and read the narrative. The narrative picks up where the video lesson left off; think of it as the rest of the story. Conversational in tone, the narrative also covers important biblical themes and places them within the context of the overarching story of Bible. Mom or Dad can read the story aloud from the textbook, or you may choose to have other family members take turns reading to the group. The motions you learn from the video will go along with this story.

Let's Talk About It

Each lesson includes five review questions for the family to discuss together. This is an opportunity for everyone to reflect on what they remember from the video teaching and the narrative reading. There's also a place in your notebooking journal to write down your answers to these questions. In the textbook, this section is designated by a red "question mark" icon.

Sidebar Articles

These brief articles were written to provide context and a fuller understanding of the Bible story. Many of the subjects were selected to help students better understand and relate to what it must have been like to live in Bible times. Topics include altars, the harvest, gleaning, the walls of Jericho, anointing kings, and more. These articles are designated by a green "light bulb" icon.

Doctrine

The content of this course is nondenominational. However, each lesson includes discussion of a Christian doctrine historically agreed upon by the church. Among the doctrines discussed in this course are the fall of mankind, sin nature, worship, idolatry, sabbath rest, miracles, repentance, God's sovereignty, giving, the problem of evil, prophecy, redemption, and more. These articles are indicated by a blue "shield with a cross" icon.

Character Sketch

Each lesson includes a profile of a Bible character told from that person's perspective. Some of these profiles are humorous in tone or language, while others are dramatic or even tragic. All of the people in the Bible were real people, and we sometimes forget that. These readings will help students to consider what it might have been like to be that person—and to remember that God uses all kinds of people to accomplish His purposes. These profiles are indicated by a purple "human face" icon.

Psalms and Proverbs

Each lesson includes suggested readings from both Psalms and Proverbs. The book of Psalms is a collection of songs, poems, prayers, and worship. Proverbs is a book filled with wisdom. Reading these passages together each week will teach your family more about who God is and how to live for Him. These readings are indicated by a red-and-black "magnifying glass" icon.

Prayer

Every lesson concludes with a prayer that touches on the themes discussed in the lesson. You can pray this together and add to it as the Spirit leads. These prayers are indicated by an orange "praying hands" icon.

Weekly Rhythm for Lessons in Part 1

In order to complete The Word in Motion: Old Testament course in a single school year, you'll want to set a goal to complete one lesson each week. To help you successfully realize this goal and still enjoy margin in your family life, we suggest a four-day schedule that looks something like this:

Day 1
Watch the video
Practice the motions
Read the sidebar article
Read the character sketch
Read the memory verse
Write the memory verse in your notebooking journal

Day 2
Read the narrative and note the biblical text references
Review the memory verse
Review the motions
Discuss the Let's Talk About It questions
Answer the review questions in your notebooking journal

Day 3
Read the doctrine article
Review the memory verse
Review the motions
Do the additional activities in your notebooking journal

Day 4
Read the assigned Psalm and Proverb
Read the prayer and pray together
Review the memory verse
Review the motions
Do any remaining activities in your notebooking journal

What's in a Lesson? – Part 2, Lessons 16–30

Part 2 of this course includes Lessons 16–30 and covers all thirty-nine books of the Old Testament. Each of these lessons contains the following elements.

Video

Again, you will begin each lesson by watching the online video teaching together. Each video lesson in Part 2 of the course opens with a brief teaching to introduce one or more books of the Old Testament. Students will learn a key word for each book and a hand sign to help them remember the key word. They will also learn how Jesus can be found in every book of the Bible.

Book-About Cards

Each Book-About Card is an overview of a book in the Old Testament. In other words, this card is about the book. The information on each card includes the name of God as portrayed in the book, the human writer(s) of the book, approximate dates when it was written, the book's intended audience, the genre of the book, key characters, the key themes in the book, the Hebrew title of the book and its meaning, a memory verse, and a statement of what we can learn about Jesus from this book of the Bible.

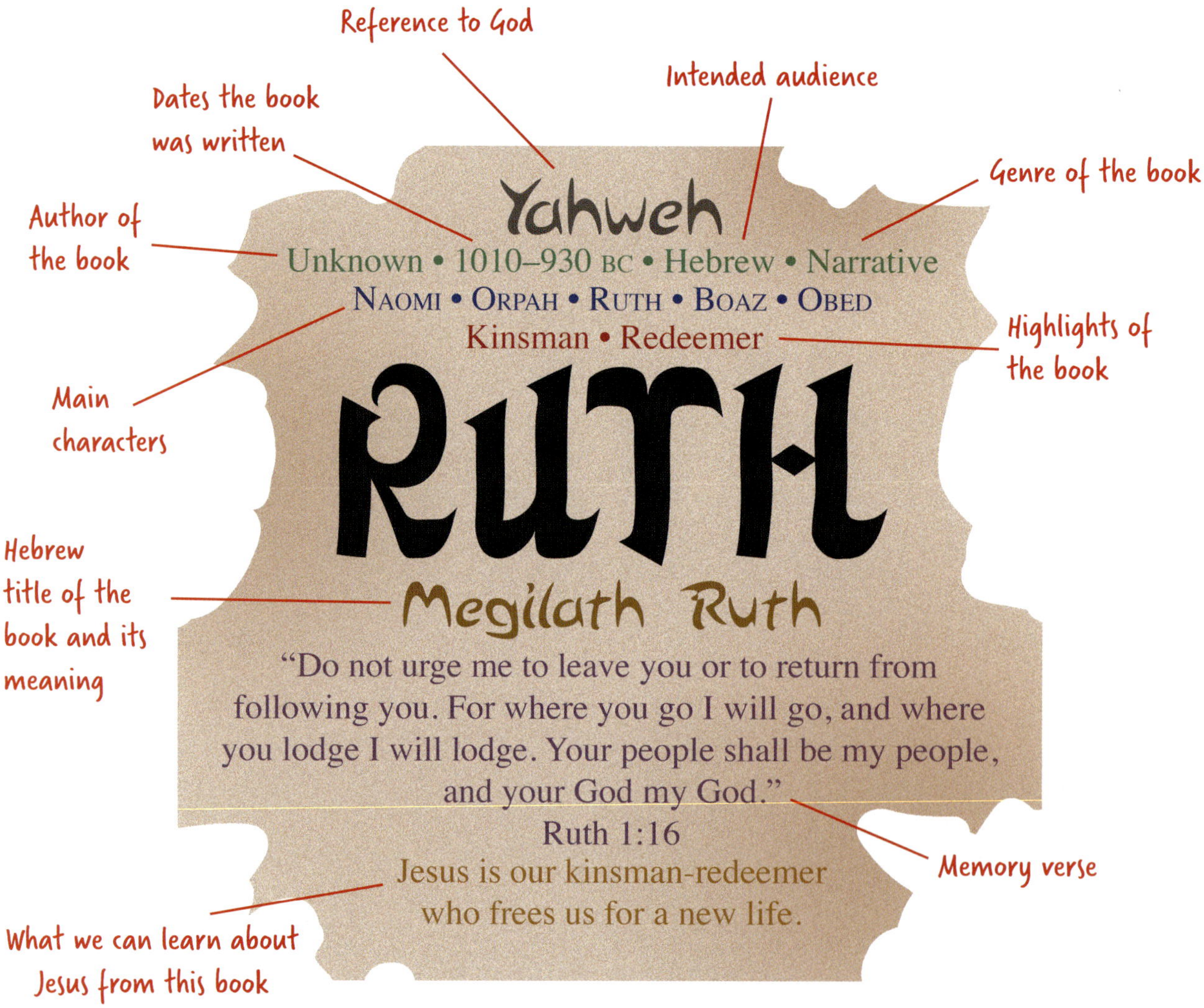

Key Word Card

These illustrations "show" the major theme of each book. In the "Quick Reference to the 39 Books of the Old Testament" found immediately after Lesson 30, you will find all of the Key Word Cards along with explanations of how to interpret each image. These images are sometimes goofy and corny, but that's the point. The purpose is to help you recognize and remember the key word and theme of each book. These illustrations, most of which feature your friend Wyatt, are designed to make the content unforgettable.

Key Chain

The key word is written on a key chain, making it easier to find than your car keys.

Take It to Heart

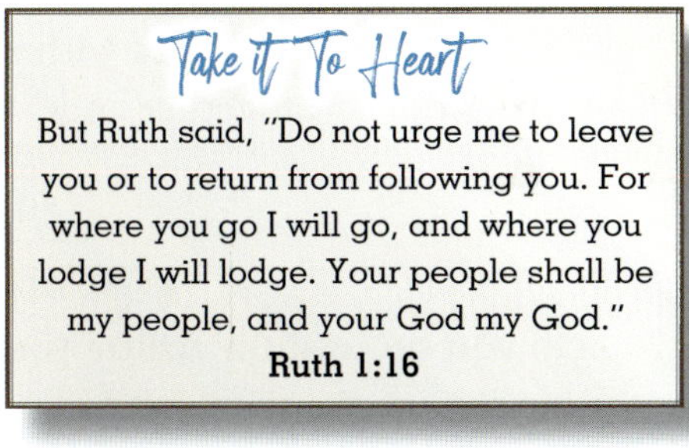

The memory verse goes with the key theme of each book of the Bible. There is a page in the notebooking journal where students will be able to practice the memory verse by copying it in their best handwriting. Memorizing God's words and hiding them in our hearts is a great way for parents and children alike to guard their hearts.

Bible Reading

Instead of a narrative that I wrote, like those you read in Part 1, in Part 2 you will be reading directly from God's Word. Take the Bible, find the assigned passages, and read them together. Don't skip this part—it's a powerful exercise. These readings represent key passages from each book of the Old Testament.

Sidebar Articles

These brief articles were written to provide context and a fuller understanding of the Bible story. Many of the subjects were selected to help students better relate to what it must have been like to live in Bible times. Topics include altars, the harvest, gleaning, the walls of Jericho, anointing kings, and more. These articles are designated by a green "light bulb" icon.

Doctrine

The content of this course is nondenominational. However, each lesson includes discussion of a Christian doctrine historically agreed upon by the church. Among the doctrines discussed in this course are the fall of mankind, sin nature, worship, idolatry, sabbath rest, miracles, repentance, God's sovereignty, giving, the problem of evil, prophecy, redemption, and more. These articles are indicated by a blue "shield with a cross" icon.

Character Sketch

Each lesson includes a profile of a Bible character told from that person's perspective. Some of these profiles are humorous in tone or language, while others are dramatic or even tragic. All of the people in the Bible were real people, and we sometimes forget that. These readings will help students to consider what it might have been like to be that person—and to remember that God uses all kinds of people to accomplish His purposes. These profiles are indicated by a purple "human face" icon.

Psalms and Proverbs

These are suggested readings from both Psalms and Proverbs. The book of Psalms is a collection of songs, poems, prayers, and worship. Proverbs is a book filled with wisdom. Reading these passages together each week will teach your family more about who God is and how to live for Him. These readings are indicated by a red-and-black "magnifying glass" icon.

Prayer

Each lesson concludes with a prayer that touches on the themes discussed in the lesson. You can pray this together and add to it as the Spirit leads. These prayers are indicated by an orange "praying hands" icon.

Weekly Rhythm for Lessons in Part 2

To help you successfully realize your goal of completing one lesson per week and enjoy margin in your family life, we suggest a four-day schedule that looks something like this:

Day 1

Watch the video
Practice the lesson's key words and hand signs
Read the Book-About card
Read the character sketch
Read the memory verse(s)
Write the memory verse(s) in the notebooking journal

Day 2

Read the Bible passage
Review the memory verse(s)
Discuss and answer the review questions in the notebooking journal
Review the key words and hand signs

Day 3

Continue reading the Bible passage, if necessary
Read the sidebar article
Read the doctrine article
Review the key words and hand signs
Review the memory verse(s)
Do the additional activities in your notebooking journal

Day 4
Read the assigned Psalms and Proverbs
Read the prayer and pray together
Review all key words
Review the memory verse(s)
Review all hand signs
Complete the remaining activities in your notebooking journal

Accessing the Videos

As I mentioned, each of the thirty lessons in The Word in Motion: Old Testament is accompanied by a four- to five-minute video teaching segment. These videos are available to stream online at Apologia's Book Extras website. To access this popular page, you will need to log in to your Apologia account or create one if you haven't done so yet.

Start by 1) going to www.Apologia.com, then 2) click on "My Account." If you already have an account, enter your username or your email and password to enter the Book Extras website. If you don't have an account yet, you can register to create one.

Once you have logged in, enter the following course password in the box and click the "Submit" button:

WordinMotionOTpassover

Under the column header "Your Book Extras Subscriptions," you should see a link for *The Word in Motion: Old Testament*. Click on the title and you will be taken to a list of all thirty video lessons. Then simply click the link for the lesson you wish to view.

Please note, these instructions are subject to change as we update the Book Extras website.

PART 1

OLD TESTAMENT Outline

In this week's video lesson, we talked about the wonder of God's creation. Some people don't think of creation as a miracle, but it is. God made everything out of nothing! There was only darkness until God said, "Let there be light," and light came into being by the power of His spoken word.

God created the universe and everything in it in just six days. At the end of each day, God looked at what He had made and saw that it was good. Everything had order and a purpose. God then made man in His own image and put man in charge of the earth and all its creatures. Adam's job was to maintain and care for what God had made.

Adam's first order of business was naming the animals. Can you imagine what that was like? Surrounded by all of God's creatures, Adam gave each one a name. A name helps us to identify a thing and often tells us something about that thing. Naming the animals must have been fun, but Adam did not find a companion or helper among the animals. Man was alone.

God knew that it was not good for man to be alone, so He made a woman, Eve, and brought her to Adam. Now God's creation was complete, and everything was perfect. The man and woman enjoyed a perfect relationship with God and with each other. There were no arguments. There was no nitpicking, no name-calling. They didn't get jealous or frustrated with each other. They simply loved one another and served one another perfectly.

Take a moment to imagine the perfection of paradise. From the radiance of each new sunrise to the chorus of birds singing God's praises, from the blossoming flowers to the trees laden with fra-

grant fruits, from the lambs and lions frolicking playfully to the bumblebees and butterflies dancing in the garden air—all was in harmony, all in perfection.

Adam and Eve lacked nothing. They didn't want for anything. They had all the beauty, all the food, all of everything anyone could ever desire. They didn't have a care. No worries, no stress.

God gave them fruit and plants for food, and it was plentiful in the garden. There was just one rule. Only one. This rule wasn't confusing or even difficult to obey. God told the man and woman they could eat any of the fruit in the garden—everything except the fruit of the tree of the knowledge of good and evil, which stood in the center of the garden.

Do you see how simple God's command was? He loves us so much and wants only the best for us. He wants us to always trust and obey Him, and so He makes His commands clear and easy to understand.

Enter the crafty serpent. As the man and woman were enjoying another day in paradise, the serpent sauntered over and struck up a conversation with Eve. "Did God actually say, 'You shall not eat of any tree in the garden'?" he asked. Eve explained that they could eat from any tree, but they could not eat or even touch the fruit of the tree in the middle of the garden, for they would surely die. (Notice that Eve was wrong when she told the serpent that God said not to "touch" the forbidden fruit. This wasn't true; God only said not to eat it.)

"You will not surely die," the serpent replied. "God knows that when you eat of it your eyes will be opened, and you will be like God, knowing good and evil" (Genesis 3:1–5).

Oddly, Eve didn't seem surprised that the serpent spoke to her. We don't know if this was unusual behavior for a snake in the early days of creation. But Eve certainly should have been alarmed by the fact that one of God's creatures was contradicting God and questioning His motives. That was reason enough to ignore the serpent and stop talking with it. Instead of ignoring the snake, however, she listened as he crafted his deception with soothing tones and pretty promises.

A new feeling came over Eve. The thought of knowing things and understanding, being wise like God . . . well, it sounded good, even if she had never felt any of these needs before. Now she started thinking she would like to be like God, apparently forgetting that she and Adam had been made in His image.

Peering now at the forbidden tree, she saw the tree was indeed lovely, and she knew its fruit would be delicious and make her wise. So Eve took the fruit and ate it, then she shared it with Adam. Adam could have refused, but he too ate the fruit, choosing his own desire over God and His love and provision.

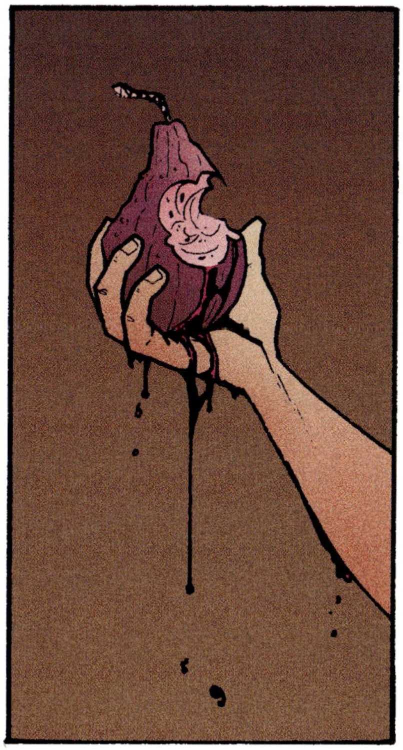

Immediately, their eyes were opened, and Adam and Eve were overcome with shame, embarrassed by their guilt and their nakedness. Never before had they known anything but peace and perfect fellowship with their Creator. Now when they heard God walking in the garden, they tried to hide from Him among the trees. They were greatly afraid, for they had rebelled against God and disobeyed His one command—the first sin.

God asked, "Where are you?" He didn't ask because He didn't know, but rather as a way of saying that Adam and Eve had disobeyed and were not where they should have been—their sin had taken them out of the light, out of a perfect relationship with God.

He called the man and woman out of hiding and confronted them with their sin. This may sound harsh, but it was actually loving of God to call them out about their disobedience. Love desires what is best for the beloved. Love forgives, but it cannot allow or overlook destructive, disobedient, or deceitful behavior.

Love has to challenge actions that may seem fun or unimportant but which are actually selfish and prideful. Love says, "I love you enough that I cannot allow you to continue to act this way." Just as your parents love you, God loved Adam and Eve enough to confront them in their disobedience.

He asked Adam, "Did you eat of the tree I told you not to eat?" Instead of confessing his guilt, Adam shifted the blame to Eve. "She gave me the fruit," he said. God then turned to Eve and asked, "What have you done?" Instead of answering the question, she pointed to the serpent. "He deceived me." The man and woman stood there pointing fingers, as they cowered under the fig leaves they had sewn together to hide their nakedness.

Then God pronounced His judgment. The serpent was reduced to crawling on its belly and eating dust, and it would forever be an enemy of the woman and her descendants. All snakes and every generation of mankind would have a basic dislike for one another.

God then turned to the woman. He pronounced that her distinctive role of mother would be marked by painful childbirth. And although she would want to rule over her husband, telling him what to do, she would need to submit to her husband's authority.

Finally, God spoke to Adam, who had been trusted with caring for God's creation and maintaining the established order. From now on, Adam's work would be much harder. Work wasn't Adam's curse—he had always worked tending to the garden, but the work had been joyful, even a pleasure. Now God cursed the ground so that it would produce thorns and thistles and Adam would struggle against the elements to grow food for his family. By the sweat of his brow he would toil, weeding and pruning, sowing and reaping—tasks that in the garden had been unnecessary.

God told them that one day they would die, as would their children and grandchildren, and their bodies would return to the dust from which Adam had been made. God made them clothing from animal skins, then He banished Adam and Eve from the garden of Eden, their perfect home.

This event—the first sin—is what we call the fall of man, or simply the Fall. Because Adam was the first human, his sin would infect all of humanity, and we live with the consequences even today.

We don't know how much time passed between God's creation of the world and the Fall. What we do know is that from the very beginning, even before Adam sinned, God had a plan to redeem us. His plan is for our salvation and spiritual growth. We will explore this plan in greater detail, but an important part of His plan is that He invites us—like He invited Adam and Eve—to trust Him and obey Him. When we come to Him, confess our sins, and repent, God chooses to forgive us and extend to us His wondrous grace and mercy.

PSALM AND PROVERB TO READ:
Psalm 104, Proverbs 1:7

6 DAYS OF CREATION

Have you ever stood in a large room with no windows and all the lights turned off? How did it feel? Genesis 1:2 tells us that before there was any light, "the earth was without form and void, and darkness was over the face of the deep." God's Spirit was everywhere, but there was nothing else but darkness.

Then God spoke and creation began. On the first day, He created the heavens and the earth. He created light and separated it from the darkness and called them day and night. And He saw that it was good.

On the second day, God created the sky. On the third day, He created dry land and gathered the water into seas. Next, He created the plants and trees and gave them seeds so they could reproduce, making other plants and trees like themselves. And He saw that it was good.

On the fourth day, God created the sun to shine its light on the earth by day, and He made the moon and the stars to shine by night. And He saw that it was good.

On the fifth day, God created all living creatures in the seas and the birds of the air. God blessed all of these creatures and told them to multiply and increase their numbers. And He saw that it was good.

On the sixth day, God created the land animals, big and small, including livestock and wild creatures. And He saw that it was good.

On that same day, God created man from the dust of the earth and breathed life into him. He created a woman from the rib of the man. Then God blessed them and gave them every seed-bearing plant and fruit tree for food, and He gave them authority over every animal on land, in the sea, and in the air.

Then God looked over everything He had made and said that it was *very* good!

He had completed His creation in six days. He rested on the seventh day and blessed it as a holy day.

What reminds you of God's act of creation? Is it the sky by day or the moon and stars by night? Is it the rocks and trees? Is it the rivers and the mountains or the desert and the oceans? Or is it the people you meet every day? All of these things should remind you of God's wonderful creation!

LET'S TALK ABOUT IT

1. Describe a time when you marveled at God's creation.
2. Identify something in creation that points to God's creative nature.
3. Name something unusual in nature that seems able to "work" only because God made it so. An example might be hummingbirds, giraffes, or other improbable creatures or natural wonders.
4. What is a parental rule you sometimes resent? Describe how it protects you.
5. Why do you think that humans are prone to disobey, especially when they're young? Why is it right that sin separates us from God?

Made in God's Image

When God created Adam and Eve, He made them in His image. The first thing many people think of when they read this in Scripture is that God must have two eyes, two ears, a nose, and a mouth. But being made in the image of God doesn't mean we physically look like Him. God is Spirit. He doesn't have a body that we can see with our eyes.

Being made in the image of God means we are like Him in more important ways. God is morally perfect, and although we aren't perfect, we do know in our hearts the difference between right and wrong. We think about things and make choices, just not in the same way that God does these things. We experience feelings and emotions. In Scripture, we read of God displaying emotions such as grief (Psalm 78:40) and joy (Zephaniah 3:17). Emotions are an attribute of God, but He doesn't change or react to circumstances like we do.

God is a spiritual being, and every human has a spirit that will exist after his or her earthly body has passed away. We seek out relationships—with God and with each other. Similarly, God is relational, and He exists eternally as three persons in perfect harmony—the Father, Son, and the Holy Spirit.

Human beings share these qualities with God. Theologians often call this teaching the Imago Dei, which is Latin for "image of God."

Adam Speaks

Every day, Eve and I rose early to work, happily tending the garden. Every night, we fell asleep beneath a canopy of stars, serenaded by the sounds of a world at peace. Our rest was punctuated by the chirping of a cricket, the hooting of a distant owl, and the low rumble of a lion. Life was good in paradise.

The garden was a botanist's dream in the midst of Dr. Dolittle's zoo. Feathered troubadours greeted us each morning with symphonies that would make Beethoven blush. The sweet nectar of the orchard beckoned us to taste its wondrous fruits. The garden was lush and its rivers clear, revealing a stunning variety of marine life. Flora and fauna bowed as we passed, recognizing us as friends and stewards of God's creation. There was plenty of food and water. Plenty to do. No complaints. It was all good!

But I messed up paradise. I brought death into this world with a single, terrible decision. The Creator had just one restriction in the garden: He singled out a tree and declared its fruit off-limits. He was very clear on this point: Don't eat it! Pretty simple.

But as we passed by that tree each day, we ventured nearer and nearer. Then one day, the serpent crept up and hissed his seductive lies. We listened. We chose to taste the forbidden fruit. We sinned against the God who had given us everything. What fools we were!

Ashamed and afraid, we tried to hide. But nobody can hide from God. Not a chance.

Now all mankind stands outside the garden. We can't go back. Because of our foolish choice, paradise is lost to us.

And yet, even as we were banished from the garden, God made a promise to all men and women out of His infinite love and mercy. He promised a child who one day would be born of woman and crush the serpent's head. This child would then create a new paradise that will forever be open to anyone who received Him.

I know now that I completely misjudged my loving Creator. We thought He was holding something back from us, so we chose not to obey Him, and the world has paid the price. Obedience is serious business with God.

A word to the wise: When you mess up, fess up! Don't blame someone else for your mistake, and don't bother trying to hide from God.

Prayer

Dear Heavenly Father,

You are the Creator of the universe, the Maker of all things: time, space, matter, and life. You spoke everything into existence. You are the Beginning of all things. You created a perfect world to worship You. Thank You for creating this world, and thank You for creating me and for loving me. Thank You for wanting a relationship with me.

Father, help me. Teach me to focus on You. There are so many distractions, so many temptations that demand my attention and would lead me astray. Don't allow me to miss Your handiwork in my life and in the world around me. As You show us Your wonders, help me to see You clearly.

In Jesus' name. Amen!

As we saw in the video, the adventure of the ark lasted many years, from Noah's first instructions from God, to the building of the ark and the gathering of the animals, to forty days and nights of rain, to the day that Noah and his family emerged from the ark onto dry ground a year later. That's substantially longer than the five minutes it took my children to play Noah and the ark when they were kids.

Have you ever taken a family road trip in cramped conditions? Did your brain ever scream, *I've got to get out of here!* or *I need some fresh air!* Or maybe you repeatedly asked your parents, "Are we there yet?" For most of my kids' childhood, my parents lived in Texas. The drive from our home in North Carolina to their door was 999 miles and took just under twenty hours. Although our fifteen-passenger van served as a kind of ark, filled with all necessary supplies and provisions, comfort mostly eluded us on the drive. By the time we arrived at Grannan and Paw's, we had to unfold ourselves from our seats. Nevertheless, after spilling out of the van and onto the driveway, we always celebrated, so glad to touch solid ground again.

I'm sure Noah and his family were exhausted from their journey by the time they finally landed in the mountains of Ararat. They must have been past ready to exit the ark, if only because of the smell! The ark may have seemed huge when Noah was building it, but it likely came to feel quite small after several months shut inside with all those animals.

Noah and his family were people just like you and me. They probably missed many things from

their old life before the flood. Once God told them the time had come to leave the ark, there must have been great anticipation mixed with apprehension about the damage and destruction they would find outside.

What they knew for sure was that God had saved them, providing shelter for them and protecting them from the floodwaters. So once outside the ark, Noah built an altar and sacrificed a burnt offering to the Lord. This demonstration of gratitude and respect toward God is beautiful and tells us something about how we all should respond to our Lord. No matter our circumstances, no matter what we've been through, our thoughts should always turn to God first. Just like Noah, we should be quick to thank Him for everything He does for us. And we should praise Him, not only for what He has done but also for who He *is*.

He is the all-powerful Creator of the universe. He spoke all things into existence. He put the stripes on the zebra and the snowcaps on the mountains. He made the sun, the moon, the planets, and the millions of trillions of stars. He exists in all places at the same time, so He is always with every one of His children. He knows everything, even our thoughts, so He is always able to help and guide us. God is holy and righteous, and He loves us perfectly. And He is faithful even when we are not.

Despite God's love and faithfulness, after Adam and Eve sinned and were expelled from the garden, mankind quickly developed a pattern of disobeying and dishonoring their Creator. God warned Adam and Eve's first son, Cain, that "sin is crouching at the door" like a monster waiting to control him, but he must learn to rule over it. But Cain failed to listen. Giving in to anger, he killed his brother Abel.

By the time of Noah, several generations later, wickedness had spread throughout the world. Everything that people thought or imagined was so evil that it broke God's heart. Noah was the only man who was faithful to God, so God chose to save him, his family, and at least one male and female of every kind of land animal and bird. All the rest He destroyed by a great flood.

Like Adam and Eve in the garden, Noah and his family were now the only people in the world. When they came out of the ark, God made a new covenant with them, much like the one he had made with the first man and woman. He blessed Noah and his family and told them to "be fruitful and multiply" and fill the earth with people made in His image. God wanted people to populate the world and spread His glory. After all, they couldn't very well care for the whole of creation if everyone stayed in one place. People would also need space to

build homes, grow food, and water their herds. God knew what would be best for mankind, but people thought they knew better.

Within a few generations after Noah, mankind had either forgotten God's instructions or chosen to ignore them. The population had grown, but people hadn't spread very far. In fact, one large group was determined to stay together in one place instead of being scattered over the face of the whole earth (Genesis 11:4). Instead of spreading God's glory, they decided to earn fame and glory for themselves. Someone had the idea to build a tower so tall that it would reach into the sky. Then others would look upon the tower and see that these people were great indeed, and they would not be forced to move to other lands.

So they began to build, brick by brick, higher and higher. Everyone was busy, busy, busy, working hard and focused on the job. They all spoke one language, and it seemed they were united in their purpose. Sadly, however, this was not the purpose God had in mind when He created them.

Mankind's purpose is to glorify God in everything we say and do. One of the most important ways we fulfill that purpose is by serving other people, not ourselves. Neither of these was the focus of this building project. They weren't building for the glory of God, nor were they serving their neighbors. No, the builders of the Tower of Babel were thinking of themselves—*their* wants and needs, *their* achievements, *their* glory.

The people were not obeying God, and He loved His creations too much to let them continue in their foolishness. So He stepped in to help mankind do what they should have been doing already. How did He do this? He confused their languages to keep them from communicating.

Suddenly, the workers couldn't understand each other. People were calling the same tool by different names and shouting instructions that made no sense to the others. Frustration quickly set in and work on the tower stopped.

The people had to abandon their ideas about the grand things they could achieve together. Their languages now separated them. Different families who spoke the same language found one another, and the various groups set out for new lands and began to fill the earth.

God has given us rules to live by that help us and protect us. We will be tempted now and then to break the rules, but isn't it good to know that when we disobey, God can step in to help us get back on the path of obedience?

PSALM AND PROVERB TO READ:
Psalm 24, Proverbs 2:1–5

LET'S TALK ABOUT IT

1. In Genesis 6:5, the thoughts of sinful people in Noah's time are described as "evil." What does Philippians 4:8 say we should think about?
2. What is something you're often hesitant to do obediently?
3. Name some character qualities exhibited by Noah. Which one would you like to improve in your own life? Why?
4. When God tells you to do one thing but you want to do something else, which one should you do?
5. What are some reasons you might be tempted to do something without God?

the FALL of MAN

God created Adam and Eve without sin, and He gave them the ability to not sin. They were free to choose whether to trust God and obey Him or to try to do things their own way. There was only one thing God told them they were not allowed to do: "You must not eat from the tree of the knowledge of good and evil" (Genesis 2:17, NIV). Now, there was nothing wrong with this tree. After all, God made the tree, and everything He made was good.

Despite the fact that all their needs were provided for and they truly wanted for nothing, Adam and Eve gave in to temptation and ate the fruit from the forbidden tree. We call this event the fall of man, or simply the Fall, for nothing was the same for mankind afterward.

As a result of the Fall, the very nature of Adam and Eve changed, so that they were not able to not sin. Every person born since that time has inherited their fallen nature. This idea is called Original Sin. It doesn't mean that eating the fruit was the first sin ever—Satan committed the very first sin when he rebelled against God—but rather, it means that all people are born with the desire to sin because the original man brought sin into the world.

Today we live in a world filled with death and disease, broken relationships, bad thinking, violence, destruction, scandal, and lies. The Fall affected the rest of creation too, and so we must deal with famine, floods, hurricanes, earthquakes, and many such events beyond our control.

In the Old Testament, God's people offered burnt offerings and sacrificed animals to cover their sin. But only the sacrifice of Jesus could cover for our sins completely and for all time and bring people back into a relationship with God.

Noah Speaks

I was just a normal guy. I wasn't the athletic type, and to be perfectly honest, I probably wouldn't have scored very high on a college entrance exam. But I lived at a crucial moment in world history. My name is Noah.

The earth in my day was in swift decline. We hadn't hit bottom yet, but we were sinking fast. Corruption, decay, and sin spread across my world like a plague. Hatred and distrust set neighbor against neighbor and ripped apart families and communities. But moral collapse is to be expected when people forget God. Our people had forgotten God, and the end was near.

During this time, my family and I continued to worship and glorify God. Although we were pressured to conform to the culture, we refused. One day, God spoke to me and said that He was going to clean up the mess we humans had made. He was going to purge the land of corruption and create a new beginning. He gave me instructions and told me to build an ark that would preserve me, my family, and every kind of animal. He would then send a flood to cover the earth, and only those in the ark would be saved.

I went to work, along with my three sons. For roughly seventy-five years, we toiled from early morning until the sun went down. Our worksite echoed with the sound of hammers as we fashioned a large boat out of gopher wood. When I wasn't pounding a hammer, I was pleading for the people to turn to God. Nobody listened. Meanwhile, animals of all kinds, many of which I had never seen before, arrived from parts unknown and entered the ark two by two when it was time.

I'll never forget the day I felt that first raindrop on my forehead. Then another. And then the heavens opened up and the springs of the earth erupted.

THE ARK

Do you think that a football field is a long distance? God instructed Noah to build an ark that was 300 cubits long—longer than one and a half football fields! The length of a cubit varied in ancient cultures, but we can estimate that the ark was between seventy-five and eighty-five feet wide and between forty-five and fifty feet high. The ark was made of cypress (also called gopher wood) and had a window, a roof, and a door on one side.

The ark was covered inside and out with pitch to keep the water out. Pitch is a sticky tar-like substance that occurs naturally in the Middle East. The ark had three decks and rooms within the decks. It was designed only to float—there was no way to steer the ark—so it drifted in the deep waters of the flood.

After spending about a hundred years building the ark, Noah was 600 years old when the rains began to fall and it was time to board. Noah and his family lived in the ark approximately one year, including the forty days it rained and the time it took for the floodwaters to recede. Can you imagine living for a year with your family inside your house with no trips to church or the grocery and no vacations?

Prayer

Dear Heavenly Father,

I praise Your name because You keep Your word. People don't always do what they say they will, but You are faithful. You will never leave me or fail me, and knowing this gives me peace and confidence during times of trial and testing. Not only are You trustworthy, but Your blessings go beyond what I could ask or imagine.

I want to honor You and glorify You both when life seems easy and when everything around me seems to be falling apart. God, teach me how to hold on to You at all times. Hold my hand when the storm rages and I'm scared. Carry me when the solid ground beneath me gives way.

Grow my faith and trust in You. Help me to live out loud during life's trials what I already know to be true: that You are faithful and true. You are my God.

I ask this in Jesus' name. Amen.

Lesson 3

ABRAHAM & ISAAC

Motions

5. Abraham
6. Isaac

Passage

Genesis 15, 21–22

Take it To Heart

Abraham said, "God will provide for himself the lamb for a burnt offering, my son." So they went both of them together.
Genesis 22:8

So far in Genesis, we have seen God make covenants with both Adam and Noah. In this week's video, we learned of a third covenant: the covenant God made with Abraham.

Have your parents ever promised you something? You knew that you could trust them, but then the time between their promise and the time it actually happened might have seemed like forever. I remember when I was in high school and my dad promised to take our family to the beach that summer. The time between his promise and the trip was only a few weeks, but to a teenager it seemed like forever!

In Genesis 12, and again in chapter 15, God promised that Abraham would be the father of a great nation. He took Abraham outside one night and told him, "Look up to the sky and count the stars, if you can. That's how many descendants you will have!" And despite the fact that Abraham and his wife had no children at the time, he believed the LORD (Genesis 15:6). Once again, God had promised something that seemed impossible, at least from our limited human perspective.

At the time of God's initial promise, Abram was already seventy-five years old. His wife, Sarah, was sixty-five. Ten years later, Abraham had a son, Ishmael, with Sarah's servant Hagar, but God made it clear that Ishmael was not the son He had promised Abraham. Another fifteen years passed, and Abraham was now *one hundred years old* (Genesis 21:5). Sarah was ninety and well past child-bearing age. Did God forget the promise He had made? Was God running late? Could He have changed His mind? No, no, and no. God knew exactly what He was doing. After all, He is perfect,

and therefore His timing is always perfect.

We need to remember that God is eternal, meaning He had no beginning and will have no end. He created time, and so He exists outside of time. He cannot be "late" or "early." He just *is*. In fact, God called Himself "I AM" (Exodus 3:14).

You and I can see only what is happening to us right here and right now, and we remember some of what has happened to us in the past. But God sees *all* of time *all* at once—past, present, *and* future. His perspective and power are unlimited, so He is able to order events perfectly to grow us spiritually and accomplish His will. This means that because our perspective is limited, God will sometimes arrange for things to happen in our lives at a time that doesn't make sense to us.

Abraham and Sarah thought God was late in keeping His promise to them. Even people who know God aren't always patient. We get restless easily. Sometimes we make rash decisions or take unwise action to help God move things along more quickly. We do things like Sarah did when she tried to help God provide Abraham with a son (see Genesis 16).

But God knows there is value for His children in waiting. He knows that as we wait, we will come to realize that He is our only hope. When God allows enough time to pass for us, we come to the end of ourselves, the end of our options, the end of our control. Then we finally arrive at the place where Abraham and Sarah arrived. It's the place where we know there isn't anything more we can do. We just can't. Only God can. Then we are finally ready to listen to God and do whatever He says to do.

After twenty-five years of waiting for the fulfillment of God's promise, Sarah became pregnant. When she gave birth at the age of ninety, Abraham and Sarah were able to give the glory to God be-

cause His mighty hand was the only explanation for this miracle. They named the child Isaac and held a great feast in celebration.

Then after some time had passed, God spoke to Abraham and asked him to do the unthinkable. God told Abraham to take his promised son to the mountains of Moriah and sacrifice him as a burnt offering to the Lord. *What?* God had fulfilled His promise to send Abraham and Sarah a son, and now He wanted Abraham to offer the boy to Him in sacrifice? It didn't make sense!

Yet there is no indication in Scripture that Abraham hesitated. No arguing, no questioning. Apparently, he believed that he could trust the One who had shown Himself faithful. So Abraham set out for the mountains early the next morning with Isaac, two of his servants, and wood for the sacrificial fire.

On the third day of their journey, they arrived at the designated place. Leaving his servants at the foot of the hill and taking with him only the supplies he needed, Abraham started up the incline. Isaac, who didn't know about God's command, walked beside his father, carrying the wood for the fire. (We don't know how old Isaac was at the time, but in order to carry enough wood for a burnt sacrifice, he must have been at least a healthy teenager.) Isaac asked, "Where is the lamb for the burnt offering?" It was a good question, and his father had a great answer: "God will provide." Abraham still trusted in God.

The Bible doesn't record the conversation between father and son when it came time for Abraham to reveal that Isaac was the required sacrifice. It simply says that Abraham bound Isaac and placed him on the altar. Think about that for a moment. Abraham was an old man, and Isaac was a

strong young man. But there was no struggle. There must have been many tears, but no wavering. Only yielding.

The son saw faithfulness in his father. He had heard the stories of God's faithfulness for as long as he could remember. He knew about his own miraculous birth. He had no doubt sacrificed and worshiped with his father many times. It wasn't just Abraham who was being tested; Isaac was, too. He submitted to being bound, trusting his father, who trusted his Father in heaven. He lay on the altar.

Abraham lifted the knife to sacrifice his son when a voice from heaven stopped him. "Now I know that you fear God, seeing you have not withheld your son, your only son. . . ." Can you imagine the relief for both father and son?

Then Abraham looked up and saw a ram caught in a thicket by its horns. So he took the ram and sacrificed it as a burnt offering in place of his son. He then called that place "The LORD will provide."

Nearly 2,000 years later, this hill would be called Golgotha, or Calvary in the Greek. On this very same hill, God would sacrifice *His* only Son, Jesus, who had never sinned. For only the sacrifice of the perfect Lamb could wash away the sins of mankind.

PSALM AND PROVERB TO READ:
Psalm 105, Proverbs 3:5–6

ALTARS

In the Old Testament, people built altars for a few different reasons. An altar might be a place of worship or a memorial of an important event or encounter with God. But most were built for the purpose of sacrifices and burnt offerings to the Lord. Animals were sacrificed on the altar because a person's sins could not be forgiven without the shedding of blood.

Noah built an altar to offer sacrifices and worship to God when he left the ark (Genesis 8:20). The first altars were constructed from a raised mound of earth or large rocks. Stone altars could be one large stone or several stones stacked together.

The altars of Solomon's temple were built with wood and then coated with metal—one with bronze and the other with gold. Each had four "horns" where the four corners were shaped to form peaks (Exodus 27:2). To the Jews, the four horns represented God's power, which extended to the four corners of the earth.

The Israelites also built altars as memorials of where they had experienced God's presence or where He had performed a miracle. For example, when Joshua led the Israelites across the River Jordan into the Promised Land, God parted the waters of the river so they walked on dry ground. After the entire nation of Israel had crossed the river, God told Joshua to gather twelve stones and build an altar as a reminder to future generations of this event.

Jesus' death was the ultimate sacrifice, and the cross was His altar. Because His sacrifice paid the full debt for our sins, God's people no longer have to sacrifice animals on an altar. Yet many churches are built with an altar at the front of the sanctuary. Why? The altar is a place to offer a spiritual sacrifice in the form of praise or thanksgiving. It is also a place to pray. Of course, you don't have to go to an altar to talk to God, but sometimes it helps to have friends pray with you when you are having a problem.

? LET'S TALK ABOUT IT

1. What promise of God have you doubted?
2. When have you tried to "help" God?
3. When do you sometimes falter in your faith?
4. Can you think of a time when God tested you?
5. What do you need to sacrifice, or give to God?

COVENANT

In the Bible, a covenant is usually an agreement God makes with human beings that defines the relationship between God and His people. In many ways, a covenant is a kind of contract, in which each side promises to do certain things to receive certain benefits. However, contracts are usually negotiated by both sides until they reach an agreement. Biblical covenants are not negotiated. Instead, God makes a covenant with whom He chooses, and He alone sets the terms of the agreement: If His people obey, they receive certain blessings; if they disobey, they receive certain curses or penalties.

Both God and the Old Testament person representing His people would take a binding oath when entering into a covenant. Often, this would include the shedding of blood to symbolize the penalty for breaking the oath.

The Bible tells of covenants God made with Adam, Noah, Abraham, Moses, and David. Each of these covenants revealed more of God's promises and pointed to the coming Messiah, Jesus Christ, whose person and work fulfilled all the requirements of the covenants. Today, it is only through faith in Jesus that we can receive all the benefits of keeping God's covenant promises.

Covenants between people and kingdoms were common in Old Testament times. They often took the form of a powerful king agreeing with a weaker kingdom to acquire their lands without destroying them. The powerful king offered protection and benefits if the weaker kingdom obeyed him. Otherwise, the weaker kingdom would be conquered through violence and receive no benefits. Because this was such a common idea at the time, it was easy for the Israelites to understand the kind of relationship they had with God.

Isaac Speaks

About a year before I was born, my parents, Abraham and Sarah, were visited by three strangers. As they sat down for a meal of bread and meat and milk, one of the men said that he would return in a year to find Sarah nursing a son. Mother was quite old at the time, and she laughed to herself at the thought of giving birth at her age. But is anything too hard for the Lord?

Just as the stranger foretold, I was born the following year. My parents named me Isaac, which means "laughter." My mother says that every time she calls my name, she is reminded how she laughed when she heard the promise of God. She likes to say, "God has brought laughter to my life, and everyone who hears about this will laugh with me."

When I was a young man, my father woke me early one morning and said, "Come, my son. We must travel some distance from here to sacrifice a burnt offering to the Lord." We saddled the donkey, gathered wood for a fire, and headed for the mountains of Moriah. I thought it odd that we did not bring a lamb to sacrifice, but I said nothing.

On the third day of our journey, we stopped within sight of our destination. Father hefted the wood onto my shoulders, and he took up the knife and a lighted torch. As we climbed the mount, my curiosity got the best of me. "Father," I said, "we have the fire and the wood, but where is the lamb for a burnt offering?" My father was silent for a moment. He did not look at me but said only, "God will provide for Himself a lamb for the offering, my son. He always provides."

When I learned that I was to be the sacrificial lamb, at first I was greatly afraid. But then a deep peace came upon me. I trusted my father, and he had taught me to trust God. So I lay down on the altar, and Father bound me with ropes. I did not struggle.

As my father raised the knife, I closed my eyes. But the knife never came down. An angel of the Lord had stayed my father's hand. Then the silence was broken by the bleating of a ram, its horns caught in a thicket nearby. My father set me loose, and together we sacrificed the ram to God.

I learned that day and have never forgotten: The Lord is faithful, He is just, and He always provides.

Dear Heavenly Father,

You are the giver of all good things. You provide for my every need, and I lack for nothing. Thank You for the many ways You meet my needs, wants, and desires. My time, treasure, and talents are from You. Each and every breath I breathe is from You. You walk with me, granting me strength, wisdom, peace, and joy as I abide in You and walk in Your light according to Your truth.

Thank You for going ahead of me and coming behind me. Thank You for knowing what I need even before I know I need it. Father, open my eyes to see each and every gift from You, the big and the small. Most of all, thank You for the gift of Jesus and eternal life with you.

Help me to be forever grateful and to gladly tell others of Your amazing love.

I ask this in Jesus' name. Amen.

Lesson 4

JACOB & JOSEPH

Motions

7. Jacob
8. Joseph

Passage

Genesis 25, 27–50

Take it To Heart

"As for you, you meant evil against me, but God meant it for good, to bring it about that many people should be kept alive, as they are today. So do not fear; I will provide for you and your little ones." Thus he comforted them and spoke kindly to them.
Genesis 50:20–21

What's your favorite ice cream? Favorite pizza? Favorite book? I enjoy talking with my children about their favorite things. It's also an interesting way to get to know a new friend. Most people are comfortable answering such questions, but sometimes it's hard to identify a favorite. For example, I don't think I have a favorite kind of music or a favorite tree. What about you?

While having a favorite flavor of ice cream is fine, having a favorite child isn't. We met Jacob in our video teaching time this week. Sadly, this issue of favorites was characteristic of his family. As a child, Jacob had been his mother's favorite. As an adult, Jacob had a favorite wife, Rachel, and consequently, she gave birth to his favorite son, Joseph. When it comes to people, especially family, playing favorites is dangerous. You must remember that God loves us all. He has no favorites. He loves every one of us the most, and that's the kind of love we should have for others.

The Bible tells us that Jacob had twelve sons, but Joseph was clearly his favorite. And Jacob's partiality wasn't exactly a secret among the family. Everyone knew about it, especially after he gave Joseph a very special gift: a beautiful coat of many colors. The lavish

gift angered Joseph's ten older brothers, and they hated him because he was their father's favorite. Jealousy brewed among the brothers, and they were unable to speak a kind word to Joseph, who was now seventeen years old.

Jacob was not wise to favor Joseph and treat him so much better than his other sons. Every time the older brothers saw the coat, they were reminded that none of *them* was Father's favorite. Can you imagine the tension, the awkwardness in Jacob's home? This was not a happy family, laughing around the dinner table and enjoying each other's company. Jacob's family wasn't thriving; they were fighting.

Then Joseph had a dream. It wasn't a regular dream about flying like Superman or being chased through a field. No, this was a prophetic dream, and it told Joseph that one day he would rule over his brothers. It wasn't his fault he dreamed the dream, but he made the mistake of telling the dream to his brothers, and they hated him all the more.

Then Joseph had another dream in which the sun, the moon, and eleven stars bowed down before him. It didn't take a prophet to know what this dream meant, and his father scolded him for telling everyone about it. "What kind of dream is that?" his father asked. "Do expect your mother and me and your brothers to bow before you?"

These dreams were the last straw for the brothers. They had had enough of their little brother. So when Joseph was sent by his father to check on his brothers, who were tending the flocks, the brothers spotted him from a distance and plotted to kill him. Now that's a dark turn in the story, but Jacob should have seen it coming.

Reuben, the oldest of the brothers, tried to talk the others out of killing Joseph. He convinced them to seize Joseph, tear off his coat, and throw him into a pit. Reuben was secretly planning to later save the boy and take him back to their father unharmed. But when Reuben returned to rescue him, he found that the other brothers had sold Joseph to a passing caravan of slave traders. They *sold* their brother. That is what it looks like when jealously is allowed to go unchecked.

To cover up their evil deed, the brothers first killed a young goat. Then they ripped Joseph's coat—the colorful coat that they despised—and dipped it in the goat's blood. They then took the bloody coat to their father and led him to believe that a wild animal had killed Joseph. Grieved by the loss of his favorite son, Jacob tore his clothes and dressed himself in sackcloth. He mourned and wept for a long time. Yet the brothers were unmoved in their resolve. In spite of their father's anguish and despair, they kept the secret of what they had done.

That's how lies work. Maybe you tell a teeny, tiny "white lie." No big deal. No one will find out, right? But then you have to tell another lie so that the first one makes sense. The next one is bigger than the first two combined, but what else can you do? The whole story has taken on a life of its own by now, and you're no longer sure what the truth *is*, much less how all the lies began.

Can you imagine it all? First, the brothers lied about finding Joseph's coat. There must have been a funeral, so did they lie at the funeral? Did they pretend to miss him? Did they mourn his death? What about their wives and their friends? Did the brothers lie to them too? See how quickly lies can swirl into a tornado of destruction? Telling the truth is *always* the better option.

Meanwhile, Joseph was trying to make his way in an entirely new country. Take some time to read the rest of his story in Genesis 39–50. He was sold as a slave to the house of Potiphar, an Egyptian official. He served Potiphar well, and God blessed Potiphar's house because of Joseph. Then Joseph was falsely accused of a terrible crime and sent to prison, but his ability to interpret dreams led to his release and his ultimate rise to power as the most powerful man in all of Egypt next to Pharaoh. A few years later, when his older brothers find themselves at the mercy of the now-mighty Joseph, does he have them thrown into prison? Does he have them killed? No, he forgives them, saying, "What you intended for evil, God meant for good."

There are many similarities between the story of Joseph and the life of Jesus almost two thousand years later. Joseph was despised by his brothers; Jesus was despised by the Jewish leaders. Joseph was sold as a slave by his own brothers for twenty pieces of silver; Jesus was betrayed by his own disciple for thirty pieces of silver (Matthew 26:14–16). Joseph forgave the unforgivable when he had the power to avenge himself on his brothers; Jesus could have called down twelve legions of angels to protect Him, but instead He went to the cross so that we would be forgiven for our sins (Matthew 26:53). Despite his awful circumstances, Joseph trusted God and remained obedient to His will; Jesus trusted His Father and was obedient to the point of death (Philippians 2:8).

PSALM AND PROVERB TO READ:
Psalm 16, Proverbs 4:23

LET'S TALK ABOUT IT

1. Have you told a lie or tried to deceive someone? Do you need to ask someone to forgive you?
2. Why is it wrong to play favorites in a family?
3. Why is hatred dangerous? What does Jesus say in Matthew 5:44 about how to treat someone who hates you?
4. Why do you think Joseph always worked hard for his masters, even though he had been unfairly sold as a slave and then wrongly imprisoned?
5. Why did Joseph forgive his brothers after all they had done to him?

TORN CLOTHES

How do you feel when you accidentally tear your clothes? Can you think of a situation when you might tear your clothes on purpose?

In Bible times, clothing was expensive and time-consuming to make because each piece of clothing was sewn by hand. There were no machines for making clothes quickly. So each person owned very few pieces of clothing.

Yet people sometimes tore their clothes as an expression of grief or deep sadness. Reuben was one of the first people in the Bible to express grief by tearing his clothes. The other person was Job (Job 1:20). Reuben tore his clothes when he realized his brothers sold their younger brother, Joseph, into slavery (Genesis 37:29–30). Then their father, Jacob, tore his clothes in grief when he was tricked into believing that wild animals had killed Joseph (Genesis 37:34), whom he loved more than all his brothers.

People did not tear large holes in their clothes, but only a small portion of the clothing. By damaging such a valuable possession in public, the person showed the depth of pain and sorrow for the death of someone or the hurt from a painful event.

Sometimes, in addition to tearing clothing, grieving people wore a coarse, scratchy material called sackcloth, which was made from goat's hair and was similar to our modern-day burlap. They might also shave their heads or put ashes on their heads to show their sadness.

What do you do when you are sad? Do you go to your room alone, or do you share your feelings of sadness with the people around you?

Hebrews, Israelites, or Jews?

Have you ever noticed that the same street can change names depending on what part of town it's running through? You can be driving down 3rd Street one minute, and without turning, the next minute you're on Franklin Avenue. A few minutes later you look up and find you're on Highway 42! This can be confusing at first, but really the different names provide you with additional information that can be helpful. In a way, that is what's going on with the proper nouns *Hebrews, Israelites,* and *Jews*. They're at once the same and different.

The word *Hebrew* first appears in the book of Genesis in reference to Abraham. Scholars aren't certain where the word *Hebrew* came from, but many believe it has roots in the idea of "crossing over." Crossing over to where? In Genesis, the name refers to Abraham's journey to Canaan. What did Abraham cross over? Among other things, he crossed a few borders as well as the Euphrates River. Water crossings would later mark a number of critical events in the history of the Hebrew people, including passing through the Red Sea and crossing the Jordan River into the Promised Land, as we will see in the next few lessons.

The word *Hebrew* also might come from the name of one of Abraham's ancestors, Eber, which would mean that it refers to a race of people. There is also some archaeological evidence in Egypt that the word may refer to a nomadic people who wandered from place to place. All these ideas fit and might even be talking about the same thing.

What about the word *Israelite*? The name of Abraham's grandson Jacob was changed to Israel when God blessed him. Jacob's descendants later became the twelve tribes of Israel, who were enslaved by Egypt after the death of Joseph. When Moses freed the Hebrew slaves and led them into the wilderness, God formed a covenant with Moses and created a nation. At first, the people of this nation, called themselves Hebrews, but by the time of King Saul they called themselves Israelites or "the children of Israel."

After Israel was divided into two nations, Israel and Judah, the word *Jews* would come to refer to the people of Judah. Both nations descended into idolatry, but of the two, Judah was more faithful to the Lord. To the people of Judah, being "Jewish" meant keeping the faith that had been revealed to them. Hundreds of years later, the New Testament writers would often use the word *Jews* to refer to those who were trying to keep the religious law.

Although there are exceptions and overlapping usages in Scripture, *Hebrew* generally refers to ethnicity, *Israel* usually means God's covenant people, and *Jews* refers to people protecting the religious law.

Joseph Speaks

I guess you could say that I was Dad's favorite, but don't envy me. Being the favored son in a large family can get you into heaps of trouble. I deeply loved my father, but my brothers were incensed by all the attention he gave me. For a long time they were content with giving me wedgies and playing nasty little tricks on me. Then our father gave me a wonderful gift, an amazing coat of many colors, and my brothers' resentment grew serious.

And then there were the dreams. I kept having these dreams that told me I would one day rule over my brothers. Maybe I shouldn't have shared my dreams with them, because their jealousy quickly turned to rage. They called me "Little Joe, the Dreamer," but there was nothing playful about the way they said it.

One day, when I was seventeen, Father sent me to the fields to check on my brothers and report back to him. When they saw me coming, they devised a plan. After stripping me of my beautiful coat, they threw me into a pit. Yes, I admit there were times I had been a pest, but I didn't deserve this treatment. When a caravan of merchants passed by on their way to Egypt, my brothers told them I was a slave and sold me to them.

As a slave in Egypt, I worked hard as if I were working for God. I was placed in charge of my master's house, and the Lord prospered everything I put my hand to. But then I was falsely accused by the master's wife and sent to prison, but still I believed that God had plans for me. Again I worked hard as if I were working for God, and soon I was placed in charge of all the prisoners.

When I turned thirty, the Lord arranged for me to interpret the dreams of the mighty Pharaoh, and I found myself placed in a position of honor and power. In Pharaoh's dreams I had seen a great famine approaching, but God showed me how to prepare the nation. When the famine hit seven years later, I was able to feed all of Egypt and the lands beyond because of what God had shown me.

You won't believe who showed up a few months later wanting food. My brothers! If you had been in my sandals, what would you have done to them? How would you have repaid them for all they had done to you? But I knew that everything that had happened to me was just as God had planned it. What my brothers had meant for evil, God meant for good, to provide food for the people in the midst of famine. So I chose to forgive them. If you think revenge is sweet, you should try forgiveness.

Prayer

Dear Heavenly Father,

Thank you that I am one of Your children. I know that You love me completely, more than any earthly person could ever love me. I feel like I'm Your favorite child, and yet I know You love everyone the most. Help me to love everyone in my family equally and deeply.

Father, teach me about forgiveness. You have forgiven me of so much. So many times I have let you down, so many times I have disobeyed, yet You forgive me every time! Forgiveness is not always easy for me, but I can do all things through You in Your strength. When I forgive other people, You are glorified, and I want my life to glorify You!

In Jesus' name, I pray. Amen.

Lesson 5

MOSES

Motions

9. Moses

Passage

Exodus 2–11

Take it To Heart

God said to Moses, "I AM WHO I AM." And he said, "Say this to the people of Israel: I AM has sent me to you."
Exodus 3:14

Moses' life is clearly divided into three parts, each lasting forty years. In the video, we discussed his first forty years, during which Moses grew up as a prince of Egypt. As the adopted son of Pharaoh's daughter, he wanted for nothing. He was given the best of everything Egypt had to offer—the best food, the best clothes, the best education. After killing an Egyptian who was beating a Hebrew slave, Moses fled from Egypt and everything familiar to him. Soon, he found himself in the land of Midian, and it couldn't possibly have been more different from the life he'd known as a prince.

In the first forty years of his life, Moses had gone from the palace to the plains, from opulence to obscurity, from prince to pauper. He became a shepherd and married Zipporah, a daughter of Jethro, and Moses watched over the flocks belonging to his father-in-law. Like I said, this was a huge life change. Yet he seemed to have settled into this new lifestyle when God came to meet Him. By this time, it had been another forty years since Moses fled Egypt. Now he was eighty years old, and

Midian was his home. No longer a prince of Egypt, he was a working man, a husband, and a father of two sons.

Being a shepherd wasn't always easy; the job had its challenges. The animals were smelly and often stubborn. They were given to falling into ditches and getting themselves lost, but Moses had learned over time how to lead the flock, how to find food and water for them, how to protect them from predators, how to bind up their wounds, and how to carry them when necessary.

There was a peace here too. Yes, there were occasional dangers like wolves. But the stillness, the breeze and the birds, the sun and the stars, the wildflowers and the water rippling in the brook—these granted refreshment. Moses had come to know the wilderness as well as he'd known the palace.

But he couldn't have known what had happened back in Egypt. A new pharaoh had come to power, and God's people cried out to be delivered from their chains. The Bible says that God heard their groaning and remembered His promises to Abraham, Isaac, and Jacob (Exodus 2:24). Does this mean that God had forgotten? No, of course not. God knows everything. But He had allowed His people to be oppressed by the Egyptians so that they would call upon the Lord and grow in their knowledge of Him. Although it may seem as if Moses had wasted the last forty years of his life watching over a bunch of sheep, God had been at work preparing Moses for a very important job.

One day, as he was leading his herd near Horeb, the mountain of God, Moses saw something strange. There in the distance was a bush that was on fire, but the bush did not burn up. The bush seemed unaffected by the flames. As Moses moved in for closer look, the voice of God called to him,

As Moses moved in for closer look, the voice of God called to him, "Moses! Moses!"

"Here I am," Moses said.

God told him to remove his sandals because the place where he stood was holy ground. God then introduced Himself: "I am the God of your father, the God of Abraham, the God of Isaac, and the God of Jacob."

Moses shrank from the presence of the Lord and covered his face.

The Lord went on. "I have seen the oppression of my people, and I have heard their cries of distress. I know they are suffering. You must lead my people out of Egypt."

The God of the universe was sending him *where?* Moses hadn't given a thought to Egypt in years, and now God was sending him back to confront Pharaoh? Moses had made a life in Midian, and he was content to be a shepherd the rest of his days. So Moses started making excuses, hoping to change God's mind. "Who am I that I should go to Pharaoh and bring the children of Israel out of Egypt? I am nobody."

The Lord replied, "I will be with you." Then He told Moses that the king of Egypt would not let the people go easily. In fact, Pharaoh would not be moved unless forced by a mighty hand. So God would strike the Egyptians with many miracles and wonders. Only then would Moses be allowed to bring God's people out of Egypt.

When Moses expressed doubts that the Hebrews would believe the Lord had spoken to him, God told him to throw down the staff he was holding, and it turned into a snake. God instructed him to pick up the snake by its tail, and it turned back into a staff.

Then Moses said, "But I'm not very good with words. I get all tongue-tied."

God said, "I will help you speak and will teach you what to say." He would even reunite Moses with his brother, Aaron, who was known to speak well.

Finally, Moses pleaded, "Lord, please! Send anyone else but me." God had called to invite Moses to participate in the deliverance of His people from bondage, and Moses simply didn't want to do it.

Can you understand that? Was there ever a time when you knew what God wanted you to do, but you just didn't want to do it? Maybe like Moses, you are comfortable with your life and the way you spend your time, and God's plans would change all that.

Moses was definitely out of his comfort zone. But when Aaron showed up, having been summoned by God to this meeting on the mountain, Moses knew he would be going to Egypt. So he picked up his staff and went out to meet his brother.

When Moses returned to his former country, there was no ticker tape parade, no banners hanging from the pyramids, no cheering crowds lining the streets to welcome him home. Egypt was different now, and so was Moses, for he had spoken directly with Almighty God. Forty years earlier, Moses had run away from Egypt, afraid for his life. But now he returned, fearless and bold, declaring the will of God. Moses was on a mission, and he walked with real purpose.

After meeting with the elders of the Hebrew people and telling them what God had said, Moses and Aaron went before Pharaoh and demanded that he let God's people go. It was an audacious demand, for the Egyptians had become dependent on Hebrew slave labor. They weren't just going to free their slaves because this eighty-year-old shepherd asked them to, not even if his brother *could* turn his staff into a snake. Besides, even the palace magicians could do that, although there was a little embarrassment when the snake that had been Aaron's staff swallowed up the snakes of the magicians. No, Moses would have to come up with something much more impressive if he wanted to be taken seriously.

Just as the Lord had said, He then brought ten great plagues upon the Egyptians. These plagues wreaked havoc on the Egyptians, their land, their cattle, and their homes. Each of the ten plagues specifically showed that God was superior to one of the many idols the Egyptians worshiped. In each instance, Pharaoh would relent and ask Moses to end the plague, only to change his mind once the plague had departed. The Bible refers to this as the "hardening" of Pharaoh's heart.

As you read the story of the plagues in Exodus 7–10, remember that only God is worthy of our worship—God alone and no other.

PSALM AND PROVERB TO READ:
Psalm 90, Proverbs 5:1–2

BASKET WEAVING

You have probably used a backpack to carry your books, a bucket to carry sand or water, or a plastic bag to carry groceries. The shape and size of any container often depends on the kind of items you want to carry.

In the Old Testament, palm leaves, straw, reeds, bulrushes, peeled twigs, and grasses were commonly used to weave baskets. The shape of the basket depended on what it was to be used for. Large and deep baskets were made to carry grain from the field. Large, flat baskets carried bread and food. A jar-shaped basket made from clay and straw was often used to store wheat, barley, and oats. Most baskets were constructed with handles.

When Pharaoh gave the order to kill all Hebrew boys by throwing them into the Nile River, Moses' mother wove a basket of papyrus large enough to hold a child and waterproofed it with tar and pitch. She placed Moses in the basket and set it adrift in the river. Little did she know that her basket was carrying the man who would one day deliver the Israelites from bondage.

Are you seeking God's plan for your life? He may use something unique in your life to fulfill His plan just as He used the basket in the life of Moses.

LET'S TALK ABOUT IT

1. Name some of the ways God prepared Moses to carry His message to Pharaoh.
2. How does the story of Moses' birth show that God uses even the most difficult events in our lives for His good purposes? What other events from the life of Moses show that God is always in charge?
3. How did Moses respond to God's call on his life?
4. Describe a time when you knew what God wanted you to do, but you were either afraid or not interested in obeying God. What excuses did you make to God? What did you finally choose to do?
5. Whom did God give to Moses to help him deal with his fears? Whom has God given you to help you face your fears?

the plagues on egypt

Moses, like all prophets, was given signs to perform in order to show he had the authority to speak for God. The plagues of Exodus are especially interesting miracles because they reveal so much about who God is. Instead of delivering His people with one swift blow from His mighty right hand, God carries out His plan in a way that demonstrates His sovereignty and power while at the same time judging Egypt for its idolatry.

Almost every plague attacked a different Egyptian god. The Nile was associated with several gods, so to turn it to blood showed the superiority of Yahweh. Gods that took the form of a frog and a cow were attacked. Gods of the sky, the sun, crops, medicine, and life were attacked. The death of the firstborn attacked the supposed deity of Pharaoh. Although Egypt's court magicians were able to imitate the first two plagues, they could not replicate the third and admitted the superiority of the God of the Hebrews.

In 1828, a document written by an Egyptian priest in the thirteenth century BC was discovered in Egypt. The document, known as the Ipuwer Papyrus, contains a possible reference to the plagues. It describes plagues that turned the Nile to blood and made it undrinkable; killed trees, crops, and fish; consumed the ground with fire; made cattle wander; and brought darkness over the land. The document also says, "He that lays his brother in the ground is everywhere," and that all Egypt cried out with grief.

The ten plagues were signs that showed God to be almighty, in full control of nature, and the only real God. It took Pharaoh a long time to figure this out, and his heart never really did soften. How many signs and miracles from God do you think it would take to make you believe?

Jochebed Speaks

I am mentioned by name only twice in the Bible (Exodus 6:20; Numbers 26:59), but I played an important part in setting an entire nation free from slavery. You see, I gave birth to a baby who was destined to change all the world. Some people say that what I did after my son's birth was heroic, but my act is only one example of the faith of godly women throughout history. My name is Jochebed (pronounced Yo-shuh-bed).

Soon after Joseph and his brothers died in the land of Egypt, a new king who knew neither Joseph nor his God ascended the throne. In the years that followed, the descendants of Jacob (who was also called Israel) multiplied so fast that the king felt threatened by their numbers. He began imposing greater burdens on them, but the children of Israel grew greater in number. Pharaoh feared that the Hebrews' sheer number could one day overwhelm his kingdom, so he decreed that all their baby boys must die. They were to be thrown into the Nile River and left to drown.

But when I gave birth to a baby boy, I refused to kill him. I hid him for three months until it just wasn't practical anymore. Knowing I could no longer protect him from Pharaoh, I wove a basket out of river grass, waterproofed it, and set my baby inside. I then set the basket afloat in the Nile. My daughter, Miriam, hid and watched as Pharaoh's daughter, who had come to bathe in the river, found the basket and the tiny child inside. Although she realized the child was a Hebrew, the princess decided to adopt him as her own. When Pharaoh's daughter agreed that someone would need to nurse the child, Miriam suggested me. I'm crying just thinking about how good and gracious God was to me and my son!

Although he was raised and educated in Pharaoh's palace, one day he would free our people and bring the Egyptian king to his knees. That boy was Moses, my son and one of the greatest revolutionaries the world has known.

I don't mind if you never heard of me before today. I'm content. While nursing my child, I looked into the face that would one day look upon God. I held the hand that would someday hold a shepherd's staff as he parted the Red Sea. I preserved an infant who would later preserve a nation.

Prayer

Dear Heavenly Father,

You are the Great I AM. You are and always have been. You created all things and hold all things together. And yet with all of Your strength and might, You love me! You sought me and prepared me to be about Your business. You even put people in my life to help me do Your will.

You delivered me from sin and are there to rescue me whenever I begin to wander away from You. You pursue my heart for Your glory, and You desire a relationship with me.

Father, continue to teach me to trust You and You alone. Do not allow me to put my faith in anyone or anything but You. Do not allow me to worship anyone or anything but You. For You alone are worthy of my praise, and my heart is Yours always. I love You!

In Jesus' name, I pray. Amen.

Lesson 6

PASSOVER

Motions

10. Passover

Passage

Exodus 7–14

Take it To Heart

Then Moses called all the elders of Israel and said to them, "Go and select lambs for yourselves according to your clans, and kill the Passover lamb. Take a bunch of hyssop and dip it in the blood that is in the basin, and touch the lintel and the two doorposts with the blood that is in the basin. None of you shall go out of the door of his house until the morning."

Exodus 12:21–22

God had told Moses from a burning bush, "The king of Egypt will not let you go unless compelled by a mighty hand. So I will stretch out my hand and strike Egypt with all the wonders that I will do in it; after that he will let you go" (Exodus 3:19–20). So when Pharaoh refused the Lord's command to free the children of Israel, God did as He promised and struck Egypt with a series of plagues.

First, the Lord turned the Nile to blood, so that no one could drink its waters. Then He sent swarms of frogs, gnats, and flies upon the land and into the people's homes. He then sent a disease that killed all the livestock belonging to the Egyptians, while not a single animal belonging to the Israelites was killed.

These plagues frightened Egypt's people, but still Pharaoh's heart was hardened against God, so he would not let the Hebrews go. So the Lord caused boils to break out on all the people and their animals. Then He sent a storm more devastating than any in the history of Egypt, and hail struck down the people, animals, plants, and trees. God then sent locusts to cover the land and destroy every plant that had survived the hailstorm. Then a heavy darkness fell upon the land of Egypt for three days, so that the people were too terrified to move about because they could not see one another. And yet Pharaoh still refused to let God's people go.

So Moses went to Pharaoh and announced God's final plague against Egypt: That night, death would come to Egypt and the firstborn child of every Egyptian family would be killed, including Pharaoh's own son. Meanwhile, death would "pass over" the people of Israel, and their children would not be harmed. After this, Pharaoh would beg God's people to leave, and they would finally go.

It was on this day that the feast of Passover was instituted by God among the Hebrews. Pay close attention here, because the Passover is profoundly important in the story of God. This is an example of why it is important to study the Old Testament—because its history and symbols help us to understand everything that will happen in the New Testament. In this lesson, we will focus on four major symbols of the Passover: the lamb, the blood, the judgment, and the feast.

First, God instructed Moses to tell the Hebrew families to each choose a lamb without spot or defect. It couldn't be a lamb that was sickly or lame, but rather a healthy lamb that would symbolize purity and innocence. This lamb would live with the family for a period of time. A perfect lamb would have great value, be loved, and therefore be a worthy sacrifice to offer.

Second, the family was to kill the lamb and dab its blood on the doorframe of their home. This would be a sign that the people in this house trusted God, and all who dwelled there would be spared from death.

It's important to remember that the concept of a blood sacrifice wasn't new. When Adam and Eve sinned against God, their sin brought death to creation. Their perfect bodies began to age and decay, and disease and death became inevitable. Thus the third Passover symbol of God's judgment was established: Death is the penalty for sin. Think back to when Adam and Eve were naked and afraid. God killed animals and used the skins to clothe them and cover their shame (Genesis 3:21). Their son Abel would later sacrifice the firstborn of his flock to God. As we have seen, Abraham and Noah both offered sacrifices to honor God. Now death was about to visit Egypt, and in order for God's people to be saved, there would have to be a blood sacrifice. So each family killed a spotless, perfect lamb and placed the blood of the lamb on their doorframe. Many hundreds of years later, the Lamb of God, Jesus, would be sacrificed, and His blood would cover the sins of all who believe in Him.

As the fourth major Passover symbol, Hebrew families were instructed to prepare a specific meal, including roasted lamb. This was to be an annual feast that God's people would celebrate for centuries to come. In this way, future generations would remember God's deliverance and protection and great love for His people, and they would learn to trust and obey Him.

Each part of this meal was significant. Bitter herbs represented the harshness of slavery and would tell future generations of the cruelty and pain of the Hebrews' oppression under Pharaoh. The Passover bread, which was made quickly, was to be unleavened because they wouldn't have time to prepare bread with yeast, which would need to rise. (Unleavened bread is like tortillas or flat bread.) Furthermore, the Hebrews were to eat the meal dressed and standing, ready to go, with their sandals on and staff in hand. "In haste," the Bible says (Exodus 12:11). This wasn't to be a leisurely meal. This was a meal intended to give the people strength for the first part of their journey out of Egypt. So in each house, God's people ate in anticipation, anxiously awaiting word that it was time to leave.

Shortly after midnight, Moses was summoned to the palace. With the death of his son, Pharaoh wanted the people of Israel to go and go quickly. God gave His people favor with the Egyptians, who gave the Israelites their silver and gold jewelry on the way out. Finally, they were free! But exactly where were they going?

The way God took them wasn't the quickest possible route. But He wasn't lost, nor did He take a wrong turn. God knew what He was doing. Yes, the plagues demonstrated His power and sovereignty to Pharaoh and the Egyptians, but they also showed His power, protection, and provision to the Hebrew people. Now God would again show Himself mighty to His chosen people.

Scholars disagree on the number of Israelites leaving Egypt, with estimates ranging from a few thousand to a few million. Most translations of Scripture say there were 600,000 men of fighting age, plus women and children (Exodus 12:37). Given the size of the crowd, they needed more than a flag on a stick to follow as they headed into the wilderness. So God led them in a pillar of cloud by day and a pillar of fire by night, making it clear which way they were to go.

When it came time to camp, the Israelites stopped at the Red Sea. Here God revealed to Moses that Pharaoh was not quite done with them. Desperate rage had driven Pharaoh to pursue them with his army and 600 chariots. And when the Israelites found themselves trapped between Pharaoh's army on one side and the Red Sea on the other, they panicked. They were not prepared to fight an army, and they didn't have any boats to cross the water. But God hadn't brought them out of Egypt to be recaptured by Pharaoh. Yes, God had led His people to a location where there was no way of escape—no way *except* by His almighty hand.

So Moses said to the people, "Fear not, stand firm, and see the salvation of the Lord. . . . The Lord will fight for you, and you only have to be silent" (Exodus 14:13–14). Then God told Moses to stretch out his hand with his staff and divide the sea. And the waters parted! As Pharaoh's army struggled to get past the pillar of cloud that protected the Israelites from behind, God's people crossed the Red Sea on dry ground, with a wall of water on their right and on their left.

"Dry ground." That's a detail we often overlook when reading this story. Not only did the waters part, but God made the seabed completely dry. Had the sea floor been wet, it would have been impossible for all the heavy wagons and carts to pass through the mud.

Once the Hebrews were safely on the other side, the pillar of cloud moved out of the way and Pharaoh and his army hurried to cross the sea floor as God's people had done. Then the Lord instructed Moses to stretch out his hand again, and the waters rushed back, drowning Pharaoh's entire army.

There could be no doubt of God's supremacy over all creation and the enemies of His people. The Bible records in Exodus 14:31, "Israel saw the great power that the Lord used against the Egyptians, so the people feared the Lord, and they believed in the Lord and in His servant Moses." And the people joined in a song of celebration that you can read in Exodus 15.

Unfortunately, the people lacked focus, and their "awe" of God Almighty faded quickly. Before long, they were actually missing Egypt! They missed the familiar and forgot the misery. They wanted deliverance to be easy, but it couldn't be. They needed to learn to trust God and follow Him. After all, they had been in Egypt for a few hundred years, and they had grown used to Egyptian ways, Egyptian foods, and Egyptian idols. As the story continues, we will see just how Egyptian the Israelites had become.

PSALM AND PROVERB TO READ:
Psalm 118, Proverbs 6:16–19

THE EXODUS

Do you ever notice the exit sign when you enter a building? The exit sign tells you the direction for the way out. An exodus is a large number of people leaving a place. The original Greek word *exodos* literally means "the road out."

The Egyptians had held the descendants of Abraham, Isaac, and Jacob captive for a little over 400 years. Day after day, they made bricks from mud and straw for Pharaoh's building projects. Long ago, God had promised Abraham that his descendants would have a new home in Canaan, but generation after generation the people of Israel waited and prayed for God to send a leader who would free them from bondage.

God heard His people's cries, and He chose Moses to lead the Israelites from slavery to freedom. Moses took God's message to the Pharaoh, saying, "Thus says the Lord, the God of Israel, 'Let my people go.'" But Pharaoh did not listen, so God sent ten plagues against Egypt, one after another. After each of the first nine plagues, Pharaoh refused to let God's people go.

The tenth plague was the most severe, killing the firstborn male of every animal and every Egyptian family, including Pharaoh's own son. Finally, he relented and freed the Israelites from slavery. So the great exodus out of Egypt began.

But Pharaoh changed his mind and led his army out to recapture the Hebrews by the Red Sea, where they had encamped. So God instructed Moses to stretch out his staff over the sea. The waters parted and the Israelites crossed the sea on dry land (Exodus 14:16). When Pharaoh's army attempted to follow them across the dry seabed, God closed the waters and destroyed the Egyptian army.

Have you felt trapped in a seemingly impossible situation? How did God help you find your way out?

LET'S TALK ABOUT IT

1. Which of the ten plagues seems the most destructive? Which one most clearly demonstrates God's power? Which one is the scariest?
2. An idol is anything that is worshiped in place of the one true God. The Egyptians worshiped frogs, the sun, and many other things. What are some things we worship today instead of God?
3. What are some of the forms idol worship takes in our society?
4. How do we know that God is far more powerful than modern idols? What are some ways He shows off to us in creation?
5. What is worship? Why should we worship God?

idoLAtry

Worship means saying that someone (or something) is worthy of our respect and reverence, and that we should bow down and serve that person (or thing). Anytime we worship anything other than God, or worship Him in a way He does not want to be worshiped, we are committing idolatry. In the Bible, God tells us not only that He should be worshiped but *how* He should be worshiped. Not all worship is acceptable to God. And when we worship Him in a way that is not acceptable, that too is idolatry.

One of the ways people have committed idolatry is by making and worshiping images of so-called gods. This was done often in biblical times and still happens today. Usually, the idols people worship are images of false gods, which displeases God and is expressly forbidden in Scripture (Leviticus 19:4; Exodus 20:3–6). But people are also warned against creating and then worshiping images of the God of the Bible. To worship a mere image of God is to worship what was created instead of the Creator; we must never worship something finite instead of Him who is eternal. God does not forbid us from making images of Him, but He does forbid the worship of them.

However, the object of your worship doesn't have to be a physical idol for idolatry to happen. All idolatry requires is a sinful heart that places someone or something above God. Some people love money or power or physical beauty or their reputation above all other things, including the Lord. Anytime we seek to find our identity and value in something other than God, we are committing idolatry.

Aaron Speaks

Moses was my younger brother by three years. And yet, I played second fiddle to him all my life. Everywhere I went, I was introduced as "Moses' brother." Living in his shadow was wearisome and frustrating. And sometimes I found myself growing angry and jealous.

My life choices weren't all that good either. You can read in Numbers 12 about the time I criticized Moses for marrying a woman from Ethiopia. Big mistake. And then I criticized his leadership, and that didn't go over well with God. In no uncertain terms, the Lord told me and my sister, Miriam, that He would not tolerate our criticism of His chosen leader.

Probably the worst was when Moses was on Mount Sinai receiving the Ten Commandments directly from God. He had been gone a long time, and the people began complaining and asking when or if Moses would return. In his absence, they demanded an idol to worship, like the Egyptians had. So they brought me their gold, and I built them a golden calf. When Moses returned from the mountain, he took one look and . . . well, I had seen my brother angry before, but not like this. God was very unhappy too.

Yet in spite of my foolishness, my jealousy, and my weakness, the Lord called me into ministry. Previously, God had called me to be a spokesman for Moses. Now God called me to be a spokesman for *Him*. He made me his high priest! I thought God had no time for someone like me, but was I ever wrong!

Do you sometimes think you are a failure? That you're beyond forgiveness? No one is beyond God's help and healing. I speak from experience, for I witnessed His great love in my life. If God could use me, He can certainly use you. What are you waiting for? Ask Him.

Prayer

Dear Heavenly Father,

You have set me free from the slavery of sin, and I am forever grateful for the sacrifice of Your Son that made this possible. But like the Israelites, I sometimes complain and wander and return to my old, sinful ways. Please remove my desire to enjoy the pleasures of sin for a season and remind me that in Your right hand there are pleasures forevermore!

Help me to walk in Your ways, enjoy freedom from sin, and desire to be in Your presence every moment of every day. Help me to remember everything You have done for me. May I never forget that You are the one and only God.

In Jesus' name. Amen.

Lesson 7

The Law, the Tabernacle, Offerings & Feasts

Motions	Passage
11. Law	Exodus 20:3–17
12. Tabernacle	Exodus 25–27
13. Offerings–Feasts	Leviticus

Take it To Heart

"Speak to all the congregation of the people of Israel and say to them, You shall be holy, for I the Lord your God am holy."
Leviticus 19:2

Moses went to the top of Mount Sinai to meet with God, and it was there that God gave him the Ten Commandments, as we discussed in the video. Additionally, God gave Moses instructions regarding the construction of the tabernacle.

Do you know what *foreshadowing* is? Foreshadowing is a device that writers use to give a hint of what is coming later in the story. Sometimes an author presents information in passing that will later become significant and central to the story. It's often easy to miss the significance of certain details until later, when one of those "ah-hah" moments happens and suddenly it all makes sense. Today we're going to discuss an example of foreshadowing in the Bible.

The Bible is made up of sixty-six books written by forty different authors over a span of about 2,000 years. The word *Bible* comes from a Greek word meaning "book," covers a variety of topics, people, and events that took place over a wide range of locations. Yet the Bible all comes down to one central theme—a theme that is woven through every word of Scripture. The one and only God, sovereign Creator of the universe, is the true author of this masterpiece, the story of His love for mankind, and His central character is Jesus Christ.

Every book of the Scriptures points to Christ. Although Jesus doesn't appear in human nature until the New Testament, His life and His sacrifice are at the center of the story and its ultimate meaning. Throughout the Old Testament, we catch glimpses of Him. Adam, Noah's ark, Joseph, Moses, the Passover lamb—all these point to Christ. And as we continue our journey through the

Old Testament, we will see many prophecies about the coming Messiah centuries before He is born in Bethlehem.

All of this brings us to the Tabernacle, an Old Testament structure that foreshadows a New Testament truth. Up to this point in the story, God has been without a dwelling place among His chosen people. The tabernacle, an elaborate tent built according to God's own design, will serve as a portable dwelling place for the Lord until the Israelites settle in Canaan. Later, in the New Testament, God will dwell with mankind in the form of Jesus, who will also be known as Immanuel, a Hebrew name that means "God with us."

The design and building of the tabernacle can be found in Exodus 25–27. It's amazing how specific God was in His planning. Like the plans He gave to Noah regarding the ark and its dimensions, the details God provides for the tabernacle are precise—its measurements, the materials to be used in its construction, the design of the engravings, the colors in the tapestries, and much more.

Our God is a God of detail. He cares about particulars that you and I may not even notice. The rings that held up the curtains, the oil for the lamps, the poles for carrying the ark—all of it mattered. Each of the items to be placed in the tabernacle had a purpose and symbolized an aspect of worship or the character of God. Many people think only the big things matter, that the little things aren't that important. We tend to believe that if we focus on the big stuff, we can neglect the small stuff. But that's not true. There is nothing about us that God doesn't know. There is nothing He doesn't care about, nothing that He can't redeem. Besides, those small things add up to become big things.

The tabernacle was divided into three areas: a courtyard, which was open to all; the holy place, where the priests served daily; and the Holy of Holies, where the high priest went once a year. The courtyard was where the people came to offer their sacrifices. The holy place was where the priests sprinkled the blood from the sacrifices, offered incense, and kept the lampstand burning. The Holy of Holies was where the ark of the covenant was kept. The presence of God dwelled there, between the wings of the cherubim atop the ark. God explained all of this to Moses on Mount Sinai.

Meanwhile, back at base camp, the people of Israel were growing impatient and restless. In fact, they started to long for the homes they left back in Egypt, forgetting the centuries of bondage they

endured there. They also seemed to forget how God had raised up a deliverer and brought them out of slavery, how He had allowed them to plunder the wealth of Egypt, how He had parted the Red Sea and destroyed the armies of Pharaoh, and how He had miraculously provided water and manna in the wilderness.

Instead, the people went to Moses' brother, Aaron, and demanded that he make them an idol to worship. Unbelievably, Aaron agreed to their request. He collected their gold earrings and other jewelry and used the gold to fashion a golden calf for the people to worship. This was the scene that Moses found when he came down from the mountain, bringing with him the two stone tablets on which the Lord had inscribed His commandments. In his anger, Moses threw down the tablets and broke them. Then Moses destroyed the golden calf that Aaron had made and ground it to powder.

Moses asked the Lord to forgive the children of Israel, and shortly after these events, God renewed His covenant with them. In Exodus 34, He gives the law to Moses once more on two new tablets that Moses carved out for this purpose. Now it was time to build the tabernacle for the Lord.

The first step was to raise a contribution for the building. Sound familiar? Today, many churches begin their building campaigns with a fundraiser. This was the original building fund. Moses put out the call, as the Lord commanded him, and the people brought everything needed for the building of the tabernacle and the construction of its furnishings—gold and silver and bronze, yarns and linen, fine animal skins, acacia wood, oil and spices, and precious stones. Later, the people were told to stop bringing contributions because they had enough. Can you imagine a situation today in which a ministry actually had to send out an e-mail asking people to stop giving because they had already given more than enough?

After construction was completed, the tabernacle was dedicated and the priests consecrated for serving God. Then a cloud settled upon the tent of meeting, "and the glory of the LORD filled the tabernacle" (Exodus 40:34). What a sight that must have been!

God's story continues in Leviticus, in which the tribe of Levi is set apart to serve as priests. Here the Lord also establishes various offerings, some that are required and others that are voluntary. He also institutes the feasts—times set aside for His people to commemorate and celebrate the Lord's goodness. Here again we read of God's lovingkindness, His desire to fellowship with us, and His invitation for us to participate in His story.

PSALM AND PROVERB TO READ:
Psalm 19, Proverbs 7:1–4

MAGIC

When the Bible warns against magic, as in Deuteronomy 18:11–12, it isn't talking about someone pulling a rabbit out of a hat or escaping from handcuffs. That's a kind of entertainment in which someone pretends to have astounding abilities, but the audience knows the magician is just pretending. Although it is a form of deception, it's no different from special visual effects in movies that make impossible things appear to happen.

The kind of magic warned of in the Scriptures is done by a "wise man" or sorcerer who tries to control events or people through the use of supernatural power. The power used to work their "miracles" is demonic, whether or not the sorcerer acknowledges that fact. And even though their signs and wonders might truly be amazing, they are used to deceive people and turn them from the one true God to worship a false god instead.

For example, when Moses and Aaron went before Pharaoh and performed miracles to prove they spoke for God, Pharaoh's magicians made their staffs turn into serpents too. They did this to show that their pagan gods were just as worthy of worship as the God proclaimed by Moses. But do you remember what happened next? The snake that had been Aaron's staff swallowed the snakes of the magicians, proving the God of the Hebrews was the one true God.

LET'S TALK ABOUT IT

1. Why did God give a list of commandments to His people? How were these commandments supposed to help them love God?
2. What was the purpose of the tabernacle? What is it about the tabernacle that should make us think about Jesus?
3. Where did the Israelites get all the gold and supplies to build the tabernacle? What does this tell you about the wisdom of God's plans?
4. What kind of skilled craftsmen were used to build and decorate the Tabernacle?
5. God created the world, and we are created in His image. How can we be creative for His glory?

Worship

Worshiping God means to give Him glory, honor, and praise. It is a way of saying that God is worthy of being the focus and foundation of every part of our lives, including our thoughts, actions, and words. Of course, everything we do should bring God glory, but most of the time "worship" refers to a dedicated time of glorifying God in His presence. Very often we worship with other believers so that we may offer praise together and encourage each other as we do so.

Even though God wants us to worship Him, we cannot do it in any way we choose. God has revealed the ways He wants to be worshiped, and not all worship is acceptable to Him. In fact, it is only through Jesus Christ that we can stand before God and offer worship that is pleasing to Him.

Although it's true that God wants us to worship Him, that doesn't mean God *needs* us to worship Him. God is perfect and does not need anything, and He doesn't gain anything from our worship that He didn't already have. He is the same whether we worship Him or not. However, because God has been so merciful toward us, so gracious and loving, it is only right and proper that we should worship Him with praise and thanksgiving.

Joshua Speaks

My father had an odd name, but he gave me a wonderful name. I am Joshua son of Nun. I was born during the years of bondage to Egypt. My name was significant to an enslaved people because it meant "Yahweh is salvation." My Hebrew name, Yehoshua, was shortened to Yeshua. This same name would be given many centuries later to a poor child who would draw all men to Him and save them from their sins. You know that child better by the English translation of the Greek version of His name: Jesus.

Soon after the Israelites were set free from their Egyptian chains, Moses chose me to be commander of the Israelite army. Years later, God appointed me to be leader of the Hebrew nation upon the death of Moses.

As commander of the army, I repulsed an Amalekite attack and proved myself a worthy warrior, earning the confidence and support of the people. When twelve men were selected by Moses to spy out the land of Canaan, I was chosen to represent the tribe of Ephraim.

Upon returning from our mission in enemy territory, ten of the twelve spies were terrified by what they had seen, saying, "The land is inhabited by giants, and we are nothing but grasshoppers in their presence." Only Caleb and I spoke with faith, knowing the Lord would fight for His people. The ten spoke of giants, but the two of us spoke of God.

Sadly, the people sided with the ten and attempted to stone me and Caleb for trying to get them killed. Because of their faithlessness, God proclaimed that none of their generation would ever enter the land that had been promised to their fathers. Only Caleb and I would live to see this land, take possession of it, and reap the many promises of God.

Prayer

Dear Heavenly Father,

You are faithful! You love me and are kind to me even when I have not been faithful to You. Your lovingkindness reaches above the heavens, to all generations, and goes on forever! Thank You, Father, for the promise of heaven. You promised Your chosen people a land flowing with milk and honey. You wanted to bless them beyond what they could ever ask or imagine, to provide for their every need. But they doubted You and feared their enemies. They did not trust You to do what You said You would do. Even though You showed Yourself mighty with ten plagues and brought the Israelites safely through the Red Sea, they forgot.

Father, help me to never doubt You. Do not let me forget Your wonderful deeds. Remind me every day of all You have done in creation and in my life. I know You are my Deliverer, my Savior, and my Redeemer. Help me to trust only in You and worship You alone. No idols or golden calves for me!

In Jesus' name. Amen.

Lesson 8

Spying, Dying, Second Law

Motions

14. Counting–Spying
15. Wandering–Dying
16. Second Law

Passage

Numbers 1, 13–14
Deuteronomy

Take it To Heart

"Send men to spy out the land of Canaan, which I am giving to the people of Israel. From each tribe of their fathers you shall send a man, every one a chief among them."
Numbers 13:2

Have you ever been sent to the corner for a time-out? A time-out is a quiet period for calming down and thinking about your misbehavior. Taking a time-out can also be a good way to pause, calm down, and consider the situation more objectively before taking action.

I once took my sons on a field trip to a police station. Seeing the officers in their uniforms with their badges, tasers, and guns caused my high-energy boys to be on their best behavior. One of the officers showed us a holding cell and allowed the boys to go inside and look around. A holding cell is where police temporarily keep people who are suspected of having broken the law. It's a kind of waiting room where arrested persons stay until they can be further questioned or processed.

A holding cell is kind of like an adult time-out. Did you know there are time-outs for adults? Sometimes God sends adults to a time-out to think through a situation, understand our disobedience, and recognize God's faithfulness, His love, and His grace. He once sent the Hebrew people to a time-out for forty years! But instead of a holding cell, the children of Israel wandered in the wilderness all that time.

Why were the Israelites sent into a forty-year "time-out"? Because of their disbelief.

In the time since the people left Egypt, God had provided for every one of their needs. The Lord personally guided them by day, appearing as a pillar of cloud, and by night, when He appeared as a pillar of fire. When the pursuing Egyptian army trapped the people with their backs to the sea, God parted the waters of the Red Sea so the people could cross to the other side on dry land, and then He drowned the Egyptians when they attempted to cross the dry seabed.

When the Hebrews hungered, God provided them manna from heaven for food. When they thirsted, He provided them water. When they fashioned for themselves a golden calf to worship, God showed them compassion and mercy and did not abandon them to their sin. He also made it so that the people's shoes and clothes did not wear out the whole time they were in the wilderness! God took good care of His people, even though they were often stubborn and disobedient.

The Israelites had seen God's power that delivered them from bondage. They had heard His thundering voice on the mountain as He gave His laws to Moses. They had seen His faithfulness and provision in the wilderness. Nevertheless, the people did not believe when God said He would give the Promised Land into their hands, and this unbelief cost them dearly.

When Moses sent twelve spies to scout out the land of Canaan and report their findings, two of the spies, Joshua and Caleb, called it "an exceedingly good land" and said, "If the LORD delights in us, he will bring us into this land and give it to us, a land that flows with milk and honey" (Numbers 14:8). They believed that if God was on their side, no one could stand against the armies of Israel. Unfortunately, not everyone felt this way.

Ten of the spies reported seeing giants in the land and said, "We are not able to go up against the people, for they are stronger than we are." They also claimed that Canaan was "a land that devours its inhabitants" (Numbers 13:31–32). After hearing this news, the people of Israel wept all night. The next day, they rebelled against Moses and tried to stone Joshua and Caleb for trying to get them all killed.

God was furious at their disbelief, but Moses prayed for the people and asked the Lord to forgive them once more. The Lord agreed to forgive their sin, but He declared that none of this generation of men would ever again see Canaan, except for Joshua and Caleb because they had spoken in faith. Instead of entering the land promised to their forefathers, the faithless generation of Israel would wander the wilderness for forty long years until everyone twenty-one years or older had died.

During the next forty years, the people had time to think about all that God had done for them, how faithful He had always been. Indeed, God continued providing for all their needs despite their disobedience and unbelief. I'm sure the Israelites wished they had trusted Him more, that they had feared God more than they had feared men.

The important lesson here is that there are consequences for our lack of trust and obedience. Do you ever doubt God's promises? Do you fear the insults and threats of unbelievers more than you respect and love God? Where you stand will be revealed in the choices you make and how you live each day. If you are focused on God and His Word, if you obey His commands and stand firm in your faith, if you are content in every circumstance, then your actions will show that you trust God and love Him.

Sadly, however, we are too easily worried by money problems, job issues, relationship turmoil, political conflicts, weather trends, and unknown future challenges. We grumble and complain. We trade insults with others. We give in to temptation. We forget all that God has done in our lives. We begin to question the truth of His Word. Such actions reflect our disbelief and lack of trust in God.

If you find yourself in a place where you have not been trusting God, stop and repent. Turn from your disbelief and give Him your whole heart once more. Rededicate yourself to His Word and His ways and choose to be content in every circumstance.

God is always faithful to receive and restore those who return to Him. Late in his life, after the unbelieving generation had passed away, Moses counted the people of Israel once more and found just about the same number of fighting men that had left Egypt forty years earlier. God had preserved His people during their time-out.

Moses would now give the Law to the new generation, just as he had given it to their parents. We refer to this as the "second law," because it's the second time Moses gave the law to God's people.

In the book of Deuteronomy, as he was about to pass the baton of leadership to Joshua, Moses presented three sermons in which he pleaded with the people to remember and obey. He urged them to choose life and not death, blessing and not cursing. He implored them to listen to the commands of the Lord and follow them always.

It's important to recognize that Moses himself wasn't allowed to enter the Promised Land because of his own disobedience. This is another example of foreshadowing in the Old Testament. God's grace in Christ alone can lead us to the gates of heaven and into our Promised Land. God allowed Moses to see the land but not cross over into it, and Moses died on the mountain at the age of 120.

PSALM AND PROVERB TO READ:
Psalm 90, Proverbs 8:33

MANNA

You probably eat a few different kinds of food each day. But how would you like to eat the same food day after day after day? As you have learned, the Israelites wandered in the wilderness for forty years because they disobeyed God. Nevertheless, God provided them food each day of those forty years.

He sent them manna in the morning and quail to eat in the evening. Each morning a layer of dew appeared on the ground. When the dew was gone, thin flakes appeared on the desert floor like frost on a cold morning. The Lord commanded each person to collect an omer (a little more than two quarts) of manna each day. Any manna that was not eaten that day spoiled and smelled terrible. God wanted the Israelites to trust Him to provide for their needs every day. On the sixth day of the week, each person in the family gathered *two* omers of manna so they would have food for the Sabbath day when they were not allowed to work or gather.

Families baked or boiled the manna, which was white like coriander seeds and tasted like wafers made with honey. This recipe will give you an idea of how manna might have tasted:

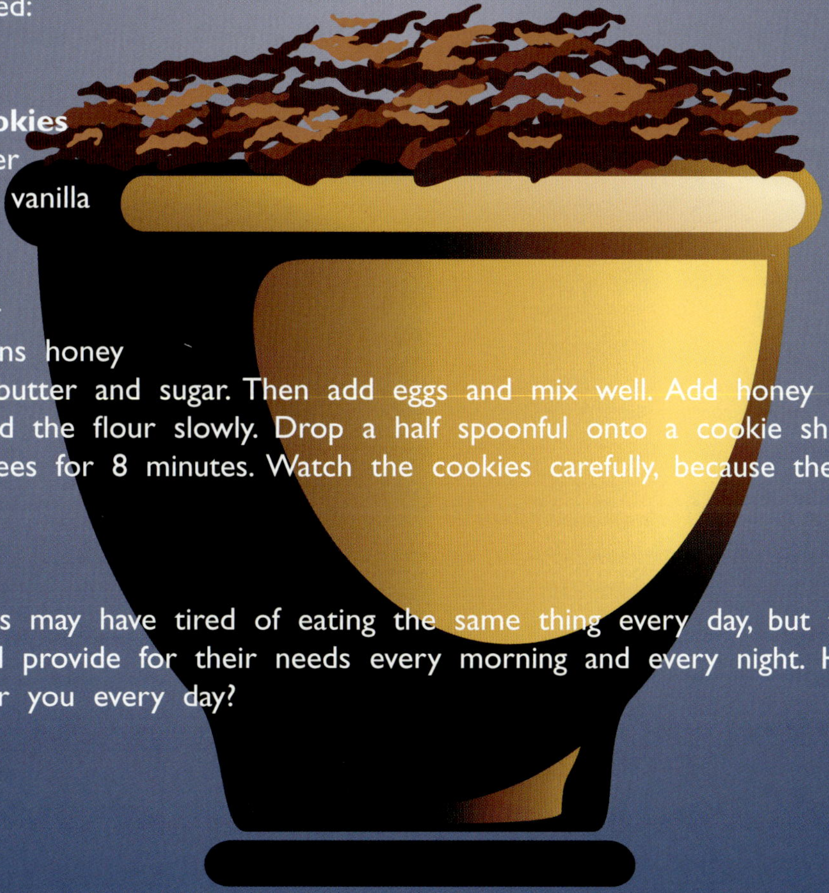

Manna Cookies

½ cup butter
½ teaspoon vanilla
1 cup sugar
2 eggs
2 cups flour
2–3 teaspoons honey

Cream the butter and sugar. Then add eggs and mix well. Add honey and vanilla, and then add the flour slowly. Drop a half spoonful onto a cookie sheet and bake at 400 degrees for 8 minutes. Watch the cookies carefully, because they will burn quickly.

The Israelites may have tired of eating the same thing every day, but they learned that God would provide for their needs every morning and every night. How does God provide for you every day?

LET'S TALK ABOUT IT

1. What are some ways you can focus on God instead of on your problems?
2. Have you ever been given a time-out? If so, were you mad or were you sorry and repentant?
3. How do you feel when someone else, maybe a brother or sister, is being punished for their disobedience? What can you learn from other people's disobedience?
4. How do you feel when you see someone trust and obey without complaining or asking questions? Why?
5. If you were a parent, what would cause you to discipline one of your own children by sending him/her to a time-out?

the Sabbath day

The fourth of the Ten Commandments reads, "Observe the Sabbath day, to keep it holy, as the LORD your God commanded you. Six days you shall labor and do all your work, but the seventh day is a Sabbath to the LORD your God" (Deuteronomy 5:12–14).

After the six days of creation, God established a day of rest that He called the Sabbath. Even though the commandment to keep the Sabbath holy was not explicitly given until Moses received the law, the Sabbath had clearly been established from the beginning of creation as a day of rest to be set aside from the rest of the week for all time.

Isaiah 56:2 tells us, "Blessed is the man who does this, and the son of man who holds it fast, who keeps the Sabbath, not profaning it." The Sabbath is a blessing to us in several ways. The day of rest refreshes us physically, reminds us of God's sovereignty as we remember the six days of creation, allows time for moral and spiritual instruction, and acts as a sign of the covenant between God and His people.

After the resurrection of Jesus Christ, Christians began honoring the Sabbath on the first day of the week (Sunday) rather than the seventh day of the week (Saturday). This change reflected Jesus' teaching that He is the Lord of the Sabbath and that His resurrection marks the new creation. Just as the original creation was memorialized at its completion by the Sabbath day, the new creation is now memorialized by the Sabbath after the finished work of Christ.

Caleb Speaks

I was one of twelve spies sent by Moses on a reconnaissance mission behind enemy lines. One man was selected from each of the twelve tribes; I was chosen to represent the tribe of Judah. Our objective: Scout out the land of Canaan and report what we saw there to Moses and the people.

We entered this strange new land from the south, crossing the desert, passing through the hill country, and descending into the valley of Eschol. And for forty days we explored this land that God had promised to our forefathers. Then we returned to make our report.

All twelve of us saw the same things: a fertile land, vast harvests, and the descendants of Anak, who were a fierce, warlike people. They were huge, like giants in the land! But I knew our God was much bigger, and I said to the people, "Let's go at once to take the land. We can certainly conquer it!"

But ten of the spies disagreed with me. "Sure," they said, "the land flows with milk and honey. And the grapes, pomegranates, and figs are larger than any we've ever seen. But we can't go up against the people who live there! We are like grasshoppers compared to them. They are far stronger than our people, and we cannot hope to defeat them! The land will devour anyone among us who goes to live there."

The people trembled and wept as they listened to this, for their fear was greater than their faith. Looking into their faces, I watched as their dreams of the Promised Land died.

Joshua couldn't listen to any more of this faithless talk. He jumped up and tore his cloak, and I did the same. We told them the land we explored was wonderful and it was ours for the taking. If the Lord was pleased with us, His chosen people, He would lead our armies, and the oversized inhabitants of the land would be helpless before us.

Now I have a question for you. If you had been there that day, would you have stood with the majority, or would you have stood with Joshua and me? When someone ridicules your faith, do you have the courage to stand? I did! And God blessed me beyond my fondest dreams.

Prayer

Dear Heavenly Father,

As much as I don't like to be disciplined, I know that You love me enough to discipline me when I go astray. This reminds me that I am Your child. But You do so much more for me than I deserve. You bless me with healthy food, clothes, and a place to call home. God, help me to always trust You and obey You without complaining or delaying. Help me remember to always choose life instead of death, blessing instead of cursing. I know that Your ways are always best for me. I believe that You have prepared a place for me in heaven, and I look forward to spending eternity with You!

In Jesus' name, I pray. Amen.

Lesson 9

Joshua & the Twelve Tribes

Motions

17. Joshua
18. Divide–Conquer
19. Twelve Tribes

Passage

Joshua

Take it To Heart

Thus the Lord gave to Israel all the land that he swore to give to their fathers. And they took possession of it, and they settled there.
Joshua 21:43

When I was a kid, Follow the Leader and Simon Says were two of my favorite games. It was great fun doing goofy things like trying to hop on one leg while patting my head at the same time or rolling down a hill or playing leapfrog just because it's what Simon said. I remember laughing during these games. Of course, the actions we were imitating weren't supposed to make sense. There was no strategy involved. It was all about being silly and just having fun.

As we saw in the video, the people of Israel followed their leader, Joshua, across the Jordan River and into the Promised Land. They knew they would have to defeat the land's inhabitants, yet they didn't just sharpen their swords in preparation for battle. Instead, they obeyed God's unique battle plan to overthrow the walled city of Jericho. They trusted that He would show Himself mighty to their enemies.

Remember, these were the children of the generation that left Egypt. This new generation probably didn't remember much about their parents' experience in Egypt, but they all knew the stories of what had happened. Finally, after more than 400 years in bondage and another forty years wandering in the wilderness, God's people were standing in the land He had promised to Abraham.

Now the Canaanites, the people who lived in this land, worshiped idols. Do you know what an idol is? An idol is a false god, usually a statue that's been crafted to look like an animal or a person. Remember, we were made to worship. However, God created us to love and honor *Him*, not just whomever or whatever we want. But after sin entered the world, people began to worship things

other than God. That kind of worship is pointless because idols are only man-made objects that have no power.

Worshiping God is one way we acknowledge His power, goodness, and authority over our lives. As wonderful as God is, it seems silly to think we would worship anyone or anything else. And yet many people choose not to worship God because they refuse to recognize Him as their Creator and King who has every right to tell them how to live. Rebellious people don't want to obey God; they only want to obey their own selfish desires.

Remember what is at the core of sin. Look closely at the word. Do you see it? "I" is at the center of S-I-N. As people living in a fallen world, we don't like being told what to do. We would much rather do whatever we feel like doing. We don't want to exercise self-control, we don't want to think of others first, and we don't want to share or be kind or give up our rights. We want to be the master of our own universe. Satan uses these selfish desires to draw us away from worshiping God. Today, people worship all kinds of idols—money, possessions, power, fame, actors, singers, sports teams, and even ideas. An idol can be anything that is given an unhealthy place in a person's life.

God wants only what is best for us, and He knows we will suffer if we give something else first place in our lives ahead of Him. But when we are obedient to worship Him, when we lift up His holy name in joyous praise, we are putting ourselves in the safest possible place: under His authority.

Now back to our story. The number one obstacle for God's people in the Promised Land wouldn't turn out to be the massive walls of Jericho or the giants that had been reported by the faithless spies. No, the greatest challenge the Israelites would encounter in this land would be the idols of the people who lived there.

Because God made worship so central to who people are, He knew that His chosen people could be easily led astray into worshiping other gods. He knew that priests of Baal and Asherah, the false

gods of the Canaanites, would require sacrifices of the Hebrews' sons and daughters. He also knew that these so-called gods were utterly powerless and incapable of loving, protecting, and blessing His people.

So God warned the people against idolatry, saying, "You shall not make for yourself a carved image, or any likeness of anything that is in heaven above, or that is in the earth beneath, or that is in the water under the earth. You shall not bow down to them or serve them, for I the LORD your God am a jealous God" (Exodus 20:4–5). Nevertheless, the Israelites and their leaders would fall into the idolatry trap time and time again.

But that would come later. For now, this was a heady time for the descendants of Israel. The doubting generation had passed away, and God had anointed a new leader in the battle-tested Joshua. With the ark of the covenant going before them, the people marched into the Promised Land. God instructed them to drive the pagan nations and their false gods out of Canaan, so starting with the walled city of Jericho, the Israelites divided and conquered the land over the next seven years. First they conquered the southern half of Canaan, and then they conquered the north.

Once they had taken nearly all the land in Canaan, God told Joshua to cast lots to determine which part of the land would go to which tribe. You might notice that there remained a few unconquered territories in Canaan, such as the region of the Philistines, but God assured Joshua that the Israelites would be able to defeat their enemies as long as they were faithful to fight.

Two of the tribes of Israel, Reuben and Gad, had been given land to the east of the Jordan at their own request. The tribe of Manasseh, which descended from one of Joseph's two sons, was given a portion that straddled the Jordan, part to the east and part to the west of the river. Nine of the tribes—including that of Joseph's other son, Ephraim—each received a portion of the land west of the river in Canaan. Only the tribe of Levi was not given a portion of land, for the Lord God of

Israel was their portion.

Take some time and review the twelve tribes of Israel. How many of them can you name? There's a map in your notebooking journal of where each of the tribes was located in the Promised Land. You will want this information for future lessons.

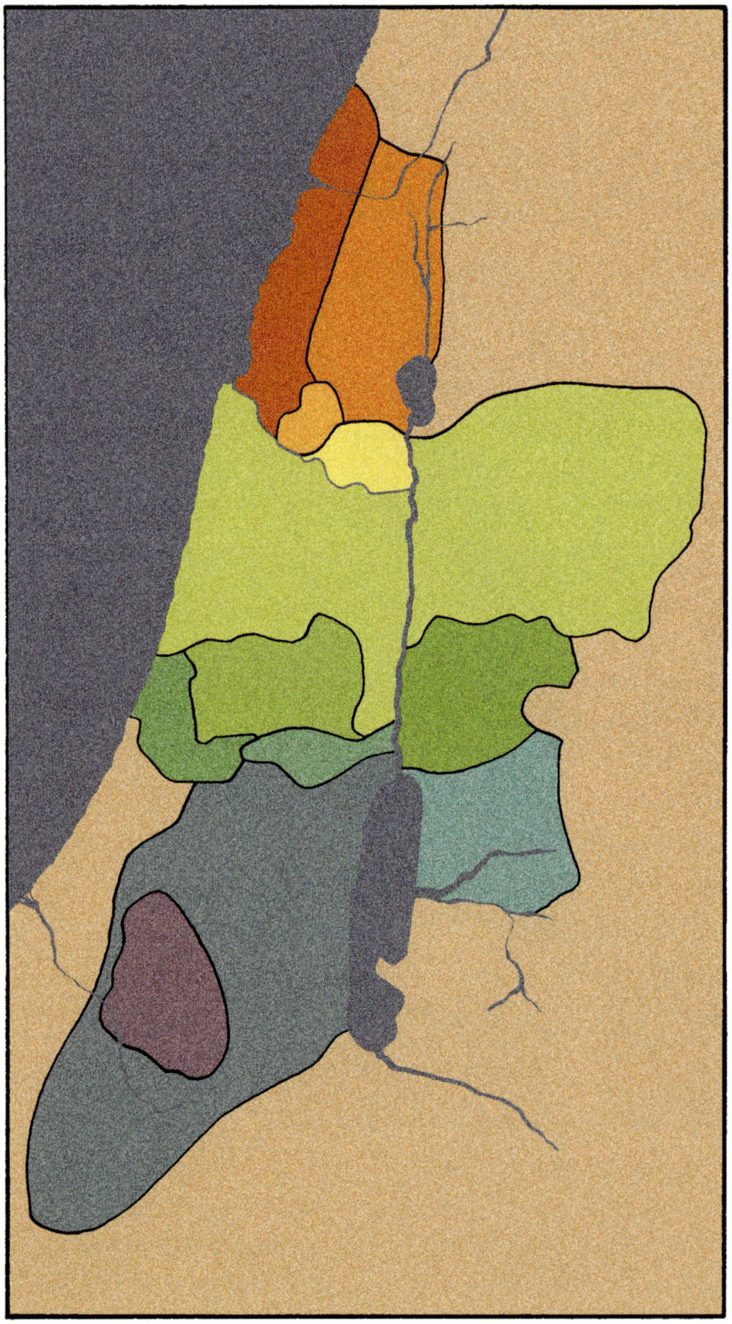

PSALM AND PROVERB TO READ:
Psalm 85, Proverbs 9:10

JERICHO

Why did the founders of your city choose its location? Many cities are built near a river, rich farmland, or a major highway.

Jericho, one of the oldest cities in the world, was centrally located in Canaan, with ideal access to trade routes between the neighboring city-states. Its natural protection included Mount Nebo to the east, the Central Mountains to the west, and the Dead Sea to the south. The Jordan River provided natural irrigation, and the underground tributaries from the Central Mountains created an oasis in the desert. Natural springs provided lush green vegetation, including a vast grove of palm trees. The double walls surrounding the city made it humanly impossible to enter other than by the gate. Jericho seemed to have everything it needed to flourish.

Yet Jericho was a wicked city. God does not look at outward appearances but at the hearts of people (1 Samuel 16:7). Jericho was beautiful on the outside, but inside it was home to idolatry, perversion, prostitution, and child sacrifice.

God wants and expects us to be filled with love, joy, peace, kindness, and compassion. What does He see in *your* heart?

LET'S TALK ABOUT IT

1. What was the significance of the ark of the covenant going across the Jordan River and into the Promised Land ahead of the Israelites?
2. Review God's battle plan for the city of Jericho. What are some reasons God wanted the Israelites to march around the city?
3. What is worship? What does it mean to worship something?
4. Do you give God first place in your life? You can know where your priorities are by making a list of your activities and how much time you spend on each one. So how do you spend your time?
5. What is an idol? It's easy to identify a statue like Buddha as an idol, but what are some other modern examples of idols? Are there any idols in your life?

Mercy

Mercy is when God shows compassion and is good to us even though we are unworthy of His goodness. There is nothing we can do to earn God's favor or deserve any good thing from God. The sinful nature each of us is born with affects every single part of our being so that we would never choose the things of God willingly. There is no good thing in us that makes us loveable to God in any way. We deserve only His wrath.

But God still chooses to love us, to call us out of our slavery to sin, and to make us His people. Instead of giving us justice, which would be to punish us for our sins, He shows us mercy by giving us salvation through the sacrifice of His Son, Jesus Christ. While we were still sinners and enemies of God, He became sin for us in order to save us (2 Corinthians 5:21). This amazing truth is mercy at its most powerful! It is only through God's mercy that we can be saved. Without it, we would be hopeless, left with God's moral law but without the ability to keep it perfectly.

We can share God's wonderful gift of mercy by showing compassion to others, by doing good to those who do not deserve it, even our enemies (Luke 6:27–36). But even this could never earn good standing with God. Instead, we do it because of what God has done for us. Show others mercy because it was given to you so richly.

Rahab Speaks

Early in life I made some bad choices. Really bad. When I look back on the lifestyle I chose for myself, I cringe. Mine was a godless generation in a land of iniquity, and my choices in life were a reflection of the times. Yet I have no one to blame for my sins but myself.

My home was a city called Jericho, in the land of Canaan, north of the Dead Sea. Jericho was a fortress with high, thick walls imposing to every pilgrim and impregnable by any army. At least, that's what we thought.

There had been much talk in the city of a nation now encamped on the eastern bank of the Jordan River. Their people followed a God who had shown Himself mighty on their behalf, drying up the waters of the Red Sea before them when they came out of Egypt. He delivered into their hands the Amorite kings Sihon and Og, whom they utterly destroyed. Now we heard that God had given them the land of Canaan as their inheritance, and we trembled in fear, for this God was indeed Lord in heaven above and on earth below.

One day, two spies from this nation slipped unnoticed into our city, though word of their presence spread quickly. Every citizen and soldier was put on alert, so the spies went into hiding, and of all places they chose my house. I knew the Lord had given them the land and Jericho could not withstand their God, so I took them up to the roof and hid them under stalks of flax I had set out to dry. When darkness fell, I let them down by a rope through the window, for my house was part of the city wall. In return, they promised to spare my family if I would remain silent about their mission and tie a scarlet cord in the window to mark my house as one to be spared.

Several days passed and, at first, nothing happened. The gates remained locked and the city secure. Then early one morning I awakened to cries of an army approaching from the east. But the Israelites did not attack. Instead, for the next six days, once a day, they marched silently around the city while the priests of the Lord sounded seven trumpets. The citizens of Jericho could only laugh, mocking the Israelites from atop the high walls.

Then on the seventh day, they marched around the city seven times, and on the seventh time the priests sounded a single long blast from the trumpets and the people of Israel gave a loud shout. Then the walls of Jericho came tumbling down!

I thank the God of Israel for sparing my life and my family. I had no idea I would play such an important part in the history of God's people. I'm humbled to know that my name actually made it into the genealogy of the promised Messiah.

Prayer

Dear Heavenly Father,

You alone are worthy of my devotion and worship. All other gods are false. You are the only God who exists. I know I shouldn't have idols in my life, so help me to keep my thoughts and desires centered on You alone.

When I think of all that You have done throughout history, I see that You have a plan for Your people. As one of Your beloved children, I want to stick close to You, listen to Your word, obey You without hesitation, and enjoy the blessings that come from a life in tune with Your will. Today and forever, help me to serve You, follow You, and love You!

In Jesus' name, I pray. Amen.

Lesson 10

Judges & Ruth

Motions

20. Judges
21. Deborah
22. Gideon
23. Samson
24. Everyone Did What Was Right in His Own Eyes Except Ruth and…

Passage

Judges 2, 4–8, 13–16, and 21:25
Ruth

Take it To Heart

Then the Lord raised up judges, who saved them out of the hand of those who plundered them.
Judges 2:16

We introduced the judges and discussed Deborah in this week's video. The events of Judges are a study of comparisons and contrasts to the story of God and His people to this point. For example, Gideon's story contains echoes of the stories of the call of Moses and of Joshua and the fall of Jericho. Where does God find Gideon when we first meet him in Judges 6? When the angel of the Lord appears, Gideon is threshing wheat in a winepress so that he is unseen by Israel's oppressors, the Midianites. He is farming, not fighting, and hiding the fruits of his labor at that. Nevertheless, the angel addresses Gideon as though he is a great warrior: "The Lord is with you, O mighty man of valor."

You might remember that Moses had run away from Egypt and was herding sheep in Midian when the Lord first appeared to him from the burning bush. Gideon is called to deliver Israel from the hand of the Midianites, much as Moses was called to deliver Israel from bondage in Egypt. Gideon questions and tests the Lord because he thinks God is talking to the wrong guy, much as Moses protested his lack of speaking skills and tried to talk his way out of the assignment.

Much as Joshua and the Israelites took Jericho not by fighting but by marching in circles, shouting, and playing a mean trumpet, Gideon is told to defeat the Midianites in battle by taking with him *far* fewer men of Israel than were willing to fight. He starts with 32,000 volunteers (some more reluctant than others) but ends up going into battle with just 300 men against a host of Midianites numbering tens of thousands! And instead of equipping his army with the finest swords and shields, Gideon is told to outfit his men with trumpets, torches, and empty jars!

By now you're probably noticing something unusual about how God chooses to move in the lives of His people. In Isaiah 55:8–9, God says that His ways are not our ways. His attack plan for the city of Jericho was certainly unusual. We don't know for certain whether the people behind the walls were scared or humored by the Israelites' silent marching. The people of Jericho may have been afraid because it was so odd, maybe even a little eerie, and yet it had to have seemed silly that the Israelites were marching around the city instead of building a siege ramp.

The battle plans of both Joshua and Gideon are excellent examples of how God doesn't do things in a way that we might feel comfortable doing them. Instead, God characteristically does things in a way in which He alone gets the glory. His plans often don't make any earthly sense, so that when He moves, when He answers prayer, when He intervenes in our circumstances, He does so in such a way that the overwhelmingly positive results can *only* be explained by His divine intervention. When things seem impossible, the odds insurmountable, the obstacles overwhelming, God shows up and shows off! Praise the Lord!

You can always count on Him to act on your behalf, but you must not insist that His actions make sense to you. God isn't obligated to explain Himself or His ways to you, me, or any of us. He's God and we're not, and it's that simple. And once we accept this order of things, we no longer have to fret or panic or worry. Rather, He invites us to simply rest in Him, trust Him, worship Him, and join Him in what He is already doing. Oh, and if He ever tells you to take up the trumpet, just do it.

Another pattern we see develop in the book of Judges is notable and worthy of discussion. It's easy sometimes to read the Scriptures and want to criticize the choices God's people made so long ago, but the sad truth is that we make many of the same bad choices. This pattern begins with **sin**, which leads to **servitude**. Israel then cries out to God in **supplication**, and God sends **salvation** in the form of a judge. There is a period of **silence** until the next sin begins, and the cycle repeats. Over the course of three centuries, Israel repeated this cycle a total of seven times.

Consider Samson, a truly tragic character. Like Isaac, Samson's birth was promised and foretold

by an angel (Judges 13). This happens only four times in the Bible, twice in the Old Testament and twice in the New Testament. Not only was Samson's birth promised, but his parents were required to raise him in an unusual way, as a Nazarite. His life was to be dedicated to God even while in his mother's womb. This meant that his hair was never to be cut, nor was he to eat or drink of anything made from grapes (wine, for example). Nor was he to eat anything unclean, as defined in the law of Moses. What was the big deal about this child? The angel of the Lord said that he would take the lead in delivering the Israelites from the hands of the Philistines.

There is every indication that his parents did as the angel instructed them, but despite their best intentions, Samson was willfully stubborn and reckless. He also allowed his arrogance and pride to get the best of him at times. Although physically strong and gifted by God, he failed to use his talents for God's glory. And he had a weakness for women, which ultimately led to his capture and enslavement by the same Philistines he was sent to defeat. Nevertheless, God used Samson to destroy Israel's enemies.

Samson is one of the Bible's good examples of a bad example. In other words, Samson did not act in a way that we should seek to imitate. Quite the opposite, in fact. We need to study Samson's life because it is a profound lesson in what not to do. It's the tragic tale of a man who squandered God's gift. God made Samson strong—unusually so. But instead of using God's gift for God's glory, Samson used this blessing for his own selfish purposes.

Samson allowed himself to be ruled by anger, revenge, and lust, and these weaknesses eventually led to his downfall. Aggravated by his strength and arrogance, his enemies, the Philistines, persuaded a woman named Delilah to manipulate Samson into revealing the secret of his strength. It's strange to read how Delilah pouted and whined to get Samson to tell her his secret. It's even stranger that he fell prey to her trap and allowed himself to be captured, blinded, and enslaved.

Although we often think of him as a hero in the end, Samson's was a life selfishly wasted. Nevertheless, he did fulfill the prophecy that he would begin to deliver Israel from the Philistines. Samson didn't choose to honor God, but God still used him to destroy the Philistine rulers.

During much of the period covered in Judges, the nation of Israel seems to be in free fall. God's people have lost their way. They have abandoned their love of God and no longer seek or serve Him. It's as though they're adrift at sea.

This brings us to one final contrast. Enter the story of Ruth. During the time of the Judges, at one of those points in the cycle when the Israelites were reaping the consequences of their disastrous choices, there was a famine so severe that at least one family decided to flee the Promised Land in search of food. Elimelech took his wife, Naomi, and their two sons and went to Moab.

So begins the story of a woman whose life becomes a shining example of good. Ruth and Orpha, both Moabites, become the wives of Elimelech's two sons. Then tragedy strikes and all three of the men die. Despair overcomes Naomi. With her husband and two sons dead, she decides to return to her homeland, to a familiar place.

She asks her two daughters-in-law to return to their families. Orpha complies, but Ruth is determined to stand by Naomi. Her resolute statement of loyalty found in Ruth 1:16–17 is often quoted at weddings. Ruth chooses to serve Naomi, and so the two make the difficult journey to Canaan together. Upon arriving back in Bethlehem, Naomi's grief lingers and she asks to be called by a new name, Mara, which means "bitter."

Ruth continues to serve her mother-in-law faithfully, going out to find food by gleaning in the fields. Gleaning was a custom among the poor. They would walk behind the hired harvesters to gather the precious bits and pieces that remained for their own tables. Gleaners were often widows, the elderly, and those who had no other means of supporting themselves. In fact, the law of Moses commanded landowners to intentionally leave portions of their fields unharvested to provide for the poor in this way (Leviticus 23:22).

We have seen over and over how God is sovereign and in control of all things, and Ruth's story is a beautiful example. Ruth sets out to glean in any field that will have her, but she soon finds herself gleaning in Boaz's field. As it happens, Boaz is the next of kin to Naomi and, therefore, Ruth. Talk about a love story! Boaz sees Ruth across a barley field ripe for harvest, her face flushed from her work and her hands full of grain, but Boaz is stricken and immediately asks the foreman who she might be. He recognizes her name and her story, and he invites her to remain in his fields and eat at his table and blesses her for her loyalty to Naomi. He even orders his workers to intentionally drop some barley as they harvest so that Ruth can gather some for her mother-in-law with a minimum of effort.

The long and short of it is that Naomi later advises Ruth exactly what to do so that Boaz will realize his role as her kinsman and redeemer and choose to marry Ruth. And they do get married, a Moabite woman and an Israelite man. And it is through their family line that the great king David will be born and, eventually, Jesus the Eternal King. Ruth is one of just five women named in the lineage of Christ.

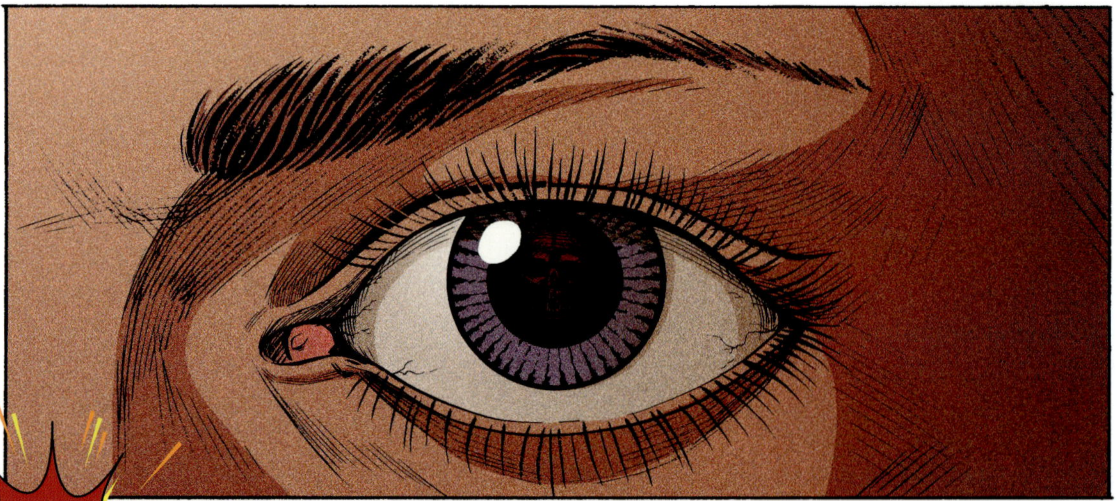

PSALM AND PROVERB TO READ:
Psalm 46, Proverbs 10:19

BARLEY HARVEST

Israel had seasons for harvesting a variety of crops. Harvesting means to gather a crop from the field once it has ripened. The summer harvest included grapes, dates, figs, and pomegranates, whereas olives were harvested in the fall.

The barley harvest plays a key role in the story of Ruth and Boaz. A chewy grain with a slightly nutty flavor, barley was a staple of the people in Bible times and was most often used to make bread. John 6:9–13 tells the story of a little boy who had five small barley loaves and two small fish. Jesus blessed the barley loaves and fish and used it to feed 5,000 men and their families, with twelve baskets of leftovers!

Barley, which tolerated harsh growing conditions, was planted in the fall and harvested in the spring. Because the barley ripened before the wheat, it was harvested first. Newly harvested grain could not be eaten until the first fruits of the grain had been offered as a sacrifice for the Jewish festival of unleavened bread. Since barley ripened before the wheat, the offering for the festival of unleavened bread was barley.

Barley continues to be an important crop in many parts of the world because it can grow in several different climates, from the Arctic Circle to tropical climes. Today, we know that barley is good for improving digestion, lowering cholesterol levels, and keeping a healthy heart. It is most often used in soups or stews today and not for making bread as in biblical times.

LET'S TALK ABOUT IT

1. Deborah is an excellent example of a strong woman doing God's will. What other examples of strong women honoring God in word and deed can you think of?
2. Where was Gideon hiding when the Lord came to him? How do you see Gideon change from the beginning of the story to the end?
3. In what ways did Samson cooperate with God's will? Why can we say he was a strong-weak man?
4. What are some ways Ruth served Naomi? How did God use Ruth? How did God bless her?
5. How does anyone forget God and start doing whatever evil they want to do?

SIGNS

A *sign* is another word for "miracle," which is when God acts in an unusual way to reveal something. There are several places in Scripture when people ask God for a sign that will guide them in making an important decision. Sometimes the people asking already have faith. Other times, unbelievers are asking to see a sign before they choose to believe (though many of these same people would find a reason *not* to believe a sign if they saw one).

Asking for a sign is a way of testing God, which is something He commands us not to do. In Deuteronomy 16:6, He says, "You shall not put the LORD your God to the test." Jesus quoted this verse when Satan tempted Him to prove that He was the Son of God. When the Pharisees asked Jesus for a sign, He rebuked them. When King Herod questioned Jesus, hoping to see one of His famous miracles, Jesus refused to answer him.

And yet, sometimes in the Bible, believers asked for a sign and God gave it to them. One of the most famous examples is when Gideon asked God to reveal His will—not once, but twice!—by leaving a fleece out all night and to be made wet or dry come morning. God could have rebuked Gideon and still required him to do what God commanded, but instead He gave Gideon a sign. Twice!

It is easy—and tempting—to want to do what Gideon did, but that is not how we are called to live. When God opens up an opportunity for you, you should pray for discernment so that you make a wise decision, but you don't need to ask for a fleece. God's response to Gideon was the exception, not the rule.

Gideon Speaks

The sun rose gently across the landscape. Already, little puffs of dust moved across the landscape as a reminder that the rains were scarce and every harvest was precious. The smoke from distant villages reminded me the Midianites were back. This time they had brought friends, a blood-thirsty horde who came wreaking havoc and pain on God's people. They destroyed our crops and took our livestock, reducing us to starvation.

Like frightened sheep fleeing a lion, we sought refuge in the hills and any dark hole we could find. Peering out from my own hiding place, a broken-down winepress, on this morning I spotted a visitor approaching in the distance. This stranger moved like one on a mission; this was not a social call. I went out to confront him, and he paused, glanced at me, then sat down under an oak tree. Only then did he speak. He brought a message from God: Somebody had to do something about the Midianites, and that someone was to be me—Gideon.

The stranger began by addressing me as a valiant warrior. What a joke! Warriors don't hide in winepresses when the enemy is at the gate. Besides, I was young and had no sword. I bore no hard-won scars as evidence of my courage and sacrifice. What battles had I fought? Where were my trophies of war? Yet the stranger insisted, "Go save Israel."

It took some convincing, but I finally yielded. Following the Lord's commands, I faced the enemy hordes with only a handful of men. We were outmanned, outmatched, and outclassed. But we had a secret weapon: the God of Israel. My little band of faithful men crushed the enemy, though armed with little more than kazoos and flashlights. God gave us the victory!

Today, the Lord still uses individuals and families and nations who put their trust in Him. If God calls you to go to battle for Him, will you go? Remember, as Moses taught my people, He goes before you (Deuteronomy 31:8).

Prayer

Dear Heavenly Father,

You made me to do good things for Your glory. I want to dedicate my life to fulfilling Your specific plans for me. Help me to always follow You, obey Your commandments, and enjoy sweet fellowship with You. I know You will give me everything I need to accomplish any task You give me, now and in the future. Help me to always be ready to say yes to You and be humble along the way. Please give me strength, confidence, courage, and perseverance for the battles that undoubtedly await me. But remind me that You are by my side and will never leave me nor forsake me.

In Jesus' name. Amen.

Lesson 11

SAMUEL & SAUL

Motions

25. Samuel
26. United Kingdom
27 Saul–No Heart

Passage

1 Samuel 3:4 and 8–31

Take it To Heart

And the LORD came and stood, calling as at other times, "Samuel! Samuel!" And Samuel said, "Speak, for your servant hears."
1 Samuel 3:10

Just the other day I was in Target when childish demands interrupted my peaceful shopping experience. A couple of aisles over from me a toddler was screaming, trying her best to manipulate her mom. She wanted the sugary cereal, not the healthier alternative that mom had placed in the cart. She wanted the one with the cute cartoon she'd seen on television, and she didn't care who knew it!

Bless her heart, the mom—in contrast to her daughter—spoke in low tones, trying to negotiate a deal with as little attention as possible. But the little rebel, her diplomatic skills being less developed, refused to engage in hushed whispers. Compromise wasn't her goal. She wasn't interested in hearing about the negative side effects her preferred choice could have on her teeth, or how sugar might affect her body and mind. She didn't care about the contrasting nutritional value of the two cereals. Despite her mother's best efforts, the daughter just kept yelling, "I want Sugar Pops! I want Sugar Pops!"

I didn't know the mom or her daughter, but I prayed for them both as I continued my shopping. I prayed for the mom to be strong and not buckle to her daughter's demands just because she was willing to yell louder. I prayed that the other shoppers would stay out of the situation and keep their advice to themselves. I prayed that God would forgive me for all of the times I make demands on Him instead of trusting Him. I generally don't yell out loud, but He hears my silent screams.

Do you know what it's like to want something and make demands on God? Have you ever wanted something that "everybody else" had? Can you think of a time when you've ignored God's

blessings because they didn't meet your own selfish desires? Yeah, me too.

In 1 Samuel, we find another instance in the Old Testament where you and I might be tempted to be overly critical of how the Israelites behaved. As you read today's story, remember how easy it is to choose selfishness instead of waiting on God and His perfect timing. From the beginning, God had instructed His people to fill the earth with His glory, to be holy as He is holy, and to live lives that were set apart for Him. God's people were never meant to be like everyone else. His children were supposed to be different.

This should have been the pinnacle of Israel's history. The time they'd long awaited had arrived: They were in the Promised Land. But instead of carrying out the responsibilities that accompanied the conquest of Canaan, God's people started looking around at the other nations. And the other nations looked pretty cool.

When we begin comparing our lives with those of our neighbors, we tend to forget how blessed we are and how faithful God has been. Instead, we take notice of our neighbors' manicured lawn, their shiny new his-and-her automobiles, their fancy swimming pool—the things we wish we had. That's what happened when the Israelites started looking around. The other nations seemed to be having more fun, they ate whatever they wanted, and they had kings. It was the king thing that really made them jealous. Oh, the Israelites had God, and He had done some amazing things. But He was invisible. No royal robes, no ceremonies, no crowns, no thrones, no nobles. Israel wanted a king like everybody else had.

Just to be clear, what Israel had was better than a king on earth. The Maker of heaven and earth was their King. In fact, He was King of the universe! But the people wanted a king they could see—a king that other nations could see.

"We want a king! We want a king!" they cried (perhaps whining a bit). Meanwhile, the people began to stray once more, drifting away from God. They wandered off, taking wives from the nations around them and following after their false gods.

The people's demand broke the heart of Samuel, the prophet of God. He took the people's demand for a king personally. But God said to him, "They have not rejected you, but they have rejected Me from being king over them." God had been a faithful and loving sovereign to His people. He knew that they didn't understand all that it would mean for them to have an earthly king.

Samuel tried to warn them, but the people were thinking like that little girl in Target—they wanted what they wanted. They weren't interested in hearing about the consequences of what they wanted. They didn't care what the cost would be in taxes or property or even the lives of their sons and daughters. They wanted what everybody else had, and they wanted it now.

So God granted their request, and Samuel anointed Saul to be Israel's first earthly king. Saul certainly looked the part. As the tallest, most handsome man in Israel, he looked like a king the people could be proud of.

But all too quickly, Saul began thinking too much of himself. He didn't fully obey Samuel, who was God's prophet. Saul started to do what he wanted to do, regardless of what God commanded.

Obedience matters. And obedience especially matters when you're in a position of leadership. God had entrusted the role of earthly king to Saul, but he thought only about himself instead of seeking God. As a result, Saul was soon rejected by God.

This is when we get our first glimpse of David, the future second king of Israel. Saul had led the Israelites out against the Philistines, but the Philistines brought with them a fighting machine that Israel wasn't prepared to face. You know this story, but try and read about it with fresh eyes and ears. The biblical account is found in 1 Samuel 17. Go ahead. I'll wait.

Did you notice anything new as you read the story this time? What did David do when he arrived at the frontlines of the battle? Where had David been before he was sent on this errand? What was his job for the family? Why did he even show up at the battlefront?

This was Saul's first introduction to the strapping teen who delivered to him the head of Goliath. David was full of the passion of youth, confident in God, and ready to stand against the enemies of Israel. But instead of being inspired and challenged by David's attitude, Saul became jealous. He saw that the fighting men respected David for his bravery and courage, and the women sang of his deeds. Saul's envy grew and festered until it became an inner rage. Twice the king tried to kill David with a javelin, missing both times, and David was forced to flee from the king and his best friend Jonathan, Saul's son.

Saul's jealousy turned to resentment, which became hatred. And it drove him to hunt for David in the wilderness for years. Twice David had an opportunity to kill Saul but refused because Saul was God's anointed one. Saul didn't deserve David's mercy, but David spared Saul out of reverence to God—not because of anything Saul did, but because of who God is.

Eventually, Saul died in battle. It was a sad end to an unnecessarily bitter life. Saul could have chosen to obey God completely. He could have chosen to follow David's example of love and devotion to the Lord and learn from it rather than letting it become a point of contempt.

Saul had no heart. And like Samson, Saul is a good example of a bad example.

PSALM AND PROVERB TO READ:
Psalm 31, Proverbs 11:2

ANOINTING A KING

Have you ever been chosen for something special? Perhaps a sports team, an orchestra, a stage play, or a weekend with a friend? How did you feel to be chosen?

God chose Israel's kings. The prophet Samuel was sent by God to anoint Saul as the first king of Israel. Samuel poured oil over Saul's head, which represented God's blessing on Saul's life. As king of Israel, Saul listened to God for a while. But then he started making decisions that were not pleasing to God, so Israel needed a new king.

The Lord told Samuel to anoint a new king, whom he would find among the sons of Jesse. Samuel went to Jesse's home and met each of his sons. They were pretty impressive, but God said to Samuel, "The Lord sees not as man sees: man looks on the outward appearance, but the Lord looks on the heart" (1 Samuel 16:7).

God chose Jesse's youngest son, David, to be the next king. Samuel anointed David, which signified God's blessing upon him. David waited fifteen years between the time he was anointed and the time he began the job God had chosen him to do. While he waited, he trusted God and tended his father's sheep. During this time, he also killed a bear and a lion, slew a giant, and even served as a musician in King Saul's court.

Did you know that God chose you too, before the earth was created? God has a plan for your life, but if you don't know the plan yet, remember that David trusted God and served Him while he waited. Are you patiently trusting God to reveal His plan for your life?

LET'S TALK ABOUT IT

1. Take a look at 1 Samuel 1:11. What vow did Hannah make? Describe how she kept her promise to God.
2. Can you think of someone who you admire? What are some things you like about that person?
3. What is jealousy? How can you guard against becoming jealous of another person?
4. Some people call jealousy the "green-eyed monster." Can you think of why this description might be appropriate?
5. What are some of the dangers of comparing yourself to others? What are some things you can do to avoid comparing yourself to others?

Jesus is Prophet, Priest, and King

In the Old Testament, God dealt with His people by appointing individuals to three different offices. Prophets were the messengers of God, and God spoke through them. Priests performed the religious duties and ceremonies required by the law to keep the people in favor with God. And kings governed the people and protected the nation as commander of its armies. Most of the time a person served in only one office. Moses was unusual in that he was both a prophet and a military leader (before Israel had kings).

Each of the three offices had a deeper meaning that wouldn't be made fully clear until much later. All three offices pointed to Christ. Jesus spoke for God, and that makes Him a prophet. His sinless life and His work on the cross paying for our sins fulfilled all the requirements of the law, which makes Him a priest. What the Jewish priests did, making sacrifices at the temple, was temporary and had to be repeated over and over. But Jesus' sacrifice was once and for all, good for eternity. As God the Son, Jesus is sovereign over all creation, which makes Him a king.

So Jesus is Prophet, Priest, and King.

Saul Speaks

Yes, it's true. I was a handsome young man from the tribe of Benjamin. Tall in stature, a powerful leader, and commander of men, I was loved by my people. I was advised in matters of state and war by a prophet of the Lord. From the beginning I had everything going for me, yet my story is one of the greatest tragedies found in the Bible. Through my poor judgment and impulsiveness, I managed to snatch defeat from the jaws of victory.

I came to the throne at the age of thirty and reigned over Israel for forty-two years. During those years I brought victory and hope to the people, whose nemesis was the brutal Philistine nation. But during a military crisis involving the Philistines, my character flaws began to surface. When the prophet Samuel was delayed several days and didn't show up to make an offering before battle, I presumed to make the offering myself. A big mistake!

Later, I failed to carry out God's explicit command to completely destroy the Amalekites, and God sent Samuel to confront me. Earlier that day, I had gone up to Carmel to erect a monument to my victory. When Samuel found me and asked why I disobeyed the Lord's commands, I lied and said I had done everything as commanded.

Then things went from bad to worse. The evidence against me was overwhelming. Instead of repenting, I began one of my famous tirades to justify my actions. Ultimately, I blamed the people for my mistakes. Samuel then gave me the crushing news: My throne would be given to another. Scared and paranoid, I spent the next several years watching for and even hunting the man who would take my place as king.

My downfall mirrors the history of mankind. When will people learn? When will they love God enough to obey His commands? And when will they stop trying to cover up their own rebellious hearts?

Prayer

Dear Heavenly Father,

I know You are *God*, and You are in charge over everything. And You are my King. Although You put people in charge of governments and nations, I do not seek an earthly king. My only desire is to be in Your courts, in Your kingdom, working in Your service for Your glory. Help me to keep my eyes and my desires fixed on You. Use me to bring about Your sovereign will on earth. May I enjoy all the blessings and fullness of life that come from being in Your presence, now and forevermore.

In Jesus' name. Amen.

Lesson 12

DAVID

Motions

28. David–Whole Heart

Passage

2 Samuel

Take it To Heart

"The Lord is my rock and my fortress and my deliverer, my God, my rock, in whom I take refuge, my shield, and the horn of my salvation, my stronghold and my refuge, my savior; you save me from violence."

2 Samuel 22:2–3

I love the Bible. I love the stories of the many different people God called and loved and forgave. And I love how "real" the people in the Bible are. They are actual historical figures whose lives are retold in Scripture. They're not cleaned up; they're unedited. The stories in the Bible are like photographs that haven't been retouched or photoshopped. These are real-life snapshots.

God used farmers, shepherds, merchants, prophets, priests, and kings. He used fathers, mothers, servants, handmaids, and soldiers. Some were humble, some were joyful, and some were depressed. Whatever their position, their attitude, or their responsibilities, God invited each one to be part of His plan and used them as threads to weave the tapestry of His story.

None of us have to be perfect to be used by God. We don't even have to get our act together before we can come to Him. And that's really good news because none of us are perfect. "All have sinned and fall short of the glory of God" (Romans 3:23). Yet God draws us to Him, and we respond. We can choose to participate in what He is already at work doing—glorifying Himself and growing us.

David is an excellent example of a character in the Bible whose story is told, warts and all. His is a real-life testimony of God's faithfulness in the life of a man who loved the Lord but made mistakes both as a man and a king. As we talked about in the video, David was an enthusiastic young man. He was passionate about knowing God through his experiences as a shepherd whose office was God's creation. David camped under the stars with the sheep for long periods of time, surrounded by God's glory. The birds' morning chorus, the flowers' intricate design, the colors of each new dawn, the starry host of the night sky—these were his closest companions. It was here that David wrote some of his psalms.

David trusted God with his life and so was able to run onto the battlefield to face Goliath while King Saul and his army cowered in fear behind rocks. He was absolutely certain the Lord would deliver the Philistine giant into his hand, "that all the earth may know that there is a God in Israel" (1 Samuel 17:46).

Let's take a moment and review David's family tree. Do you remember Rahab and the spies in Jericho? Well, she married a man named Salmon. They had a son named Boaz, who married Ruth. Ruth had a son named Obed, and he was the father of Jesse. David was the youngest of Jesse's eight sons. A little more than a thousand years later, the promised Messiah would be born through David's descendants.

In contrast to Saul, David had a whole heart for God. Even so, he was still human. As can be true all too often in our lives, David did well to keep his focus on God during times of difficulty and trial, such as when Saul hunted him for eleven years. But once on the throne, that's when David faltered. The Bible records that it was spring, "the time when kings go off to war" (2 Samuel 11:1, NIV). But David didn't go to fight the Ammonites. He sent his army to war, but he stayed behind in the palace. In other words, there was a place where David was supposed to be, but he wasn't there. That will get a person into trouble every time.

Anyway, David stayed home and perhaps grew bored, merely wandering about the roof of the palace. (There's another red flag—boredom. That's two, if you're counting.) It was in this situation that David looked out over the city and saw a beautiful woman taking a bath. He sent someone to find out who she was. Her name was Bathsheba, and she was the wife of Uriah, one of David's soldiers. At this point in the story, David should have realized he was in over his head. Instead, he sent for the woman and spent the night with her. This is how sin so often begins, with a person in the wrong place, bored and unfocused. That's a pattern you can predict will end badly. And so it did for David.

Then he made it worse. When he learned that Bathsheba was pregnant, David tried to cover up his sin by having her husband killed on the front lines. So how did David go from being a passionate giant killer to being an adulterer and murderer? And how is it that in 1 Samuel 13:14, the prophet called him a man after God's own heart? The answer to this last question speaks to God's faithfulness, forgiveness, and redemption. In fact, it's important to understand that the story of David's life and reign is less about David and more about God, as all of our lives should be.

Although he was wise enough to write many of the psalms in the Bible, David needed someone to speak into his life and help him see his sin for what it was. In biblical times, speaking God's truth to kings was the job of a prophet. But Samuel had passed away by this time, so his successor, the prophet Nathan, confronted David. However, he did so in an unusual way. Nathan knew that the king couldn't see what he had done, so he told David a story about a man and his only pet lamb. Nathan asked David what should

be done to the wealthy man who had plenty but took the poor man's lamb and killed it to feed his own guests. David was enraged by the sin of the wealthy man and the heartbreak of the man from whom the lamb was stolen. He said, "As surely as the LORD lives, any man who would do such a thing deserves to die!" Nathan replied to the king, "You are that man!"

We all have blind spots—sinful habits, thoughts, attitudes, and words that we cannot see for what they are. We skip merrily through life, assuming everything is okay when it's not. Even worse, some blind spots are sins we ignore on purpose. In those cases, we choose to turn a blind eye because we're embarrassed or ashamed or guilty and we don't want to face our sin. David's sinful behavior with Bathsheba was a blind spot.

The good news is that David immediately saw the error of his ways and repented. Soon after, he wrote Psalm 51, which includes a confession and a plea for God's cleansing and forgiveness. David wrote, "Against you, you only, have I sinned and done what is evil in your sight" (Psalm 51:4). Please don't misunderstand what he was saying. When we injure a family member or a neighbor, it is indeed a sin, but it is sin mainly because the action of injuring another person violates the law of God. David understood that his sin was horrific because it was an affront to a holy God.

Too often we don't understand the significance of our sin, nor do we recognize our need for forgiveness and cleansing. We minimize and rationalize our sins and even pass laws to "legalize" our sins and make them seem perfectly normal to the rest of society. But David's understanding and the humility of his confession illustrate why Scripture calls him a man after God's own heart.

You need to know that God is holy. That means He has never sinned and cannot ever sin. It also means that because people are made in God's image, we too were made to be holy. He also made us to worship Him alone, and sin is evidence that we're worshiping other things. If we will choose to follow Jesus, study His Word, and seek to obey Him in all things, our hearts will be more in line with the heart of God too.

PSALM AND PROVERB TO READ:
Psalm 23, Proverbs 12:19

GIANTS

Have you ever seen a giant? The tallest professional basketball player ever was about seven feet, nine inches tall. Robert Wadlow, the tallest person who lived in the past hundred years, was eight feet, eleven inches tall. According to I Samuel 17:4, the Philistine warrior Goliath measured six cubits and a span. By modern calculations, Goliath stood over nine feet tall!

For forty days and forty nights, Goliath taunted the Israelite armies with a challenge, saying, "Choose one man to come down here and fight me! If he kills me, then we will be your slaves. But if I kill him, you will be *our* slaves!"

Who dared accept this gigantic challenge? David, a mere boy, volunteered to fight Goliath. The Lord had previously protected David, helping him to kill both a lion and a bear trying to steal his father's sheep; he trusted the Lord would protect him again. Goliath sneered at the boy in contempt as he entered the field of battle, and the giant came at him with a sword, a shield, and a massive spear. However, just one stone from David's slingshot struck Goliath's forehead and felled the seemingly unconquerable enemy.

Do you have giant problems like a particular temptation to do wrong, a bully in your neighborhood, or someone with whom you can't get along? David trusted the Lord and overcame his giant. You too can always trust the Lord to help you overcome your biggest problems.

LET'S TALK ABOUT IT

1. David spent many days working as a shepherd outdoors in God's creation. What attributes about God do you think he learned during those times?
2. Do you ever find yourself choosing to be where you're not supposed to be or doing what you're not supposed to be doing?
3. Do you often find that you are bored? Why might you be at greater risk of sinning when you're bored? How can you determine to spend your time more wisely?
4. The Bible challenges us to keep our focus on God (Isaiah 26:3; Psalm 119:2; Colossians 3:2; Matthew 6:33; Hebrews 12:1–2, etc.). What are some ways you can guard your eyes and keep your focus on God?
5. What does it mean to repent? Why is it important to practice repenting?

repentance

In the days before Jesus began His public ministry, John the Baptist came preaching to the Jewish people, "Repent, for the kingdom of heaven is at hand" (Matthew 3:1–2). Nathan and all the other prophets before John preached a similar message of repentance. What does it mean to repent? To repent means that you understand you have sinned, you're sorry for your sins, and you confess them to God and choose to live in obedience to Him.

The word *repentance* is translated from a pair of Hebrew words meaning "to feel sorrow" and "to return." To repent means to turn your back on sin and turn toward Jesus. It means hating your sin, or at least loving Christ and God's Word more than your sin. And it means to act on that belief by changing how you live.

Repentance is the act of faith done in response to God's work through His Son and the leading of the Holy Spirit. Many people can point to a very specific time when they turned from their sinful lives to embrace Christ. Yet as believers in Christ, we are still in the process of being made holy. Although we have genuinely repented, sometimes we can fall back into a sin we need to repent of again.

The good news is that it is Christ's work that saves us, not our own. You and I don't have the power to turn from sin on our own. Instead, repentance, and the true change in our lives that follows it, is a response to what God has done for us. We repent *because* we are saved, not in order to be saved.

David Speaks

My name is David. I was a shepherd, and the Lord was my shepherd. I was the youngest of the eight sons of Jesse, a man of some importance in the town of Bethlehem. My job as the youngest brother was to watch over my father's sheep.

One day when I was a teen, as I was in the fields tending the sheep, Samuel the prophet arrived at our home. Our neighbors were afraid that Samuel had come with a judgment from the Lord, but he was there in search of a king. Dad paraded my seven older brothers before the prophet, but the Lord told Samuel that Israel's new king was not among them. Then Samuel turned to my father and asked, "Are all your sons here?" Dad said, "Well, there is the youngest, but he is keeping the sheep." The prophet told him to send for me. When I arrived, the Lord told Samuel, "This is the one. Anoint him."

I would not be made king over all of Israel until I was thirty years old. So I had to be patient and wait, but when the time came, I was ready. My army was renowned for their deeds in battle. Men wrote songs and poetry about me, and women sang in the streets, telling of my victories. Yet I was merciful, twice sparing the life of King Saul, who had unjustly hunted me for several years. I can honestly say that I had a heart for God, and I was determined to honor the Lord and lead the nation of Israel back to faith in Him.

You see, my story is not really about me at all. My story is about the God who is mighty to save. It's about the God who helps us stand up to the giants in our lives. It's about the faithful God who never leaves us, even when we fail. It's about the God who is our strength when we are weak.

How well do you know God? Is He your companion and friend? Is He your refuge, your sword, and your shield? If not, who will equip you for all the challenges you will face in life? When the giant called Fear and his brother Failure taunt you, how will you answer them? Don't try to go it alone. Go with God.

Prayer

Dear Heavenly Father,

Thank You for Your Holy Spirit, who convicts me of my sins. Thank You that You are faithful to forgive me when I confess to You and repent of my sins. Thank You for second chances.

Thank You for my parents and friends who point me to Your truth and Your loving kindness. As I walk through each day, don't let me miss the wonder of Your creation and its everyday miracles.

Father, teach me to worship You and You alone. When I worship You, my spirit is refreshed and renewed! Help me to keep my eyes lifted and focused on You, not on my circumstances. When I am focused on You, I am reminded of Your wondrous love for me. You give me peace, strength, and confidence to face the giants in my life. And with Your help, I will overcome.

In Jesus' name, I pray. Amen.

Lesson 13

Solomon, Bad Kings & the Prophets

Motions

29. Solomon–Half Heart
30. Divided Kingdom
31. Mostly Bad Kings
32. Prophets Speak

Passage

1 Kings 2:13–12:16

Take it To Heart

Therefore the LORD said to Solomon, "Since this has been your practice and you have not kept my covenant and my statutes that I have commanded you, I will surely tear the kingdom from you and will give it to your servant."
1 Kings 11:11

This is where people trying to read through the Bible in a year often get hung up or simply dismiss the narrative as being "too hard to follow." And I admit, the two Kings books and two Chronicles books are not light reading. But reading them is well worth the effort.

God's words are living and active, and they will not return to Him void, or empty (Isaiah 55:11). That means when we study the Bible, we will be blessed by it! This portion of the Old Testament is especially important to our understanding of who God is, His love and mercy for His people, and the very real consequences of sin. Let's dare to engage our minds and dig deeper into His Word.

But first, we need to talk about one of the major themes that runs throughout the Bible: unity. Even before creating all things, God was the very model of unity. He has always existed and will always exist in the fellowship of the Father, Son, and Holy Spirit. We call this the Trinity. The three members of the Trinity each have unique roles, but they share the same essence and are always in perfect agreement. When He created mankind, God invited us all to live in perfect unity with Him and with each other.

Although we lost our ability to live in harmony when sin entered the world, the death and resurrection of Jesus Christ made it possible once more for His church to live and work in unity. In fact, the night before He died on the cross, Jesus prayed that His followers "may all be one, just as you,

Father, are in me, and I in you, that they also may be in us, so that the world may believe that you have sent me" (John 17:21). He also said, "By this all people will know that you are my disciples, if you have love for one another" (John 13:35).

In contrast, the enemy works tirelessly to destroy unity. He targets friendships, marriages, families, communities, churches, neighborhoods—any relationship in which agreement and cooperation are needed to flourish. The enemy delights in sowing deadly seeds of frustration, selfishness, pride, jealousy, and impatience. He uses a variety of weapons including gossip, slander, miscommunication, lying, rebellion, and murder. In other words, the enemy fans the flames of man's fallen nature to wreak havoc on the fellowship God wants for His children.

One of the most common tactics the devil employs to divide us is to simply distract us. Some of the ways he distracts us can seem like good things such as activities, hobbies, reading, or relaxation. None of these things is wrong in and of itself unless it takes our focus off serving God. But if we allow anything to dominate our attention so that we don't have time for God and for each other, then it has become a negative distraction.

Take reading, for example. When we get caught up in reading everything except God's Word, then it's become a distraction from His truth. Another good example is relaxation. God commands that we set aside one day a week to rest from our work. But when we allow relaxation and recreation to become slothfulness and irresponsibility, then we are allowing ourselves to be distracted from opportunities in which God wants us to participate. In this day and age of mobile phones, the internet, and hundreds of TV channels, we can easily become distracted and not even recognize that it's happened.

Worse, though, is when we lose focus because of sin. The enemy puts much effort into making sin look fun or easy or even good. He lies and tells us that the little sins don't really matter. Little sins? There's no such thing! But the enemy wants to convince us that what's truly important is taking care of our individual wants, needs, desires, and feelings. However, anytime we turn to something or someone other than God to meet our wants, needs, desires, and feelings, we've stepped into a form of idolatry, and there's nothing little about that.

Solomon was blessed by God with unprecedented wisdom and wealth, yet he allowed himself to be plagued by sinful distractions. According to God's law, the people of Israel were forbidden from marrying women and men from the surrounding nations, because they would lead the Lord's chosen people to serve other gods. And after the dedication of the temple, which Solomon built for the Lord to replace the tabernacle, God appeared to him and specifically warned him not to worship other gods (1 Kings 9:1–9). Yet just a few pages later, in 1 Kings 11, we read that Solomon "loved many foreign women" and "clung to these in love." He put his feelings and desires ahead of his love for God and took these women for his wives—700 of them! He also kept 300 concubines, or legal mistresses.

Sure enough, when Solomon was old, his wives

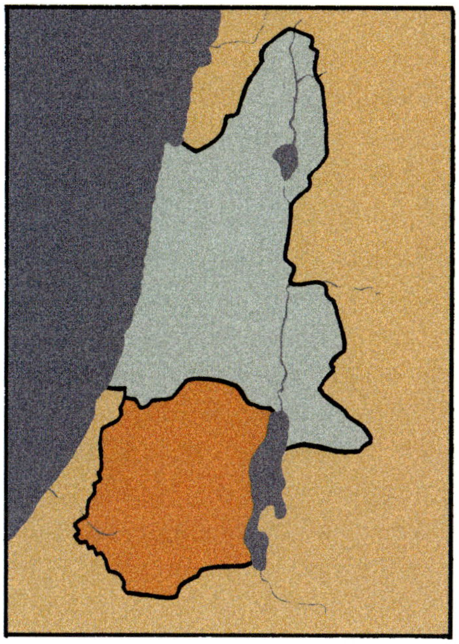

"turned away his heart after other gods, and his heart was not wholly true to the LORD his God" (1 Kings 11:4). He even built shrines in high places where the people of Israel could worship the pagan gods! And so the Lord became angry with Solomon and told him that because he had not kept God's covenant and commands, He would tear much of the kingdom away from his son and heir and give it to one of his servants.

After Solomon's death, his son Rehoboam became the fourth and final king of the united kingdom of Israel. But Rehoboam was a foolish young man. Instead of listening to the wise counsel of his father's advisors, he took the advice of his childhood friends and raised taxes on the people. Civil war resulted, and the kingdom became divided into the northern kingdom of Israel and the smaller, southern kingdom of Judah.

After the division, the southern kingdom remained under Rehoboam's rule, with Jerusalem as its capital. The kingdom of Judah consisted of only two tribes, Judah and Simeon (although they were eventually joined by the tribe of Benjamin). Solomon's former superintendent, Jeroboam, was chosen to rule over the northern kingdom, which consisted of the other ten tribes. Samaria was the capital of the northern kingdom of Israel.

Over the next 400 years, the people were consistently led astray by one bad king after another. The southern kingdom of Judah had the occasional good king, although twelve of the twenty kings of Judah are described in Scripture as having done "what was evil in the sight of the LORD." But according to God's Word, all nineteen kings who ruled the northern kingdom of Israel were bad. What characterized a "bad" king? Well, the Bible tells us that most of the leaders of the divided kingdom "did what was evil in the sight of the LORD." What does that mean? Largely, it means that these kings did not honor or worship the God of Abraham, Isaac, and Jacob. In many cases, the kings turned away from the one true and living God to follow false gods into all manner of idol worship. And the people followed their leaders into evil.

And so God's chosen people continued in their sin and rebellion. They adopted the idols of the pagan cultures around them and participated in pagan worship. They rejected God over and over and abandoned His commandments. They no longer lived as God's holy people. And in their rebellion, their arrogance and sin increased.

But the Lord is a God of great compassion and faithfulness. Throughout this period, He continued to send His prophets to warn the people and call them to turn from their wickedness and sin and worship God alone, according to His covenant with Him. The prophets of God were courageous men who mostly stood alone and risked their lives to speak against the sins of the people. They boldly proclaimed, "Thus says the LORD. . . ." The messages they delivered were often unpopular and generally ignored. But the prophets were obedient to God in delivering His messages to His people.

In addition to calling for repentance, the prophets also challenged the people to put their hope in God alone. One characteristic of sin is that it's an indication we have misplaced our hope. Instead of putting all our hope and trust in God, we often put it in people, things, money, traditions, or rituals. Nothing and no one but God deserves our hope. Hope is the confident expectation that God will do what He said He will do. Over and over, He has proved Himself faithful to His word. And that is why we can and should always put our faith and hope completely in Him.

PSALM AND PROVERB TO READ:
Psalm 2, Proverbs 13:12

? LET'S TALK ABOUT IT

1. What are some things in your life that sometimes distract you from God?
2. What are some relationships in your life that the enemy would probably like to disrupt? How can you resist the devil's attempts to divide and destroy the good relationships in your life?
3. People were made to worship, so they're always worshiping something. What are some ways we worship? Do you worship God when you're alone, or only when you're in a group or at church? Why or why not?
4. Why is it important that we only worship God? Why does it matter who or what we worship?
5. Is there a behavior, action, or attitude that you need to repent of?

BAAL

The Canaanites' religion was a series of stories created to explain things that happened in nature. They were mostly farmers, so rain—or lack of rain—was important to them. They believed that a period of drought meant the gods were unhappy. If rain came and the crops grew to provide food for the people, the Canaanites thanked Baal, god of rain, wind, lightning, and fertility.

King Ahab of Israel disobeyed God frequently and worshiped Baal. In fact, he did more to provoke God to anger than all the kings of Israel who came before him (1 Kings 16:33). God's prophet Elijah told Ahab that the Lord would not send rain or dew to water the land. After three years with no rain, Elijah summoned King Ahab and 450 prophets of Baal to Mount Carmel, where he issued a challenge to the people of Israel, who had come to watch the confrontation:

> "Let two bulls be given to us, and let them choose one bull for themselves and cut it in pieces and lay it on the wood, but put no fire to it. And I will prepare the other bull and lay it on the wood and put no fire to it. And you call upon the name of your god, and I will call upon the name of the LORD, and the God who answers by fire, he is God." (1 Kings 18:23–24)

Baal's prophets placed a sacrifice on their altar and shouted out to Baal from morning until noon, begging him to send fire and burn their sacrifice. Nothing happened. About noon, Elijah taunted them and told them to shout louder. The prophets cut themselves with swords and spears, as they were accustomed to doing, and continued to shout to Baal. Still nothing happened.

Then Elijah rebuilt the altar of the Lord with twelve stones representing the twelve tribes of Israel. He dug a trench around it and commanded the people to pour four jars of water over the sacrifice and the firewood. Elijah told them to do this three times, until the bull and the wood were thoroughly drenched and the trench filled with the overflow. Elijah then prayed to God, and God responded with fire from heaven that burned the sacrifice, the wood, the altar, and the stones and dried up all of the water surrounding it. When the people saw this, they fell to the ground on their faces and cried out, "The LORD, He is God! The LORD, He is God!" Then the rain fell to replenish the land once more.

The Israelites and their wicked king had been distracted by the beliefs of the people around them and had turned away from the Lord. Do the beliefs of your peers distract you? How do you keep your focus on God?

the temple

When God met with Moses on Mount Sinai, He gave him details for constructing an elaborate place of worship called the tabernacle. As we discussed in lesson 7, this is where God would dwell among His people. Someday the ceremonies and sacrifices of God's people would be carried out in a permanent house of worship, but the tabernacle was portable, meaning it could be disassembled and moved with the Hebrews as they moved from place to place.

After the Israelites had settled in the Promised Land and David succeeded Saul as king, an angel appeared to David to show him where the tabernacle and the ark of the covenant should be placed and where sacrifices were to be offered (1 Chronicles 21:15–28). So David built the altar for sacrifices on the same mountain where Abraham offered Isaac to God a thousand years earlier. David had long wanted to build a permanent house for the Lord and began making preparations for its construction in this location (1 Chronicles 22:1–5). But David knew he would die before the real work could begin, and so he charged his son and heir, Solomon, to build the house according to the plans the Lord had given him (1 Chronicles 28:11–19).

God had revealed to David detailed plans for every part of this house, which would be known as the temple. The temple consisted of three main parts. A massive altar and place of sacrifice stood in a courtyard open to the sky. Beyond the courtyard, inside the main building, was a large room that held a table for showbread, twelve loaves of bread that were always present as an offering to the Lord. Nearby was the seven-branched candlestick and a golden altar for incense. At the far end of this room was the doorway to a second, smaller room called the Holy of Holies, which held the ark of the covenant. The Holy of Holies could be entered only once a year, and then only by the high priest.

Sometimes called Solomon's Temple, the first temple stood for more than four centuries, until Nebuchadnezzar destroyed it and captured the Jews, taking them to Babylon. Fifty years later, work began on a second temple. It wasn't nearly as beautiful and impressive as Solomon's. Several hundred years later, around the time Jesus was born, Herod the Great rebuilt it to be as magnificent as Solomon's. Yet it stood only seventy years before it was destroyed by the Romans while crushing a Jewish rebellion.

The second temple did not contain the ark of the covenant, which was lost when the first temple was destroyed. Also, the Holy of Holies was separated by a giant curtain called the veil in place of the original, massive doors.

A few attempts were made to build a third temple, and some Jews still pray for that day. Since the destruction of the second temple, a pagan temple to Jupiter and a Christian chapel have stood where the Holy of Holies probably once was. For the last thousand years, an Islamic shrine called the Dome of the Rock has stood there.

Solomon Speaks

I was the second son of David and Bathsheba, and some say I was destined for greatness. When I was but a young man, I was crowned king over Israel upon the death of my beloved father.

Not long after, the Lord came to me in a dream and said, "What do you want? Ask, and I will give it to you!" Knowing that I lacked the wisdom I would need to rule over God's chosen people, I asked that He give me an understanding heart, that I might discern the difference between good and evil and rule justly.

The Lord was so pleased that I asked for wisdom instead of riches or a long life, that He gave me not only great wisdom but also wealth and honor beyond that of all other kings. My wisdom and fame became like magnets drawing visitors to my palace from all over the world. The Queen of Sheba came to consult with me and was overwhelmed by what she saw. She said to me, "I didn't believe what was said until I arrived here and saw it with my own eyes. In fact, I had not heard the half of it! Your wisdom and prosperity are far beyond what I was told."

I expanded the kingdom to its greatest geographical boundaries, and under my leadership the nation of Israel enjoyed its greatest prosperity. Unfortunately, prosperity and power tend to dull a person's senses over time, and I was no exception. As I aged, my judgment diminished. I surrendered God's discernment and played the fool to please my many wives from other nations. When they moved in, they unpacked their idols and continued their pagan ways. Temptation slowly ate away at my spiritual foundations until I almost destroyed the nation.

In my early days, when I was still wise, I wrote many songs and proverbs. Later, I wrote the book of Ecclesiastes, in which I depict the collapse of a life—my own—when it seeks to find peace and satisfaction in personal accomplishments and wealth and pleasure. In it, I share what I have learned about the utter futility of trying to fill the hole in our hearts and our lives with anything other than God.

At the end of Ecclesiastes, I call young and old to abandon the hollow pursuit of prosperity and pleasure and instead "Fear God and keep his commandments, for this is the whole duty of man" (Ecclesiastes 12:13). I wrote these words with a heavy and sorrowful heart, and what a fool you are if you don't heed them!

Prayer

Dear Heavenly Father,

I want to worship You and only You. I want to be in sweet unity with my family, friends, and fellow Christians. Help me avoid saying and doing things that might hurt them or cause division in the family of God. Give me wisdom and understanding and help me to stay true to You all of my days. Help me to never stray from Your ways. May the words of my mouth and the meditations of my heart be pleasing to You.

In Jesus' name, I pray. Amen.

Lesson 14

Scattered, Exiled, Returned, Temple

Motions

33. Israel–Scattered
34. Judah–Exiled
35. Judah–Returned
36. Zerubbabel–Temple

Passage

2 Kings 17–25
2 Chronicles 36

Take it To Heart

And this occurred because the people of Israel had sinned against the Lord their God, who had brought them up out of the land of Egypt from under the hand of Pharaoh king of Egypt, and had feared other gods.
2 Kings 17:7

Remember that although the nation of Israel was divided into two kingdoms, Israel and Judah, all the people of these kingdoms who were descended from Abraham and Jacob were still Hebrews and God's chosen people. Now let's review God's promise to Abraham way back in the book of Genesis:

> "I will make of you a great nation, and I will bless you and make your name great, so that you will be a blessing. I will bless those who bless you, and him who dishonors you I will curse, and in you all the families of the earth shall be blessed." (Genesis 12:1–3)

The Lord promised that He would make a great nation of Abraham's descendants. All the nations of the earth would be blessed through this nation. If they listened and obeyed and worshiped God alone, He would be their God and they would be His people.

But the nation of Israel turned away from God. They did not listen or obey. In fact, they often willfully ignored and disobeyed God's laws. They didn't walk in His ways, and they failed to remember everything the Lord had done for them. God sent His prophets to awaken and warn the people, but they refused to listen. Even when the prophets warned of the imminent destruction of Jerusalem and called the people to return to the Lord's path, they said, "We will not walk in it" (Jeremiah 6:16).

Eventually, God raised up another nation to come against His own people. Assyria and its capital city, Nineveh, were known for their wickedness. (See the book of Jonah.) The Assyrian army mounted a three-year siege of Israel's capital city, Samaria. After the city fell, God's people were scattered by the Assyrians, who had a practice of displacing and dispersing the people of nations they conquered.

God then raised up the nation of Babylon to conquer Assyria and, subsequently, the kingdom of Judah. Led by Nebuchadnezzar, Babylon besieged the city of Jerusalem. The king of Judah surrendered and was taken prisoner. The Babylonians then looted the temple and carried off its treasures. Judah's officers, fighting men, craftsmen, and young men were taken to Babylon and made to serve Nebuchadnezzar. Only the poorest people of the land remained, and some fled to Egypt in fear for their lives.

This is a tragic story. God had kept His part of the covenant with Abraham, and He had been patient with Abraham's descendants. But the Israelites chose to go their own way. You may be thinking, *Why didn't they just obey God? Why couldn't they remember how faithful and loving God had been to them?* Reading this story in our Bibles, we can see what the Israelites were unable to see. We know they were headed down the wrong path, blinded by their own pride.

Sin works that way. It's always easier to see sin in other people than to discern it in ourselves. When we disobey God, we think we have good reasons for what we've done: "It's the other person's fault." Or "I had no choice." Or "I didn't know better." Or "It was just a little sin that didn't hurt anyone." But when we read the story of Israel and Judah and the consequences of their sins, we see just how serious sin really is.

The fact is, we all sin. But God has made a way for us to turn from our sin and come back to Him. That way is called repentance. But if we continue in our sin and refuse to repent, we fall deeper and deeper into darkness and farther and farther away from God. We reap the consequences of our sin, but so do the people around us. That is an important lesson we can take away from the Old Testament account of God's judgment on His people's sin. Sin is deadly.

Getting back to the story, Judah's exile lasted seventy years. At that time, God raised up the nation of Persia to conquer Babylon. Once again, He used a pagan king to bring about His sovereign will. He stirred the heart of King Cyrus of Persia to issue a proclamation:

> "The Lord, the God of heaven, has given me all the kingdoms of the earth, and he has charged me to build him a house at Jerusalem, which is in Judah. Whoever is among you of all his people, may his God be with him, and let him go up to Jerusalem, which is in Judah, and rebuild the house of the Lord, the God of Israel." (Ezra 1:2–3)

Remember, history is His-story. Sending God's people back to their homeland wasn't Cyrus' idea but was the result of God's prompting. This was always part of God's plan.

In response to the edict, 50,000 people wanted to return to their homeland. Imagine what it must have been like for the Jewish people to return from exile. The excitement, the anticipation, the joy. But the Jerusalem they returned to was no longer the city they had left. Its walls and the temple had been completely destroyed. Jerusalem was once a beautiful, thriving city, and the people must have wondered if it would ever be that way again. Where would they even begin to rebuild?

The first thing they rebuilt was the altar. Why was this significant? Why rebuild the altar first? Think back to some of the sacrifices we've seen in our study of the Old Testament. Think all the way back to the garden of Eden. After Adam and Eve sinned, God provided for them a covering made from the skins of animals. When God entered into the covenant with Abraham, Abraham offered a sacrifice to God. And we saw the formal establishment of sacrifices in the law God gave to Moses. Sacrifice was a central part of worship to God in the Old Testament. Animals were sacrificed so that their blood would make atonement for the people's sins.

Israel and Judah had abandoned the worship of the one true God and had embraced idol worship. As a result, they experienced God's judgment by being scattered and exiled. Upon returning to Jerusalem, they rebuilt the altar and offered sacrifices upon it to signify their return to worshiping God.

Two years after God's people returned, they began to rebuild the temple, although opposition caused them to stop and restart a couple of times before finally completing it after several years.

PSALM AND PROVERB TO READ:
Psalm 94, Proverbs 14:1

UNDER SEIGE

In ancient days, a common strategy of war was for the attacking army to lay siege a town or fortress by surrounding it and camping outside its walls for an extended period of time. Not only did this tactic prevent opposing soldiers from escaping or going for help, but it also cut off their access to needed supplies such as food, water, and medicine. Eventually, if the siege remained unbroken, the opposition would be forced to negotiate or even surrender.

Sometimes it can seem as though you're under siege by the enemy of our souls and his foot soldiers. Everywhere you turn there is a point of stress, a worrying illness, a besetting sin, a family crisis, a personal attack, or a serious temptation. After a few weeks or months of dealing with such fearsome, difficult circumstances, you may be tempted to throw up your hands and surrender your once-strong position of faith and trust in God.

Time and again the Bible tells us not to be afraid—Joshua 8:1, Psalm 23:4, Isaiah 43:1, Matthew 10:31, and so on. Even as he was nearing death, Moses told the Israelites:

> "Be strong and courageous. Do not fear . . . for it is the Lord your God who goes with you. He will not leave you or forsake you." (Deuteronomy 31:6)

Throughout the Old Testament, we see examples of God fighting for His people:

> "The Lord your God is he who goes with you to fight for you against your enemies, to give you the victory." (Deuteronomy 20:4)

> "One man of you puts to flight a thousand, since it is the Lord your God who fights for you, just as he promised you." (Joshua 23:10)

Even today, we need not be fearful, whatever our circumstances. Jesus holds the victory over sin and death in this world, and all who believe belong to Him. Not only will He fight for you, but He also will use even the worst of your circumstances to grow you spiritually and mature your faith. "What then shall we say to these things? If God is for us, who can be against us?" (Romans 8:31).

LET'S TALK ABOUT IT

1. Reread Deuteronomy 30:19. Can you remember the choices Moses gave the second generation of Israelites before they entered the Promised Land?
2. What are some excuses you've used when you did something wrong? Do you find it hard to recognize sin in your own life?
3. What are consequences? Why do you think there are consequences when we sin?
4. Do you ever feel far from God? What is the best way to get back on track in your relationship with Him? How do you feel after you confess and repent of a sin?
5. How do you think the people of God felt after they returned to Jerusalem? Do you think they were mostly encouraged by the opportunity to rebuild or discouraged by how much work there was to do?

God's Wrath

God is perfectly good, holy, and righteous. Because God is good, He hates sin. Because He is holy, He cannot allow sin in His immediate presence. And because He is righteous, He must punish sin. God shows His intense hatred of sin and righteous anger against sin through His punishment of it. The Bible calls this God's wrath.

We usually think of hate and anger as bad things. After all, God is love. But sin is so horrible that hating sin and being angry about it are the appropriate responses to it. That's because all sin is an attack on God and a rejection of all that He is. Wrath is the way He protects and defends goodness, love, and justice. If God did not hate the things that attack what is good and right, He would not be worthy of our worship.

We have seen God's wrath poured out several times in this study, including the flood that destroyed the world, the plagues on Egypt, and the destruction of Pharaoh's army. Some people have thought the Old Testament shows us a God of wrath and the New Testament shows us a God of love.

Yet the fullness of God's wrath would only be revealed at the crucifixion of Christ. When Jesus died on the cross, He paid for the sins of everyone who believes in Him. This means that Jesus received the punishment we deserved for our sins—God's wrath was poured out on Him. It also means that those who reject Christ will receive God's wrath for eternity in hell.

The Prophets Speak

As you've seen throughout the Old Testament, God often used us, His prophets, to reveal His will and words to humanity. When one of us spoke, people were to listen carefully, believe, and take the words to heart.

Sometimes God's messages were meant to teach and guide the people. Other times He warned them to turn from their wicked ways or face the consequences. So when one of us came to town to deliver a word from the Lord, the message was rarely received with much enthusiasm. In fact, we were often ignored and sometimes beaten or even killed.

Some of us prophets took time to write down the messages we received from the Holy Spirit. Seventeen books in the Old Testament are the preserved writings of prophets. The books of Isaiah, Jeremiah, Lamentations, Ezekiel, and Daniel are said to have been written by "major prophets," while the other twelve are called minor. The distinction doesn't have anything to do with which of us was more important than the others. The books of the major prophets are simply much longer and have more words than those of the minor prophets.

The law of Moses warned the people against listening to "false prophets." God said, "The prophet who presumes to speak a word in my name that I have not commanded him to speak, or who speaks in the name of other gods, that same prophet shall die" (Deuteronomy 18:15–22). When a supposed prophet spoke in the name of the Lord, if the word did not come to pass, then that prophet was false and was to be put to death. Speaking on behalf of God was—and is—serious business.

The Lamb of God would also warn against false prophets who, like "ravenous wolves" in sheep's clothing, seek to lead His followers away from God (Matthew 7:15). "Such persons do not serve our Lord Christ, but their own appetites, and by smooth talk and flattery they deceive the hearts of the naïve" (Romans 16:18).

Prayer

Dear Heavenly Father,

Help me to stay far away from sin. When I am tempted, give me the wisdom and strength to flee. When I sin, help me to recognize my sin for what it is, repent quickly, and turn back to You completely and wholeheartedly.

Help me to never place anyone or anything above You in my heart. I want to worship You alone! Keep my heart tender to the things that are important to You. Help me to walk in the light of Your salvation, always being obedient to tell others about the wondrous things You have done. Let me be about Your business, always eager to worship You in ways that are pleasing and right.

In Jesus' name, I pray. Amen.

Lesson 15

Esther, Ezra, Nehemiah & Waiting for Christ

Motions	Passage
37. Esther–Queen	Esther
38. Ezra–People	Ezra
39. Nehemiah–Walls	Nehemiah
40. Wait–Christ	

Take it To Heart

"O Lord, let your ear be attentive to the prayer of your servant, and to the prayer of your servants who delight to fear your name, and give success to your servant today, and grant him mercy in the sight of this man."
Nehemiah 1:11

After Judah's seventy-year exile, there were three waves of Jews returning to Jerusalem. Zerubbabel led the first wave of exiles in the rebuilding and the dedication of the temple. The second wave was led by Ezra, who subsequently led the people in a revival. He was "skilled in the Law of Moses" (Ezra 7:6), and he "had set his heart to study the Law of the Lord, and to do it and to teach his statues and rules in Israel" (Ezra 7:10).

Once again, God's people found themselves starting over, beginning anew under a learned man sent to teach them God's law. Once again, God also used a pagan king to protect His servant. Artaxerxes, the new king of Persia, supported the work of rebuilding Jerusalem. He even provided Ezra with a letter of protection. Take a moment now to read the text of this letter in Ezra 7:12–26.

Ezra's response to this letter was to praise God for providing for His people in this way. Ezra then set about preparing the people by leading them in fasting and prayer. We would do well to remember these actions as we set our hearts and minds on worshiping God.

What is fasting? Fasting means that we choose to deny ourselves something—usually food—for a time so that we can more fully focus our attention on God. Praying is often paired with fasting in the Bible because the two work together powerfully. When we go without food, our bodies grow hungry, and that hunger drives us to seek God and depend on Him alone. Fasting and praying can also help

us to better see God for the truly glorious King of Creation that He is, and see sin for the truly hideous thing it is. When you choose to refocus your heart on God and His glory, you will be better able to hear and respond to God's call on your life.

Back in Persia, thirteen years after Ezra led the first wave of exiles returning to Jerusalem, a Jew named Nehemiah was serving as cupbearer to King Artaxerxes. Although he was not a scribe like Ezra or a prophet like Jeremiah, he held a position of honor in Artaxerxes' court. Then Nehemiah received distressing news from travelers who had come from Jerusalem. They said that the Jews who had returned to Jerusalem with Ezra were in great trouble and disgrace. They faced opposition from all sides, and the wall around the city had been torn down and its gates burned.

Nehemiah wept when he heard the news. Then he fasted, mourned, and prayed. He was willing and able to do the work, but he couldn't just resign from his job. As important as he was, he was still a servant to the king. Like all servants, Nehemiah was expected to be pleasant and display a cheerful disposition in the presence of the king, no matter what might be happening in his life. But he could not hide his sadness. The king noticed his sad demeanor and asked about its cause. Nehemiah cried out, "Why should my face not look sad when the city where my fathers are buried lies in ruins and its gates have been destroyed by fire?" God was with Nehemiah, and the king graciously responded, "How can I help you?"

Nehemiah prayed before answering. He then asked to be sent to rebuild the city. Once that was settled, the king granted all his requests, including letters to the local governors, instructing them to allow the prophet to travel safely through their territories and ordering them to provide any building supplies his people required. In addition, the king sent an army escort and appointed Nehemiah governor of Judah.

Following in the footsteps of Zerubbabel and Ezra, Nehemiah led the third wave of exiles returning to Jerusalem. When he arrived in Jerusalem, the same leaders who had harassed the people earlier were disturbed that someone had come to help the Jews. Two of the officials, Sanballat the Horonite and Tobiah the Ammonite, openly ridiculed the work and accused the Jews of rebelling against the king. They clearly didn't want to see this project finished. But God's hand was on Nehemiah, and the prophet stood up to the bullies, saying that the God of heaven would make the rebuilding efforts successful.

Nehemiah posted guards at the worksite both day and night, even as Sanballat and Tobiah plotted against the work. Meanwhile, the Jews continued working with all their strength. When they became discouraged, Nehemiah called them together for a pep talk and to remind them of the important things in life, like their families. He reminded them to not be afraid because the Lord was with them. With that, they returned to work—half of the men working on the wall while the other half put on armor and defended the workers with spears, shields, and bows.

Amazingly, the work was completed in just fifty-two days!

As the Old Testament story line draws to a close, the remnant has returned to Jerusalem, rebuilt the temple, restored worship according to the law of Moses, and secured the city by rebuilding its walls. Revival broke out among the Jews as they renewed their vows before God.

Unfortunately, in time the people's worship once again grew cold as they became impatient waiting for the Messiah to appear and restore glory to Israel. The prophet Malachi called the people back to faithfulness, assuring them that the Day of the Lord was coming and they had better get ready!

PSALM AND PROVERB TO READ:
Psalm 81, Proverbs 15:1

400 YEARS OF SILENCE

According to Jewish tradition, from the time of Moses to the days of Malachi—roughly 1400 BC to 400 BC—there was always at least one prophet in the land. Not all of them wrote books, but all were messengers sent by God. However, after Malachi died, no one else was raised up by God until John the Baptist. This 400-year gap between the Old and New Testaments is sometimes called "the silent period" because God was not speaking to His people. But that doesn't mean nothing happened to the Jews during this time.

One of the most important events was the conquering of the ancient world by Alexander the Great, whose conquests spread Greek culture from Africa to Asia. Two hundred years later, Antiochus IV tried to rid the world of everything that was not part of Greek culture, and that included turning the Jewish temple into a pagan house of worship. Outraged, the Jews revolted and took back the temple, an event commemorated annually in Hanukkah celebrations.

Because Greek culture had become so widespread, many Jews knew the Greek language better than Hebrew or Aramaic. So the scribes translated the Scriptures into Greek. We call this Greek Old Testament the Septuagint. The scribes added books that documented the history of that time, even though they didn't consider the books a part of holy Scripture.

When Christians later translated the Hebrew Bible into Latin during the early days of the church, sometimes they copied what was in the Septuagint and included these extra books. Unlike the Jews, some Christians treat these books, known as the Apocrypha, as scriptural. That's why the Bibles of Roman Catholics and Eastern Orthodox Christians contain more books in the Old Testament than do the Bibles of the Protestants, who follow the teachings of the Jews about these books.

LET'S TALK ABOUT IT

1. If you were called by God to do something important, what would you do? Who or what might try to stop you from completing your assignment?
2. Are you working on a project that needs your undivided attention? What can you do to focus on the task God has given you to do?
3. When people say hurtful words to discourage you, what is a good way to respond?
4. Have you ever seen God intervene in a miraculous way in your life or the life of a loved one? Describe the circumstances.
5. When you think about getting yourself ready to worship God, what are some things you need to do?

providence

We often think of miracles as surprising and wonderful things that happen when God does something in the world, especially when the event or its timing cannot be explained by natural or scientific laws. Although miracles are one of the ways God works, they are not the only way.

God is always at work in our world, although it is usually in ways we take for granted or that don't call attention to themselves. For example, God sustains the world every second of its existence. Scripture tells us that God upholds and sustains all things by His powerful word (Hebrews 1:3). What we call the laws of nature—time, gravity, thermodynamics, the speed of light, and so on—are really just a way of referring to some of His work.

We sometimes use the word *providence* to refer to God's provision, care, and guidance over our lives, our nations, and the whole of human history. He ordains what happens in this world. We can make our plans, but God orders our steps (Proverbs 16:9).

Sometimes we call what happens "coincidence" or "luck," but there's really no such thing. We usually dismiss "chance meetings" and seemingly ordinary events each day as a part of life and don't give them much thought. But God is at work in these "usual" things just as much as when He performs a miracle, which is when He acts in an "unusual" way.

Ezra Speaks

Although I have dwelled in Babylon all my years, my heart longs to see Jerusalem. Oh, to have lived in the time of my great-grandfather Hilkiah! He was high priest of the temple under Josiah, a king who loved God and did what was right in the eyes of the Lord. But Josiah could not fully undo the damage that was done by his grandfather, the wicked king Manasseh, who did not love God but provoked the Lord to wrath.

In his time, Manasseh persecuted and murdered God's prophets, built shrines to Baal and Asherah, and even killed his own child as an offering to idols. And so twelve years after Josiah's death, our people were exiled from the Promised Land and taken captive by the armies of Babylon, who desecrated the holy temple and pillaged its treasures.

As a descendant of the chief priest Aaron, I was meant to serve in the Lord's temple, offering fragrant sacrifices on behalf of our people. In Babylon, I served as a scribe, interpreting and teaching the law of Moses. I dedicated myself to preserving the Law so that one day, when our inheritance was restored, we would return and worship God just as He intended.

I have discovered that the more I learn and speak of the Lord and His precepts, so grows my passion for His ways. Many times in my zeal I have cried out, "Oh, how I love your law!"

Now that Babylon has fallen to the Persians, the exile of Judah is nearly at an end after seventy years, as the prophet Jeremiah foretold. God has not forgotten us! Now I will give my life to restore the people to Judah and, more importantly, turn their hearts to worship our Holy God, whose word is life and law.

Prayer

Dear Heavenly Father,

You are my refuge and my strength. You uphold me with Your mighty right hand and do not allow my foot to stumble. When I am weak, when I am overwhelmed, when I am tired, when I am vulnerable, You are always strong. Thank You for my family and for Your plan to bless our work and our service. Use me and help me to do the work and ministry You have prepared in advance for me to do. Truly, the joy of the Lord is my strength. Teach me the beauty of resting in the joy of Your salvation.

In Jesus' name, I pray. Amen.

OLD TESTAMENT *Outline*

Quick Reference to the 40-Point Outline

Story Line: Beginnings

1. Creation

2. Fall

3. Flood

4. Nations

5. Abraham

6. Isaac

7. Jacob

8. Joseph

Story Line: Wanderings

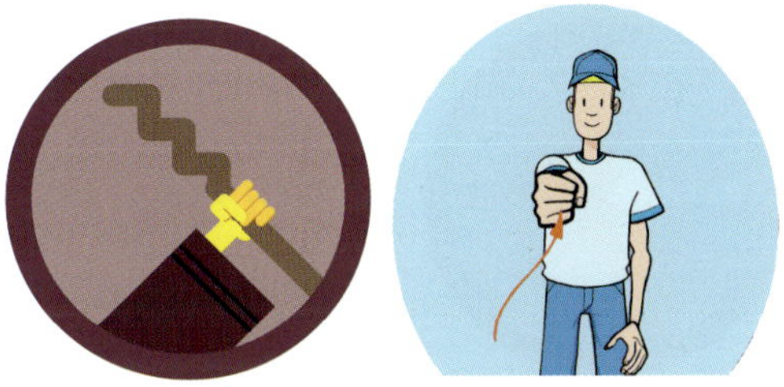

9. Moses

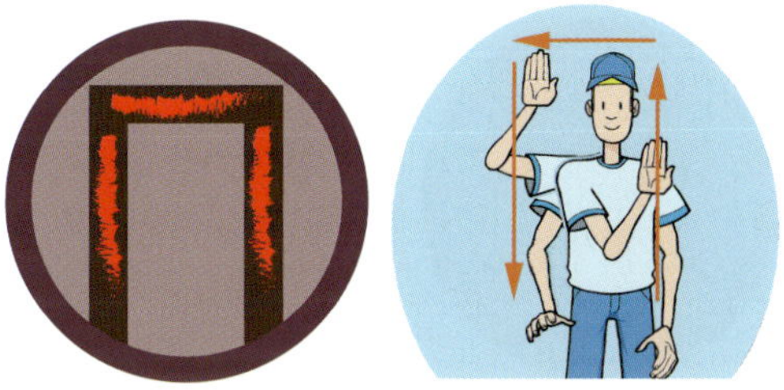

10. Passover

11. Law

12. Tabernacle

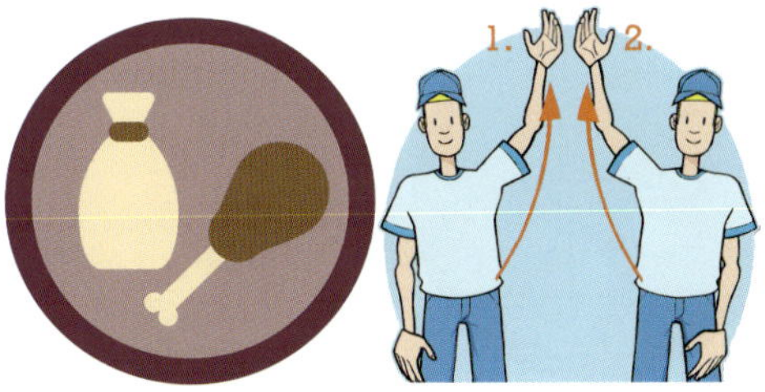

13. Offering–Feasts

14. Counting–Spying

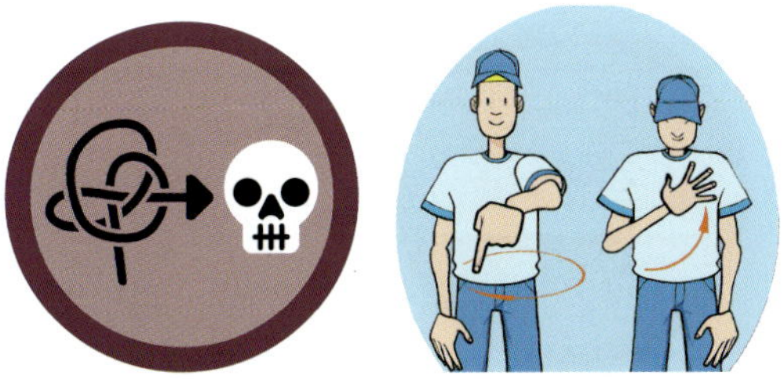

15. Wandering–Dying

16. Second Law

Story Line: Promised Land

17. Joshua

18. Divide–Conquer

19. Twelve Tribes

20. Judges

21. Deborah

22. Gideon

23. Samson

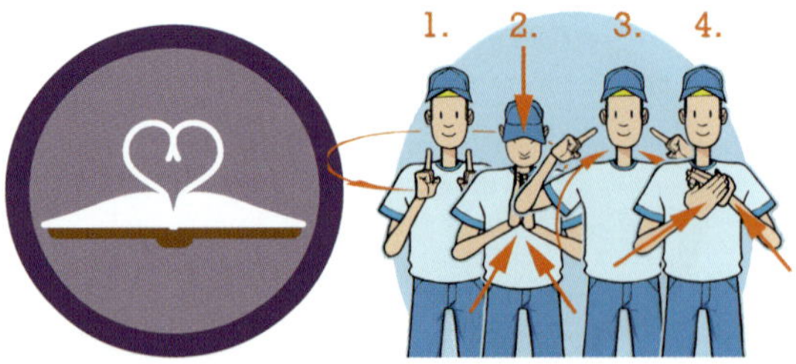

24. Everyone Did What Was Right in His Own Eyes, Except Ruth and...

Story Line: Kingdoms

25. Samuel

26. United Kingdom

27. Saul–No Heart

28. David–Whole Heart

29. Solomon–Half Heart

30. Divided Kingdom

31. Mostly Bad Kings

32. Prophets Speak

Story Line: Capitvity

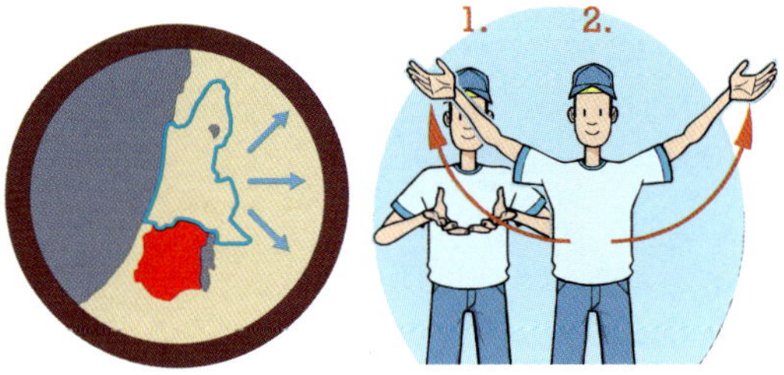

33. Israel–Scattered

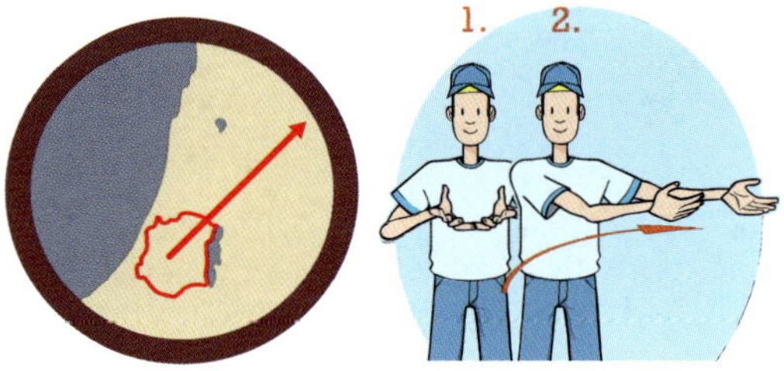

34. Judah–Exiled

35. Judah–Returned

36. Zerubbabel–Temple

37. Esther–Queen

38. Ezra–People

39. Nehemiah–Walls

40. Wait–Christ

PART 2
OLD TESTAMENT
39 Books

Lesson 16
GENESIS & JOB

Elohim

Moses • 1446–1406 BC • Hebrew • Narrative
ADAM • EVE • NOAH • MRS. NOAH
ABRAHAM • SARAH • ISAAC • JACOB • JOSEPH
Time • Light • Land • Sea • Life • Man • Woman • Marriage
Sin • Sacrifice • Redemption • Family • Work • Murder
Languages • Covenants

GENESIS

Bereshith: In the Beginning

"I will establish my covenant between me and you and your offspring after you throughout their generations for an everlasting covenant, to be God to you and to your offspring after you."
Genesis 17:7

Jesus is the Creator of the universe.

Bible Reading

Genesis 15

Key Word

Beginnings

Take it To Heart

"I will establish my covenant between me and you and your offspring after you throughout their generations for an everlasting covenant, to be God to you and to your offspring after you."

Genesis 17:7

El Shaddai

Unknown • Debated BC • Hebrew • Poetry

Job • Job's Wife

Eliphaz • Bildad • Zophar • Eluhu

Righteous • Satan • Questioning

Friends • Grief • Loss • Depression • Suffering

God's Answer • God's Sovereignty • God's Blessing

JOB

Job

Then Job arose and tore his robe . . . and fell on the ground and worshiped. And he said . . . "The Lord gave, and the Lord has taken away; blessed be the name of the Lord." In all this Job did not sin or charge God with wrong.
Job 1:20–22

Jesus is sovereign.

Key Word

Sovereignty

Bible Reading

Job 1, 42

Take it To Heart

Then Job arose and tore his robe. . . . And he said . . . "The LORD gave, and the LORD has taken away; blessed be the name of the LORD." In all this Job did not sin or charge God with wrong.
Job 1:20-22

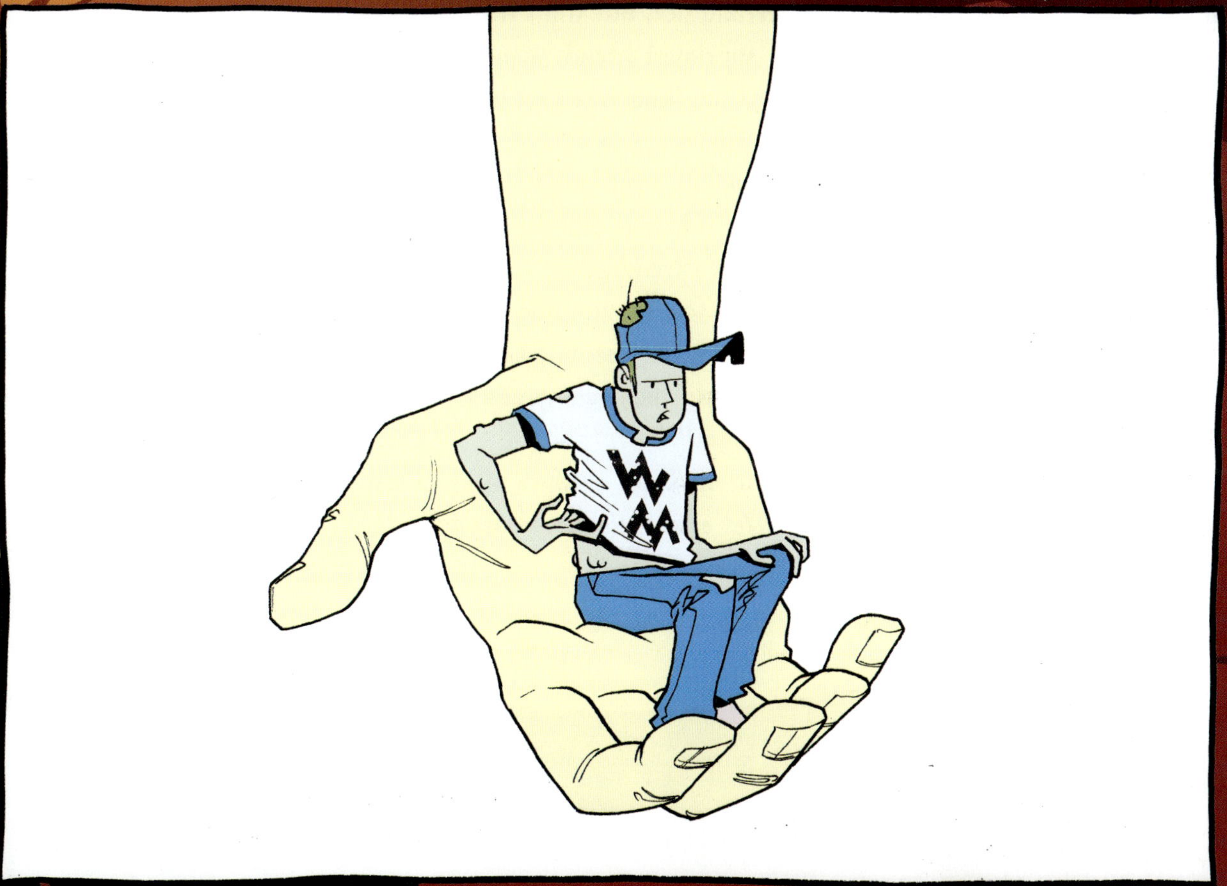

Job Speaks

My name is Job, and I was the wealthiest man in the land of Uz. I was a family man, the father of seven boys and three girls. I was a good man. Law abiding. God fearing. Well respected. I was incredibly blessed, and I gave God all the glory.

But that all changed without warning. First came the storm. Then the thieves. Finally the lightning. My wife and I lost everything that day.

My sons and daughters . . . GONE!

My servants . . . GONE!

Seven thousand sheep . . . GONE!

Three thousand camels . . . GONE!

A thousand oxen and five hundred donkeys . . . GONE!

I knew the Lord gave me these things, and now the Lord had taken what was rightfully His. Blessed be the name of the Lord! Then I became terribly sick, but still I trusted my God.

My wife urged me to curse the Lord. My closest friends suggested that I must have done something horrible for God to smite me so. I protested my innocence and sent them away. Now I was upset. I had questions, and I cried out to the Lord for answers. And then a great storm cloud approached, and God spoke to me from out of the whirlwind, saying, "I will question you, and you will answer me."

"Where were you when I made all THIS?" Then He pulled back the curtain of the universe, and I gasped at the magnificence of His handiwork. I trembled at the edge of the great sea as He showed me the giant creatures that roamed its depths. I saw the sun and moon and stars give their light in turn as they marked the days and seasons. I saw the waters become hard like stone, and I saw wastelands become grassy meadows. I saw the hawk take flight and the eagle spread its wings. I looked. I listened. And then I cried, "Lord, I know that you can do all things!"

Then in His great mercy, He restored to me twice as much as I had lost. He blessed me with seven new sons and three beautiful new daughters! Yet even if He should decide to take my life, my hope will still be in Him!

Satan

Angels are spiritual beings created by God when He made the universe. Some of these angels rebelled against God and were banished from heaven. These "fallen angels" became known as demons.

The leader of the demons is Satan, whose name is the Hebrew word for "adversary." In the New Testament, he is also called the devil. Satan did not want the position God had given him; he wanted to be God and to rule the universe in His place. In his pride, he led other angels astray, so Satan and his followers were cast out of heaven forever and will suffer eternal punishment.

Although his rebellion did not bring him to power, Satan has continued to work against God. He tempted Eve in the garden, and mankind's disobedience led to the corruption of the world. Today, Satan and his demons continue to attack God's creation by tempting and deceiving human beings whenever they can.

Satan and his demons are spiritual beings. They exist in the invisible spirit realm but can affect our physical world, so yes, the devil is powerful. But because he is a created being, he cannot be more powerful than God, the One who created him. Satan's power is always within God's control and is limited by it. Unlike God, the devil can be in only one place at a time, he does not know the future, and he is not all-powerful. Satan is the ruler of this world only because God allows him to influence it. Even then, God uses Satan's evil actions to ultimately achieve God's good purposes.

CIRCUMCISION

When God made His covenant with Abraham, He required that all males in the family and all their male descendants be circumcised. That was the outward sign of being part of God's people (Genesis 17:11–13). But the physical act of circumcision alone wasn't enough to change someone's heart. In the books of Deuteronomy and Jeremiah, God reveals that He wants the *hearts* of His people to be circumcised. Thus, the outward sign should reflect an inward truth.

In the New Testament, some people in the early church taught that new believers—including Gentiles—also had to be circumcised. There was so much controversy about this that the very first church council was called. At that meeting, the apostles agreed that circumcision was not a requirement (Acts 15). Later, Paul explained that circumcision is a matter of faith and of the heart (Romans 4:9–12).

Paul goes even further and explains that baptism is the sign of the New Covenant in the same way that circumcision was a sign of being part of God's chosen people in the Old Testament.

Prayer

Dear Heavenly Father,

You are the Lord! You have supreme authority over all things, including me, and for that I am thankful. I rejoice knowing that I live under Your loving care and lordship. Help me to walk by faith, never doubting You and always trusting that You will watch over me. Like Abraham, I want to be believe You and obey You. Like Job, I want to remember that everything I have comes from You. Thank You for providing everything I need to enjoy You in this life and forever in heaven.

In Jesus' name, I pray. Amen.

PSALM AND PROVERB TO READ:
Psalm 1, Proverbs 16:3

Lesson 17
EXODUS & LEVITICUS

Yahweh

Moses • 1446–1406 BC • Hebrew • Narrative

JOCHABED • MARIAM • PHARAOH • AARON

JETHRO • JOSHUA • MOSES

Slavery • Deliverence • Redeemer

10 Plagues • Passover

10 Commandments • Tabernacle

EXODUS

Shemot: Names

Then the LORD said, "I have surely seen the affliction of my people who are in Egypt and have heard their cry. . . . Come, I will send you to Pharaoh that you may bring my people, the children of Israel, out of Egypt."

Exodus 3:7, 10

Jesus is like Moses who leads us out of bondage and through the wilderness.

Bible Reading

Exodus 12-14

Take it To Heart

Then the LORD said, "I have surely seen the affliction of my people who are in Egypt and have heard their cry. . . . Come, I will send you to Pharaoh that you may bring my people, the children of Israel, out of Egypt."

Exodus 3:7,10

Key Word

Exit

Jehovah

Moses • 1446–1406 BC • Hebrew • Narrative
Aaron and Sons • Israelites • Moses
Sabbath • Holiness • Firstfruits
Unleavened Bread • Pentecost • Trumpets
Passover • Day of Atonement • Tabernacles
Offerings: Burnt, Meal, Peace, Sin, Trespass

LEVITICUS

Va-Yikra: and He called

"Consecrate yourselves, therefore, and be holy, for I am the Lord your God. Keep my statutes and do them; I am the Lord who sanctifies you."
Leviticus 20:7–8

Jesus is the spotless Lamb of God who was sacrificed for our sins.

Take it To Heart

"Consecrate yourselves, therefore, and be holy, for I am the LORD your God. Keep my statutes and do them; I am the LORD who sanctifies you."
Leviticus 20:7–8

Key Word

Offerings and Feasts

Bible Reading

Leviticus 16

Moses Speaks

It was just another quiet day in the fields when I found myself talking with Almighty God. I was no longer a prince of Egypt; that was almost forty years ago. Now I was just a lowly shepherd keeping the flock of my father-in-law, Jethro, the priest of Midian. I had led my flock to Horeb, the mountain of God, when I saw a miraculous sight—a bush that was burning . . . but not burning.

Then the voice of God called to me from out of the bush. He said He had a job for me to do. I tried to politely decline. I made every excuse I could think of: "Nobody's going to believe I talked with you. After all, I'm nobody special. Besides, I have this slight stutter . . ."

This made God angry! It's not wise to make God angry. "Who made man's mouth?" He thundered. "Is it not I, the Lord? Now go, and I will be with your mouth and teach you what to say." He said that my brother, Aaron, would go with me before Pharaoh, and that we must tell him to let God's people go free.

So I returned to Egypt. God led; I followed. He spoke; I listened.

Pharaoh was stubborn. But after God had struck Egypt with a series of devastating plagues, Pharaoh let the children of Israel go free. Of course, Pharaoh thought better of it and pursued us, until God destroyed his army at the Red Sea. As I said, it's not wise to make God angry.

I then led the Israelites to Mount Sinai. And I thought shepherding sheep was tough! You should try leading a couple of million people to freedom—I've never heard so much bellyaching! "Moses, are we there yet?" "Can we stop for a while?" "I'm thirsty." "Are we lost?" "I think I liked Egypt better."

Still, forty years later the mission was accomplished, and God's people entered the Promised Land. In that time, I learned that when God speaks, it's best to listen. Where He leads, follow. When He commands, trust and obey. The rewards are far greater than you can imagine!

giving & tithing

God is Lord over all things, and all things belong to Him. Everything we have comes from God. An important part of the Christian life is to give back to God a portion of what He has given to us. Giving is a form of worship in which we acknowledge that we are utterly dependent on the Lord.

In the Old Testament, giving was usually called "tithing." The word tithe means "one tenth," or ten percent. According to the law that God gave to Moses, the Israelites were required to give back to God one tenth of their income, their crops, and their livestock. These tithes were used to support the priests, pay for repairs to the temple, and help people in need. Animals were used to feed the priests and for ceremonial sacrifices. In addition to the tithe, some gave freewill offerings as well.

In the New Testament, there is no set percentage for how much to give. Part of the reason is that there were no buildings to maintain. Giving was used to support those who were in ministry full-time and to help the needy. Even though there is no definite amount for what to give, Christians are expected to give something and to do it with a glad heart.

Sometimes we mistakenly think of giving as a hardship. But giving back to God with a glad heart always blesses us (2 Corinthians 9:7). Giving transforms our hearts and helps mature us through spiritual growth, and it contributes to the establishment of God's kingdom on the earth.

Remember, although God can accomplish whatever He chooses to do without our offerings, He also chooses *how* He will accomplish His purposes. One of the ways He has chosen is through our offerings.

BLOOD

The shedding of blood is a symbol for death because when you bleed, life is literally leaving the body. Because the only just penalty for sin is death (Romans 6:23), the only way to escape this penalty is to offer a blood sacrifice in our place.

In the Old Testament, God said to Moses, "For the life of the flesh is in the blood, and I have given it for you on the altar to make atonement for your souls, for it is the blood that makes atonement by the life" (Leviticus 17:11). *Atonement* means to cover, cleanse, or purify ourselves to make us acceptable to God; in essence, we are washed by the blood.

However, the Old Testament system of animal sacrifices was never meant to be permanent. Instead, it was a picture of the sacrifice that Jesus would one day make by dying on the cross. The Old Testament system is one of the ways we can know and understand the meaning of His death and what it does for us.

Because Jesus is God, the shedding of His blood is able to pay the penalty we owe for sinning against God. He is called the Lamb of God, and His sacrifice is sufficient to cover all the sins of whoever believes in Him, once and for all time. Nothing else ever needs to be done to pay this price.

Prayer

Dear Heavenly Father,

You are Almighty, You are eternal, and You know all things. You are holy and perfect and altogether righteous. You are so much more, but it's hard to think about and remember everything there is to know about You. Help me to love You and seek You with all of my being! Remind me that sin is ugly and help me to hate sin as You do. Help me to desire only You and Your kingdom. Thank You for the sacrifice of Jesus, whose blood covers my sin and allows me to be declared righteous in Your eyes. I am so glad to be Your adopted child! Help me to live every day for You.

In Jesus' name, I pray. Amen.

PSALM AND PROVERB TO READ:
Psalm 88, Proverbs 17:27

Lesson 10
NUMBERS, DEUTERONOMY & JOSHUA

Yahweh

Moses • 1446–1406 BC • Hebrew • Narrative

MOSES • AARON

JOSHUA • CALEB • ISRAELITES

Census • Rebellion • Complaining • 12 Spies

Grumbling • Wilderness • Wanderings

Rebellion • Aaron's Staff • Bronze Snake

NUMBERS

Bemidbar: In the Wilderness

"Not one shall come into the land
where I swore that I would make you dwell,
except Caleb . . . and Joshua."
Numbers 14:30

Jesus is slow to anger and abounding
in love, forgiving sin and rebellion.

Take it To Heart

"Not one shall come into the land where I swore that I would make you dwell, except Caleb . . . and Joshua."
Numbers 14:30

Bible Reading

Numbers 14

Key Word

Wanders

Yahweh

Moses • 1446–1406 BC • Hebrew • Sermon Series

MOSES • JOSHUA • ISRAELITES

Fear • Keep • Love • Heart

Children • Obey • Blessing and Cursing

DEUTERONOMY

Devarim: Spoken words

"I call heaven and earth to witness against you today, that I have set before you life and death, blessing and curse. Therefore choose life, that you and your offspring may live."

Deuteronomy 30:19

Jesus is merciful.

Bible Reading

Deuteronomy 6

Second Law

Key Word

Take it To Heart

"I call heaven and earth to witness against you today, that I have set before you life and death, blessing and curse. Therefore choose life, that you and your offspring may live."
Deuteronomy 30:19

Yahweh

Joshua• 1406–1385 BC • Hebrew • Narrative

JOSHUA • CALEB • ISRAELITES • RAHAB • ACHAN

Victory • Obedience • Greed • Faith • Leadership

JOSHUA

Y'hoshua

"Be strong and courageous. Do not be frightened, and do not be dismayed, for the LORD your God is with you wherever you go."

Joshua 1:9

Jesus is the victorious warrior that leads us into the promised land.

Bible Reading

Joshua 1, 24

Take it To Heart

"Be strong and courageous. Do not be frightened, and do not be dismayed, for the LORD your God is with you wherever you go."
Joshua 1:9

Key Word

Conquers

The Levites & Priests Speak

The priesthood was central to the spiritual health of the nation of Israel. Our members were highly respected and our position of supreme importance, as we orchestrated corporate and individual worship and performed such tasks as intercessory prayers and sacrifices. We priests were the spiritual compass of Israel—as the priesthood went, so went the nation.

A priest was not elected by the people but appointed by God. When the Jewish people made and worshiped a golden calf at the foot of Mount Sinai, the descendants of Levi were the only tribe that did not participate. So we, the Levites, were chosen to serve God in the tabernacle and, later, the temple. But the most sacred tasks were reserved for the descendants of Aaron, brother of Moses and the first high priest of Israel.

We priests were God's representatives and served as mediators among the people. Our clothing carried the names of all twelve tribes on the sleeves, a constant reminder to us of our high calling. We served as the spiritual conscience of the nation, constantly nudging the people toward God. But our primary function was to reconcile men to God and to atone for their sins with the appropriate sacrifices.

As priests, our calling was sacred, our mission was holy, and our message was from God. Today, Jesus is your High Priest, interceding for you before the throne of the Father. The sacrifice He offers is not the blood of bulls and goats; His sacrifice is Himself. What a sacrifice! What a Savior!

Chosen by God

God not only revealed to Moses *how* He should be worshiped but also *who* should perform the ceremonies. Not just anyone could serve in the tabernacle or the temple. All those who served had to be men from the tribe of Levi. Of these, only men descended from Moses' brother, Aaron, could be priests. The other men, called Levites, served as guards, singers, musicians, and assistants to the priests.

When the land of Canaan was divided among the Hebrew tribes, no land was given to the Levites, for God was their portion. Instead, the priests and Levites were fed and provided for through offerings made by the other tribes. They lived only in certain towns that were spread throughout the land. The priests were also given special clothes to wear that set them apart from everyone else.

Levites had to be at least thirty years old and were required to retire from regular service at the age of fifty (Numbers 4:3). Priests who brought offerings into the Lord's presence could not be blind, injured, or disabled in any way (Leviticus 21:16–21). Does this mean that God does not love senior citizens or people with disabilities? No, not at all! Scripture assures us that "God shows no partiality" and "anyone who fears him and does what is right is acceptable to him" (Acts 10:34–35).

To understand these rules, we first need to remember that God is completely and utterly holy. Sinners cannot enter His presence without being destroyed. In fact, only that which is perfect and unblemished can approach Him. This means that none of us—not one—is qualified to come near to Him, for all have sinned and fall short of God's glory (Romans 3:23). And yet

God allowed certain priests to enter His presence at specified times to bring Him the offerings of His people. Why did He do this?

By choosing a specific group to carry out the priestly duties and setting strict parameters for how He was to be worshiped, God created a sign that pointed to the coming Messiah. Before the death and resurrection of Christ, priests acted as go-betweens for God and mankind; they did the work that atoned for our sins, and their unquestioned obedience is what pleased God. But now, Jesus acts as our priest. Unlike the earthly priests, Jesus kept God's law perfectly. And by offering Himself as the perfect sacrifice—the spotless Lamb of God—Jesus paid for all the sins of all the people who believe in Him.

Christ's work on the cross has made the ceremonies of the priests no longer necessary. Now, clothed in *His* righteousness, we can not only approach God, but we can spend forever in His glorious presence!

WHAT IS A SERMON?

A sermon is a talk that informs, instructs, and inspires. A good sermon informs us about a biblical truth, gives us instructions on how to live according to the truth, and inspires us to obey God.

Moses preached three sermons to the people of Israel before they crossed the Jordan River into the Promised Land. His first sermon informed the new generation of Israelites about the history of their people in the wilderness (Deuteronomy 1:1–4:40). He reminded them of all the wondrous things God had done for the nation to bring them to the land they were about to enter.

Moses' second sermon gave the people instructions for living according to the will of God (Deuteronomy 5:1–11:32). He reminded the Israelites they must worship the one true God only and observe all of the laws He had given them.

In his third sermon, Moses inspired the Israelites with the hope that even if they were unfaithful to God and lost the land they had been given, they could repent and be restored to God's favor (Deuteronomy 11:32–33:29).

A good sermon will not only teach you about the Bible and how to live according to its truths, but it will also leave you with the desire to follow God's instructions for your life.

Prayer

Dear Heavenly Father,

Thank you for Your Word, which teaches me about You. Thank You for the Holy Spirit, who reminds me what Your Word says and guides me into all truth. Help me to know and love Your ways and to recognize and reject the enemy's lies when I hear them. Help me to listen carefully to Your teaching and to study Your Word diligently. Help me to be a doer and not just a hearer of Your Word and to choose life at all times.

I ask these things in Jesus' name. Amen.

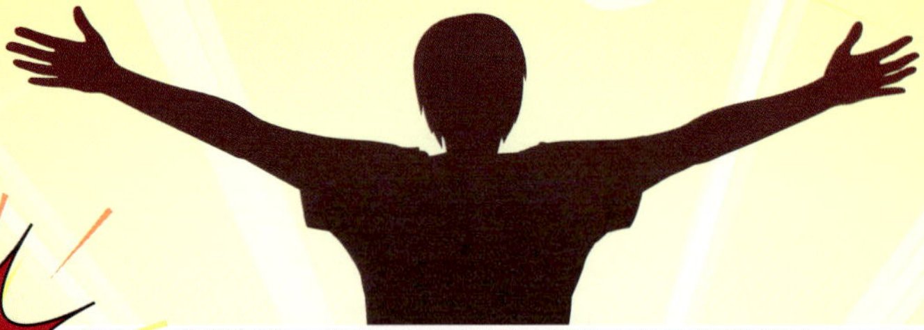

PSALM AND PROVERB TO READ:
Psalm 27, Proverbs 18:10

Lesson 19
JUDGES

Yahweh

Samuel • 1050–1000 BC. • Hebrew • Narrative

DEBORAH • GIDEON • JEPTHAH

SAMSON • DELILAH • ISRAELITES

Disobedience • Disaster • Distress • Deliverance

JUDGES

Shophatim: to judge

And there arose another generation after them who did not know the LORD or the work that he had done for Israel. And the people of Israel did what was evil in the sight of the LORD.

Judges 2:10–11

Jesus is the righteous Judge who judges all things rightly.

Key Word

Cycles

Take it To Heart

And there arose another generation after them who did not know the LORD or the work that he had done for Israel. And the people of Israel did what was evil in the sight of the LORD.
Judges 2:10–11

Bible Reading

Judges 2

Deborah Speaks

I was a prophet and judge who held court under a palm tree in the hill country of Ephraim. The people of Israel would visit me there to have their disputes decided. Yes, I was wise, but I was also tough. Most importantly, I was a servant of God who listened to His word and obeyed.

My name is Deborah, and yes, I was a woman.

For twenty years the people had been cruelly oppressed by a Canaanite king called Jabin. The king's vast army was led by Sisera, a ruthless commander whose forces were equipped with 900 iron chariots. But Jabin and Sisera were about to meet an unforeseen end.

One day, I sent for a man named Barak from the tribe of Naphtali and gave him a message from the Lord. Barak was to gather an army of 10,000 men at Mount Tabor. There the Lord would give him victory over Sisera's army. Barak responded by saying he would go, but only if I went with him. I agreed. We recruited 10,000 men from the tribes of Zebulun and Naphtali and gathered them at Mount Tabor. When Sisera heard of this, he called for all of his 900 chariots and all of his warriors and marched them to Mount Tabor.

Then I said to the Israelites, "Arise! This day the Lord will give you victory over Sisera, for the Lord is marching ahead of you." And Barak led his 10,000 men down the slopes of Tabor into battle, sending Sisera and his men into a panic. Many fled the battle, and Barak pursued them. That day, all of Sisera's army was killed, and the reign of the Canaanite king was soon ended.

Israel prevailed that day under my leadership. I was simply following the orders of my Commander in Chief. Forty years of peace followed. When you find yourself oppressed by the forces of darkness, follow my example. Listen to the Lord, obey Him, and triumph!

THE KING'S COURT

It takes wisdom to make good decisions. Before Israel had kings, God gave them judges such as Gideon, Deborah, and Samson to serve as leaders and dispense justice. Later, at the Israelites' insistence, God appointed kings to lead the people and pass judgments in difficult cases as the highest authority in the land.

The king listened to both parties in a dispute, heard witnesses, and pronounced judgment. The king's decision was final. In 1 Kings 3:16–28, we read about a difficult case in which two women living in the same house had each given birth to a baby boy. When one of the babies died in the night, the mother of the dead child switched the infants and claimed that the living child was hers. The women took their case to the wise King Solomon and asked that he decide the matter.

Solomon called for a sword and ordered that the baby be cut in half and a piece be given to each mother. The false mother said this sounded fair, but the child's true mother cried out and pleaded with the king not to harm the baby but instead give the child to the other woman. Solomon wisely recognized that a mother would never want her child to be harmed, so he gave the baby to his real mother. News of the king's judgment spread quickly and the people stood in awe, for they saw the wisdom God had given their king to administer justice.

Do you ask God for wisdom to find solutions to your problems? God knows everything, including the best way to solve every problem and dispute. And James 1:5 tells us that He will give wisdom to any of His children who ask. You can find God's answers by praying, reading Scripture, or asking your parents or pastor for help.

Sin Nature

God made Adam and Eve with the ability to obey and keep His moral law. They did not have a sinful nature. When Adam disobeyed God, his sin radically changed him so that he became unable to keep the law, even though he was still required to obey it. And because we are all descended from Adam, each of us has inherited his sinful nature.

Our sinful nature keeps us from choosing to obey God—we are unable *not* to sin. That doesn't mean we sin every time we get the chance, or in every way we can. But it does mean that sin touches every part of our lives and that nothing about us is free from the corruption of sin. It also means that we are not born sinless and then become sinners when we sin; rather, we sin because we were born with a sinful nature.

Before we were saved, we were slaves to sin (Romans 6:1–23) and could not escape our sin nature through our own power. We were hopelessly fallen and could never do enough good works to make up for our sins, for the wages of sin is death.

It is because we could never choose God on our own that we needed Jesus. Now we can be made spiritually alive through belief in Christ's perfect obedience to God and His death in our place. Now when we die, our natures will not only be free of sin, but we will be unable to sin.

Dear Heavenly Father,

I am so thankful that You are merciful and have provided forgiveness of my sins through Jesus Christ. Please keep me from doing what is right in my own eyes. Instead, please give me the desire and strength to do what is good and right in Your eyes. Give me Your wisdom and understanding so that I may live my life to Your glory.

In Jesus' name, I pray. Amen.

PSALM AND PROVERB TO READ:
Psalm 62, Proverbs 19:11

Lesson 20
RUTH

Yahweh

Unknown • 1010–930 BC • Hebrew • Narrative

Naomi • Orpah • Ruth • Boaz • Obed

Kinsman • Redeemer

RUTH

Megilath Ruth

"Do not urge me to leave you or to return from following you. For where you go I will go, and where you lodge I will lodge. Your people shall be my people, and your God my God."

Ruth 1:16

Jesus is our kinsman-redeemer who frees us for a new life.

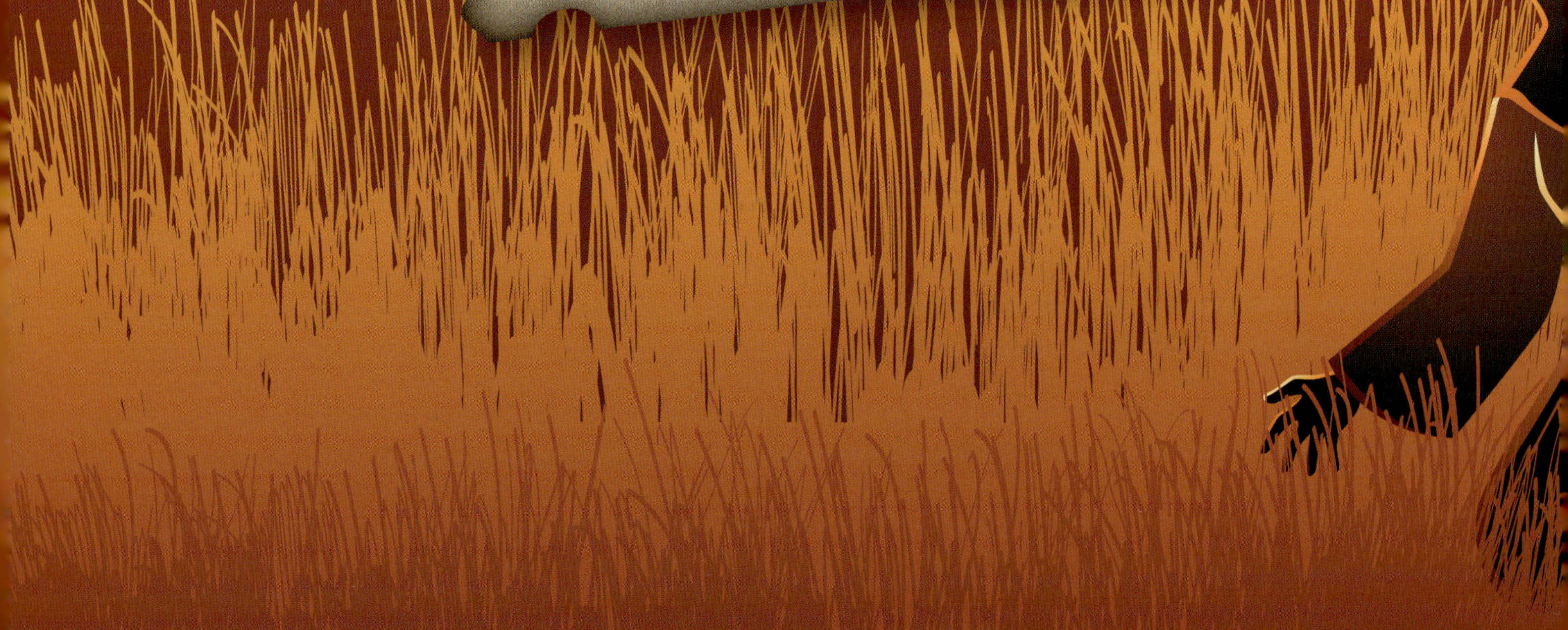

Bible Reading

Ruth 1–4

Take it To Heart

But Ruth said, "Do not urge me to leave you or to return from following you. For where you go I will go, and where you lodge I will lodge. Your people shall be my people, and your God my God."
Ruth 1:16

Key Word

Love Story

Ruth Speaks

The journey from Moab to Bethlehem was both arduous for me and unfamiliar. Every step I took moved me farther from the land of my birth and from the grave of my husband. I traveled with my mother-in-law, Naomi. Years earlier she and her husband, along with their two sons, had immigrated to my country because of a severe famine in Judah. They were refugees in my homeland. And now, I would be a refugee in hers.

It was in my country of Moab that I met her son, fell in love, and got married. Then tragedy struck. Naomi's husband died, followed by the first of her sons. And then my husband died too. Naomi was grief-stricken and determined to return to her homeland, and I chose to go with her. As we traveled, I fought back my own unrelenting grief. The husband of my youth was gone, and my future appeared dim. Tears flooded my soul. I was a widow, a stranger in a strange new land.

We arrived in Bethlehem just a few days ago, in time for the barley harvest. We needed grain for food, so with Naomi's permission, I took my place among the gleaners who walked the fields behind the harvesters and picked up leftovers. The work was hard and the temperature harsh, but I counted the opportunity as a blessing.

The owner of the field, a man called Boaz, came to survey his fields and greeted all the workers. He seemed a very kind man. Someone had told him my story of suffering and loss. When he approached me, I bowed down and thanked him for allowing me, a foreigner, to glean his fields. He offered a blessing upon me because I had been very attentive and loyal to Naomi. At the close of the day, I told my mother-in-law about meeting Boaz and how he had been so kind. Naomi told me that he was a close relative of hers and advised me regarding the customs of her people, and I paid close attention. That night, I dreamed of a wedding.

KINSMAN-REDEEMER

Have you ever attended a family reunion? Family reunions usually involve more than your parents and siblings. There are grandparents, aunts, uncles, cousins, nieces, nephews, and in-laws. Often you won't really know all the people at your family reunion, even though you're related to them in some way. A clan was like this in biblical times—bigger than an extended family, but still all related.

The clan usually chose one of the men to be their main protector, and they called that man the kinsman-redeemer. According to Jewish law, the kinsman-redeemer had a responsibility to act on behalf of a relative who was in trouble or need. For example, if a member of the clan fell on hard times and had to sell property, the kinsman-redeemer would buy the property to keep it in the family. If things got so bad that a family member had to sell himself into slavery, the kinsman-redeemer would buy his freedom.

If a man of the clan died before his wife and had no children, the kinsman-redeemer would marry the widow. Any children from the new marriage would be considered the children of the man who had died.

The book of Ruth is a beautiful story of a widow in need presenting herself to the kinsman-redeemer and asking that he cover her, protect her, redeem her, and make her his wife.

GLEANING

Gleaning is an ancient practice among the poor of picking over leftover crops after a field has been harvested by its owner. The law of Moses provided the opportunity for the gleaners to gather food for themselves and their families:

> "When you reap the harvest of your land, you shall not reap your field right up to its edge, neither shall you gather the gleanings after your harvest. And you shall not strip your vineyard bare, neither shall you gather the fallen grapes of your vineyard. You shall leave them for the poor and for the sojourner: I am the LORD your God."
> (Leviticus 19:9–10).

A landowner could be punished under the law if he didn't permit the poor to glean in his fields.

Harvesters often used a sickle, a handheld tool with a curved blade, to cut down the grain or fruit from a tree. The gleaners followed behind them to pick up any fallen grains or fruit.

Gleaning is still practiced today. Each year, the nonprofit organization Boston Area Gleaners uses volunteers to glean from local farms in order to provide fresh fruits and vegetables to the poor of the area.

Prayer

Dear Heavenly Father,

I sometimes feel like a stranger in a strange land. But I know You have good plans for me, and I believe You will provide everything I need. Thank You for every good thing that I get to enjoy. Remind me that I don't need to worry about tomorrow. Give me a grateful attitude, a trusting heart, and a mind set on following You and staying close by Your side.

In Jesus' name, I pray. Amen.

PSALM AND PROVERB TO READ:
Psalm 111, Proverbs 20:3

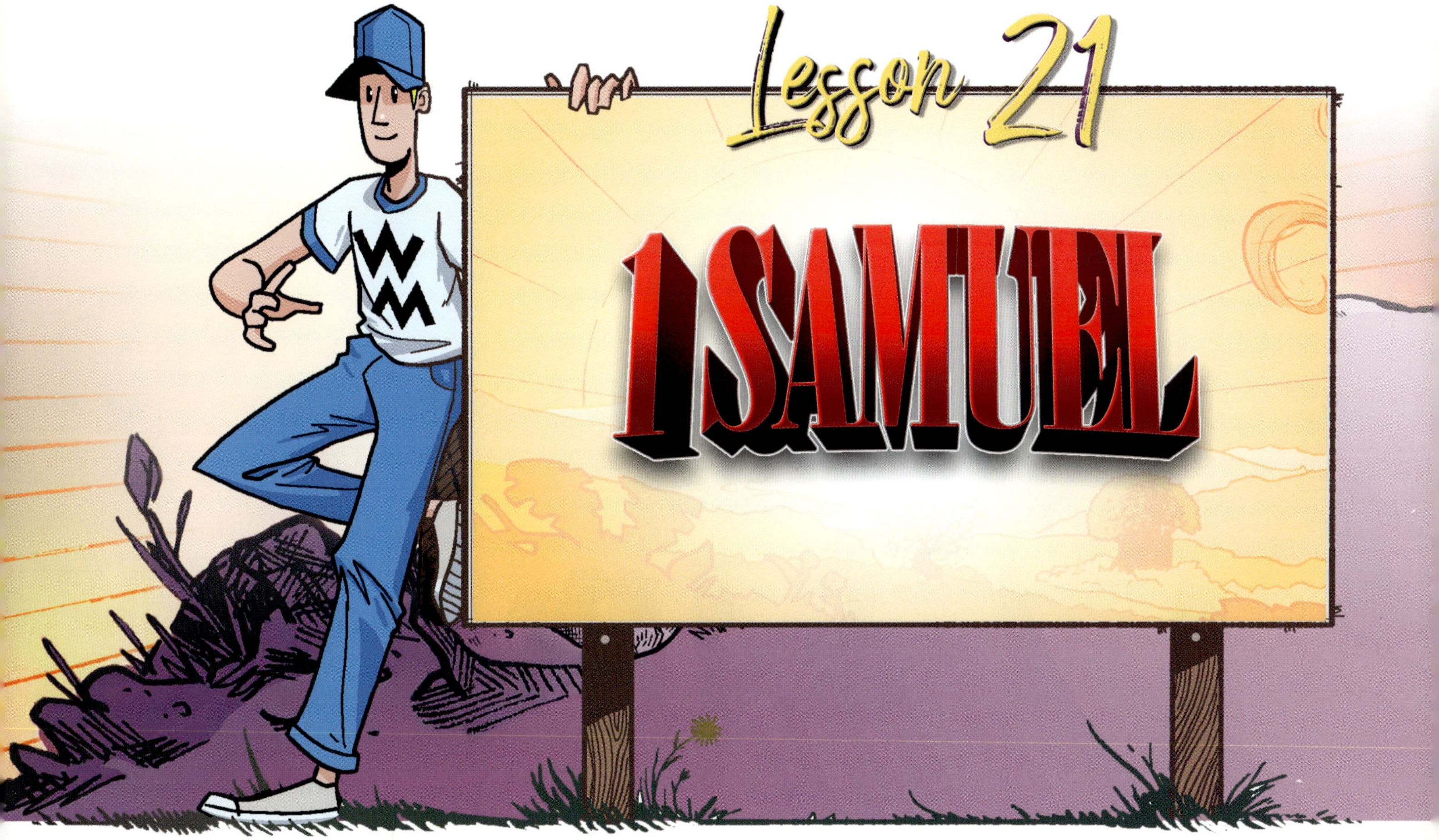
Lesson 21
1 SAMUEL

Yahweh

Samuel, Nathan, Gad • ~975 BC. • Hebrew • Narrative

Eli • Hannah • Samuel

Saul • David • Jonathan • Mighty Men

Desperate • Promise • Answered Prayer

Vow Fulfilled • Anointed • Disobedience • Boldness

Rejection • Friendship • Escape • Loyalty • Honor

1 SAMUEL

Sefer Sh'muel

And the LORD said to Samuel, "Obey the voice of the people in all that they say to you, for they have not rejected you, but they have rejected me from being king over them."
1 Samuel 8:7

Jesus is the one who calls "Samuel, Samuel."

Key Word

Saul

Take it To Heart

And the LORD said to Samuel, "Obey the voice of the people in all that they say to you, for they have not rejected you, but they have rejected me from being king over them."
1 Samuel 8:7

Bible Reading

1 Samuel 15

Samuel Speaks

My life began at a peaceful time in Israel's history. In those days a woman from the hill country of Ephraim longed for a child. Her name was Hannah, and she and her husband, Elkanah, were deeply devoted to the Lord. They were childless but hopeful. With God, there is always hope. And so Hannah prayed without ceasing for a son.

She vowed to God that if He would grant her a son she would dedicate him to the service of the Lord. God heard her prayers. Nine months later, I was born. True to her promise, when I was weaned, Hannah took me to an aging high priest named Eli. He received me, a mere child, and raised me in preparation for the priesthood. And so I grew up in the presence of the Lord.

Now messages from the Lord were rare in those days, and visions were infrequent (1 Samuel 3:1). Then one night, when the shadows from the oil lamps flickered eerily on the temple walls, I heard a distinct voice calling my name. "Samuel! Samuel!" Three times I heard the voice, and three times I hurried to Eli to ask what he wanted. But the priest had not called for me.

Then Eli realized that it was the Lord who was calling. Eli instructed me in what to do if I heard the voice again. The next time the Lord called to me, I answered, "Speak, for your servant hears." Then God revealed to me that the ministry of Eli's household was coming to an end.

Thus, I began my journey as a prophet, and all Israel recognized and confirmed that I spoke for the Lord.

fear of god vs. fear of MAN

When we think about what God is like, we usually focus on His infinite love or on how merciful and gracious He is. The Bible calls us to love Him in return with all our heart, soul, mind, and strength, but it also tells us repeatedly that we should "fear" God. How can we fear someone we love? The Bible also tells us that "perfect love casts out fear" (1 John 4:18). God is love, so how can we fear Him if He casts out all fear?

The word translated as *fear* in our English Bibles isn't quite the same thing as the fear we experience while watching a scary movie or being afraid of heights. To fear God in the biblical sense means to be awed by and have deep respect for Him. And because God is holy, righteous, and just, we are right to fear His judgment. When we fear God in this way, it is actually a form of worship because it means that we recognize and acknowledge the truth of His power, His glory, His authority, and all that He is. Indeed, we live according to His ways because we both love and fear Him.

Sometimes we fear the harm that other people can inflict upon us. But when we fear God properly, we are freed from the power someone else has over us because God is infinitely more powerful than any man (or *all* men, for that matter). By fearing God and trusting Him more than we fear or trust our worldly circumstances, we can face difficult times that come our way.

THE KING'S ROLE & RESPONSIBILITIES

Everyone has responsibilities. What are your responsibilities at home? Perhaps you are expected to clean your room, dust the furniture, mow the lawn, do homework, or babysit your siblings.

God chose the kings of Israel and gave them certain responsibilities. For example, He expected the king to study His Word daily and enforce His laws with justice and righteousness. The king was to defend the nation in battle when necessary. He had the right to take men for military service and women for domestic service. And one tenth of the harvest, flocks, and herds were collected to support the monarchy. The people were not always happy with their king, but they were expected to respect him nonetheless.

However, the king was not all-powerful, and he was not above the law. God required obedience from the king as well as his subjects. When the king did not follow the law, the high priests and prophets served justice.

Today, God requires you to act justly, love mercy, and walk humbly with Him (Micah 6:8). Your responsibility as a Christian is to treat others with fairness, compassion, and love without thinking of yourself first. Have you accepted your responsibilities?

Prayer

Dear Heavenly Father,

You are my King. Yet I am as fickle as the Israelites of old. Please help me to remain loyal to Your kingdom and Your service. Deep down inside, I want only to worship You. Help me resist the worldly temptation to go along with the crowd when other people choose to sin. Help me not to make excuses for my bad behavior, hurtful words, and ugly thoughts. Teach me to fear You in the way that is proper and appropriate. I want to be ready to answer Your call and obey right away. Help me do this for Your glory.

In Jesus' name, I pray. Amen.

PSALM AND PROVERB TO READ:
Psalm 21, Proverbs 21:3

Lesson 22
2 SAMUEL, 1 CHRONICLES & PSALMS

Yahweh

Zabud, Nathan, Gad • ~930 BC • Hebrew • Narrative

DAVID • BATHSHEBA • NATHAN

ABNER • JOAB • ABSOLAM • ISRAEL

Trouble • Covenant Victory • Sin

Confrontation • Consequences • Worship • Rebellion

2 SAMUEL

Sefer Sh'muel

"And your [David's] house and your kingdom shall be made sure forever before me. Your throne shall be established forever."

2 Samuel 7:16

Jesus is like David at his best.

Take it To Heart

"And your [David's] house and your kingdom shall be made sure forever before me. Your throne shall be established forever."
2 Samuel 7:16

Bible Reading

2 Samuel 11

Key Word

David

Yahweh

Ezra • ~450 BC • Hebrew • Narrative

DAVID • MIGHTY MEN • SOLOMON

Genealogies • God's Faithfulness • Worship

1 CHRONICLES

Dibre Hayyamim

And David knew that the LORD had established him as king over Israel, and that his kingdom was highly exalted for the sake of his people Israel.
1 Chronicles 14:2

Jesus has a permanent temple and home.

Bible Reading

1 Chronicles 17

Key Word

Editorial on David

Take it To Heart

And David knew that the LORD had established him as king over Israel, and that his kingdom was highly exalted for the sake of his people Israel.

1 Chronicles 14:2

Yahweh

Several • 1500–500 BC • Hebrew • Poetry

David

Praise • Prayer • Thankfulness
Trust • Wicked • Righteous

PSALMS

Tehillim: praises

Let everything that has breath praise the LORD!
Praise the LORD!
Psalm 150:6

Jesus is my shepherd; I shall not want.

Take it To Heart

Let everything that has breath praise the LORD! Praise the LORD!

Psalm 150:6

Bible Reading

Psalm 100

Key Word

Worship

Jonathan Speaks

I am Jonathan, and I was King Saul's oldest son. Some say I was intelligent, brave, and loyal—a warrior and a national hero. My greatest accomplishment, however, wasn't on the field of battle. Today I am known best for my friendship with a young shepherd and future king named David.

My father had been chosen by God to be the first king of Israel. He had defeated many of the nation's enemies and united the scattered tribes. King Saul was widely admired for his stature and his deeds. Yet after David's victory over the giant Goliath, the people began to sing the shepherd's praises, making more of his single victory than all of my father's. From that moment, Father kept a jealous eye on David and began plotting to rid himself of the young shepherd-turned-warrior.

But my friendship with David was unshakeable. I loved David as I loved myself, and I persisted in warning David of my father's plans to harm him. When David was forced to flee for his life and hide out in the hills, I stayed in constant communication with him. I risked my own life to save David's and even surrendered my own claims to my father's throne.

We all need a good friend in our life. Someone who knows our deepest secrets. Someone who comes to our aid. Someone who is willing to die for us, if necessary. I was that friend to David.

THE VALUE OF FRIENDSHIPS

Jonathan showed us what it's like to be a friend in need. How do you comfort a friend when he or she is sad or hurting? Do you spend time talking with your friend and share encouraging words? Do you tell your friend about how God has comforted you?

Job was blameless and upright, and he stayed away from evil. He feared God and offered burnt sacrifices to the Lord daily. And God had blessed him with a large family, good health, and great wealth. Then one day God permitted Satan to test Job.

Satan set about destroying all of Job's possessions and killing his family. When Job refused to sin by blaming God, Satan caused painful sores to break out on Job's body from the soles of his feet to the top of his head. Job wished he had never been born, yet he remained faithful to God through all of his troubles.

Job's friends Eliphaz, Bildad and Zophar heard about his troubles and came to mourn with him. They cried aloud, tore their robes, and threw dust on themselves, as was the custom for mourning. They sat on the ground next to Job for seven days and seven nights but did not speak to Job because he was so sad.

When at last they spoke, his friends began to blame Job himself for all of his troubles. Eliphaz and Bildad told Job that his troubles were evidence that he had sinned. Zophar told Job that God would surely bless him if he would repent of his sins.

Job needed his friends to be understanding and loving in his time of sadness. Instead, his friends judged him and blamed him for his problems.

Do your friends blame each other when one of them has a problem? What can you do to help your friends understand that true friends care about each other and comfort one another in both good times and difficult times?

A MAN After god's OWN Heart

We have seen that David was called in Scripture "a man after God's own heart." We have also seen that David was not perfect. So how is it that David can be an example of someone whose heart is like the heart of God?

As a mere boy, David volunteered to face the giant Goliath on the field of combat. Before he went to battle, he said to the king, "The LORD who delivered me from the paw of the lion and from the paw of the bear will deliver me from the hand of this Philistine" (1 Samuel 17:37). David believed that God would take care of him.

David loved God's law. He spent much of his time meditating on God's Word, practicing the Lord's precepts, and thinking about godly things.

During good times and difficult times, David never forgot to thank God for everything. He wrote, "Enter his gates with thanksgiving, and his courts with praise! Give thanks to him; bless his name!" (Psalm 100:4)

One afternoon, David sinned against God. He wanted another man's wife. So he had her husband killed and took her for his own. When confronted with his sin, David was devastated. He repented of his sin and was truly sorry. He asked God to have mercy, forgive him, and cleanse him from his sin (Psalm 51:1–2).

How can God use a man like David as an example of someone whose heart is like His own? David did many things right. He had great faith, he loved God's Word, he praised the Lord every day, and he kept a thankful heart. Did David make mistakes? Yes, he did. Like David, you too will make mistakes. But God is merciful to forgive when you confess your sins to Him and repent.

Dear Heavenly Father,

Give me a whole heart like King David. When I sin, let my heart be convicted quickly so that I can repent right away. And let me always run back to You. Thank You for your mercy and forgiveness when I confess my wrongdoings. Keep me close to You and help me to always walk by faith and in Your grace. I pray that You will surround me with good friends, like Jonathan was for David, and that I would be a good friend to others. Help me to be kind, trustworthy, honest, and loyal.

In Jesus' name, I pray. Amen.

PSALM AND PROVERB TO READ:
Psalm 51, Proverbs 22:1

Lesson 23
1 KINGS, PROVERBS, ECCLESIASTES & SONG OF SOLOMON

Yahweh

Unknown • 600–540 BC • Hebrew • Narrative

Solomon • Rehoboam • Jeroboam • Ahab

Jezebel • Elijah • Asa • Jehoshaphat

Humility • Wisdom • Success • Popularity

Temple • Foolishness • Women • Idols

Consequences • Division

1 KINGS

Sepher M'jakhim

So Solomon sat on the throne of David his father,
and his kingdom was firmly established.
1 Kings 2:12

Jesus is the one who charges
the ravens to feed Elijah.

Bible Reading
1 Kings 12

Take it To Heart
So Solomon sat on the throne of David his father, and his kingdom was firmly established.
1 Kings 2:12

Key Word
Solomon

Yahweh

Solomon• 1500–500 BC • Hebrew • Poetry

Solomon

Praise • Prayer • Thankfulness

Trust • Wicked • Righteous

PROVERBS

Mishlê Shlomoh: Proverbs of Solomon

The fear of the Lord is the beginning of knowledge;
fools despise wisdom and instruction.
Proverbs 1:7

Jesus is our wisdom.

Take it To Heart

The fear of the LORD is the beginning of knowledge; fools despise wisdom and instruction.
Proverbs 1:7

Bible Reading

Proverbs 8

Key Word

Wisdom

Yahweh

Solomon• ~930 BC • Hebrew • Poetic Sermon

SOLOMON

Vanity • Time • Man • Heart • Wisdom • Sun

ECCLESIASTES

Qoheleth: Preacher

Fear God and keep his commandments,
for this is the whole duty of man.
Ecclesiastes 12:13

Jesus gives our lives meaning.

ECCLESIASTES

Bible Reading

Ecclesiastes 12

Take it To Heart

The end of the matter; all has been heard. Fear God and keep his commandments, for this is the whole duty of man.
Ecclesiastes 12:13

Key Word

Vanity

Yahweh

Solomon • ~960 BC • Hebrew • Poem

Solomon • His Bride

Beloved • Love

SONG OF SOLOMON

Shir ha-Shirim: Song of Solomon

I am my beloved's and my beloved is mine.
Song of Solomon 6:3

Jesus is the wonderful bridegroom who loves His bride, the church.

Key Word

Love in Marriage

Take it To Heart

I am my beloved's and my beloved is mine
Song of Solomon 6:3

Bible Reading

Song of Solomon 7

Elijah Speaks

My name is Elijah. God called me to prophesy in some of the darkest days of my nation. Decadence abounded. Civil unrest persisted. Fear mounted. Hope had vanished. Then God commanded me to tell the king that a severe drought was coming, followed by a famine. In so doing, I pronounced God's judgment on the throne.

King Ahab was the most pompous toad that ever squatted upon the throne of a nation. His queen, the Phoenician princess Jezebel, was vindictive and ruthless. She desecrated the altars of the Lord and killed most of His prophets. At her request, Ahab built places to worship the false gods Baal and Asherah throughout the countryside. Soon the people became confused as to which god they were supposed to worship. Thus, Ahab did more to provoke the Lord to anger than all the kings of Israel before him.

For my part, I did everything God asked. I stood before the king and pronounced that the Lord would send drought and famine upon the land, earning the nickname Troubler of Israel. Ahab and Jezebel were enraged and sought to kill me. God warned me to leave Israel, so I ran and hid in a ravine near the brook Cherith, east of the Jordan. I drank from the brook, and God sent ravens to bring me bread and meat. There I waited on the Lord.

A few years later, at God's direction, I emerged from hiding and confronted Ahab once more, this time with a challenge for the prophets of Baal and Asherah. At Mount Carmel, the Lord dramatically showed the people that He alone is God. The prophets of Baal and Asherah were destroyed, and Jezebel vowed that I would pay for their deaths with my life. And so I ran a day's journey into the wilderness, in fear for my life. There under a broom tree I slumped to the ground, tired, depressed, and discouraged. Despite the great victory over the gods of Jezebel, I had run at the first threat of retaliation.

Yet it was in the wilderness that I remembered God's provision. I took refuge in the safety and security of His promises. He reminded me that serving Him sometimes comes at a very high price, but it was nothing compared to His eternal rewards. Soon my heart was emboldened to be faithful to Him for the rest of my days.

You too are going to face a few bullies in your life. When God calls you, I pray you won't run the other direction. Instead, stand confidently and speak up for God. As God did for me, He will provide!

Marriage

Marriage is when one man and one woman take vows before God to be joined together in mutual love, loyalty, and support for the rest of their lives. They are now one flesh, exclusively given to each other intellectually, emotionally, and physically. They are to commit to each other, relate to each other, complement each other, and complete each other. Together they form the core unit of a distinct family, which will hopefully be blessed with children.

Marriage is a reflection of the unbreakable bond between Christ (the groom) and the church (His bride). Christ's willingness to sacrifice Himself for the church helps us to better understand the profound and unique relationship between husband and wife.

Marriage was established by God and is therefore more than a legal contract or simple agreement between two people. Because marriage is not a human invention but was instituted by God, marriage cannot be redefined to mean anything other than what God intended it to be.

While it is true that the Bible tells of some marriages that were not as God intended them to be—Solomon's 700 wives, for example—that does not mean there are many kinds of marriages. Just because a biblical king had more than one wife does not mean it pleased God or was in keeping with His intentions for marriage.

There is a difference between what the Bible describes and what it prescribes, and God's prescription for marriage will always be between one man and one woman.

WISDOM

We live in a time that has been called the Information Age. Never in history have so many people had easy access to so much data. However, there is a difference between knowing something and how you live because you know it. You probably know many things that don't affect how you live day to day. But when you let your experience in the world be guided by knowledge and understanding, that is called wisdom.

In the Bible, wisdom has a more specific meaning. It's allowing the knowledge of God to transform how you live. There are many people who know things about God and the Bible but fail to let that knowledge transform their hearts. People who are biblically wise use God's Word to make good decisions, walk with God, and light their way through a dark world.

Being humble, discerning right from wrong, keeping God's commandments, being thoughtful and careful, and fearing the Lord are all part of being wise. This is one of the reasons why Jesus is called the very wisdom of God (1 Corinthians 1:24).

Prayer

Dear Heavenly Father,

I want to be bold like Elijah when he faced the prophets of Baal. Help me to listen carefully for Your small, still voice in order to hear Your call on my life. Then give me the confidence I need to walk in Your calling and spread Your message to the people around me. Please give me wisdom beyond my age so that I can know what to say and when to speak up. When the time is right, I pray You will prepare me to be a good spouse and honor You with a godly marriage and strong family.

In Jesus' name, I pray. Amen.

PSALM AND PROVERB TO READ:
Psalm 145, Proverbs 23:12

Lesson 24
2 KINGS, 2 CHRONICLES, HOSEA & AMOS

Yahweh

Unknown • 600–540 BC • Hebrew • Narrative

Elijah • Elisha • Shunammite • Naaman

Jehu • Jeroboam II • Hezekiah • Josiah

Manasseh • Nebuchadnezzar

Idolatry • Choices • God's Patience

Miracles • Prayer • Judgment • Captivity

2 KINGS

Sepher M'lakhim

But they would not listen, but were stubborn, as their fathers had been, who did not believe in the LORD their God.
2 Kings 17:14

Jesus is the double portion for Elisha.

Key Word

Exile

Take it To Heart

But they would not listen, but were stubborn, as their fathers had been, who did not believe in the Lord their God.
2 Kings 17:14

Bible Reading

2 Kings 25

Yahweh

Ezra • ~450 BC • Hebrew • Narrative

Solomon • Jehoshaphat • Joash

Uzziah • Hezekiah • Manasseh • Josiah

Temple • Wealth and Fame • Distractions • Division

2 CHRONICLES

Dibre Hayyamim

"If my people who are called by my name humble themselves, and pray and seek my face and turn from their wicked ways, then I will hear from heaven and will forgive their sin and heal their land."
2 Chronicles 7:14

Jesus is God with us.

Bible Reading

2 Chronicles 24

Key Word

Editorial on Judah

Take it To Heart

"If my people who are called by my name humble themselves, and pray and seek my face and turn from their wicked ways, then I will hear from heaven and will forgive their sin and heal their land."
2 Chronicles 7:14

Yahweh

Hosea • ~715 BC • Hebrew • Prophecy

Hosea • Gomer • Their Children

Sin • Judgment • Love • Forgiveness

HOSEA

Hoshea: salvation

The LORD said to me, "Go again, love a woman who is loved by another man and is an adulteress, even as the LORD loves the children of Israel, though they turn to other gods."

Hosea 3:1

Jesus is the forgiving husband who loves and pursues and forgives again.

Bible Reading

Hosea 4

Take it To Heart

And the LORD said to me, "Go again, love a woman who is loved by another man and is an adulteress, even as the LORD loves the children of Israel, though they turn to other gods."
Hosea 3:1

Key Word

Harlot

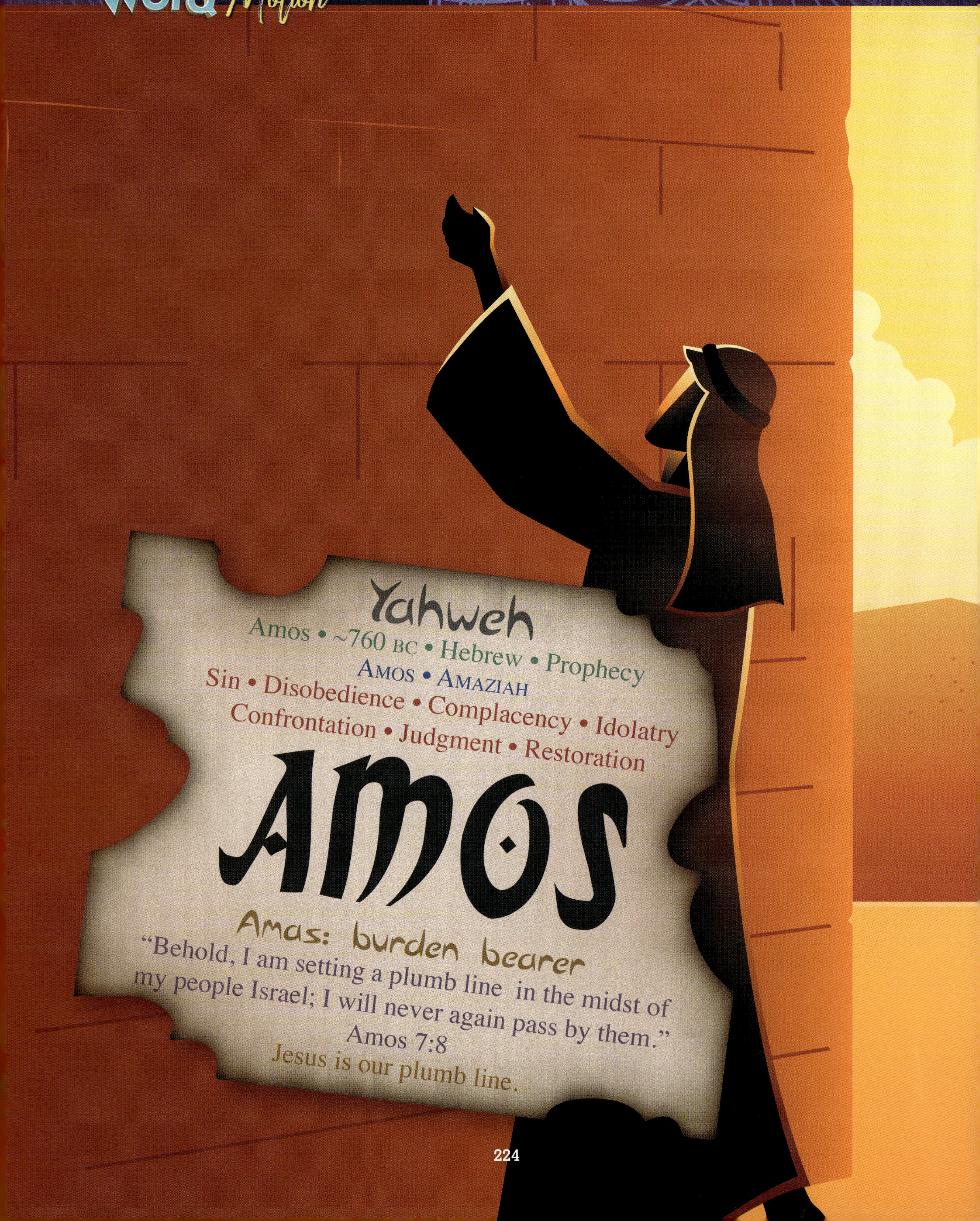
Yahweh
Amos • ~760 BC • Hebrew • Prophecy
AMOS • AMAZIAH
Sin • Disobedience • Complacency • Idolatry
Confrontation • Judgment • Restoration
AMOS
Amos: burden bearer
"Behold, I am setting a plumb line in the midst of my people Israel; I will never again pass by them."
Amos 7:8
Jesus is our plumb line.

Bible Reading

Amos 9

Key Word

Plumb Line

Take it To Heart

"Behold, I am setting a plumb line in the midst of my people Israel; I will never again pass by them."
Amos 7:8

Josiah Speaks

Some people think I had it made. After all, I became king of Judah when I was only eight years old. Sure, life was pretty great at first. I got anything I wanted—you know, plenty of cake and ice cream even when it wasn't my birthday. But after a while, I started to wonder if there wasn't something more to being king, and began to think about getting a little more serious.

That's when it happened. I had ordered that repairs be made to the temple of God when the high priest, Hilkiah, found a book. And not just any old book. This was the book of the law that the Lord God had given to Moses. I had a feeling this book might hold some answers to my questions about what I was supposed to do as king of my people.

Hilkiah gave the book to Shaphan, my secretary, who read the book to me. And my heart was pierced by what I heard. I was so upset that I tore my clothes and wept in grief. I discovered that our fathers had not obeyed anything written in God's law, and I knew that His great anger must be burning against the kingdom and its people. To begin with, how could our priests have misplaced the words of the Lord, this book of infinite worth?!?

So I gathered all the inhabitants of my kingdom, young and old, great and small, to the house of the Lord, and I read to them the entire book of the law. And when I finished, I made a covenant then and there to obey the Lord, to keep all His commands and decrees with all my heart and soul. And the people pledged themselves to the covenant I had made.

Now it was time to make a few changes. I ordered the destruction of all kinds of idols and their shrines and altars and rid Judah of any priest who had offered sacrifices to the pagan gods. Finally, I restored the feast of Passover as commanded in the law, and everyone celebrated the Passover to the Lord God in Jerusalem.

I might have started off with the easy life as a young king, but I had to grow up fast. The key was turning my heart to the Lord. If I could offer you any advice from my time as king, it would be just that: Turn your heart to God—the earlier, the better.

The Reliability of Scripture

There are more copies of the New Testament still in existence than any other ancient book. More than 5,800 original-language manuscripts of the New Testament have been discovered so far, whereas we have fewer than a dozen copies of Julius Caesar's book *Gallic Wars*, and the oldest of these was produced 900 years after the original was written! The oldest of the existing New Testament manuscripts was produced just a few decades after the original text was written.

When we compare the many copies of the Bible, none are exactly the same. So how can we know what the original text actually said? For one thing, the vast majority of differences among the manuscripts are clearly misspellings, or inserting a wrong word that sounds the same as the intended word (such as writing *four* instead of *for*). These differences are easily spotted, and therefore the original intent is not lost.

In other cases, scholars use several means of figuring out the original text. For example, they'll often depend on the oldest copy since there was less time for errors or changes to be introduced. Or they'll choose a shorter copy of the manuscript because a scribe was more likely to have added text to clarify a point than to have edited something out.

Based on the mountain of evidence in these ancient copies, scholars are certain we still have 99.5 percent of the original text as written. That leaves about 400 words we're uncertain of, and no Christian doctrine is based on these words.

As for the Old Testament, the ancient scribes had incredibly strict methods for copying that helped to keep their work as accurate as possible. Even though there aren't nearly as many copies of the Old Testament in existence compared to the New Testament, we can see how well these were copied. Scholars have compared the oldest existing copies of the book of Isaiah (from the Dead Sea Scrolls) to the next oldest copy from about ad 950, and found that their wording is the same 95 percent of the time. All this gives us confidence to know that the Bible we read today is faithful to what was written.

ADULTERY

God told the prophet Hosea to marry an adulteress. What exactly is an adulteress? When a man and woman get married, they are commanded by God to be faithful to one another. This means that the only person a husband should enjoy sexual intimacy with is his wife. And the only person a wife should enjoy sexual intimacy with is her husband. If one of them is intimate with someone else, then he or she has committed the sin of adultery. *Fornication* is another word that means much the same thing as *adultery*, but it involves two people who are not married.

Sexual intimacy was created by God for a husband and wife to enjoy together. It's not only good for the couple's relationship, but it's how God brings children into the family. But what happens when sex is removed from the intended bonds of marriage? Broken marriages, addiction to pornography, abortion on demand, sexually transmitted diseases, the objectification of the human body, sex trafficking, and more. Sexual sin destroys families, and broken families lead to broken churches, broken communities, and broken nations.

Getting back to Hosea. Why do you think God told him to marry an adulteress? Isn't it bad for a wife to be unfaithful to her husband? Yes, it is very bad. But God wanted to teach a lesson to Hosea, the people of Israel, and us. You see, the Israelites had long been unfaithful to God by running after idols and false gods, much like an adulteress is unfaithful to her husband. God wanted to show that He would take back His stubbornly wicked children (the Israelites) just as Hosea repeatedly took back his adulterous wife. That kind of steadfast love shouldn't cause us to become lazy and unfaithful. Rather, it should inspire us to worship God, and God alone, for the rest of our lives.

Dear Heavenly Father,

I pray that You will show mercy to me, my family, and my nation. I know there are many people in my country who don't worship You, honor You, or even believe You exist. Please forgive us and help us turn from our wicked ways. God, I pray that You will give a pure heart to our president, our states' governors, our cities' mayors, and all our public servants. May they choose to honor You and Your commandments in all their decisions. I pray that every marriage will honor You and that husbands and wives will be faithful to one another as Christ is faithful to His church. I know Your Word is true and reliable. It is our standard and our plumb line. Help the people of my country read it often and come to see the breadth and depths of Your love for each one of us.

In Jesus' name, I pray. Amen.

PSALM AND PROVERB TO READ:
Psalm 78, Proverbs 24:3–4

Lesson 25

Habakkuk, Isaiah, Jeremiah & Lamentations

Yahweh

Habakkuk • 615–605 BC • Hebrew • Prophecy

Habakkuk • Babylonians

Questions • Wrestling • Trust • Confidence • Deliverance

HABAKKUK

Chavaqquq: embrace

I will take my stand at my watchpost and station myself on the tower, and look out to see what he will say to me, and what I will answer concerning my complaint.
Habakkuk 2:1

The Lord is in His holy temple.
Let all the earth be silent before Him.

Bible Reading

Habakkuk 3

Take it To Heart

I will take my stand at my watchpost and station myself on the tower, and look out to see what he will say to me, and what I will answer concerning my complaint.
Habakkuk 2:1

Key Word

Watchtower

Yahweh

Isaiah • 740–680 BC • Hebrew • Prophecy

Isaiah • Yahweh • Hezekiah

Repent • Salvation • Righteousness

Peace • Comfort • Servant • Hope

ISAIAH

Yeshayahu: Yahweh is salvation

For to us a child is born, to us a son is given;
and the government shall be upon his shoulder,
and his name shall be called Wonderful Counselor,
Mighty God, Everlasting Father, Prince of Peace.
Isaiah 9:6

Jesus is the suffering servant, born of a virgin, to be the Savior of the world. And He will be called Wonderful Counselor, Mighty God, Everlasting Father, Prince of Peace.

Key Word

Groan/Glory

Bible Reading

Isaiah 53

Take it To Heart

For to us a child is born, to us a son is given; and the government shall be upon his shoulder, and his name shall be called Wonderful Counselor, Mighty God, Everlasting Father, Prince of Peace.

Isaiah 9:6

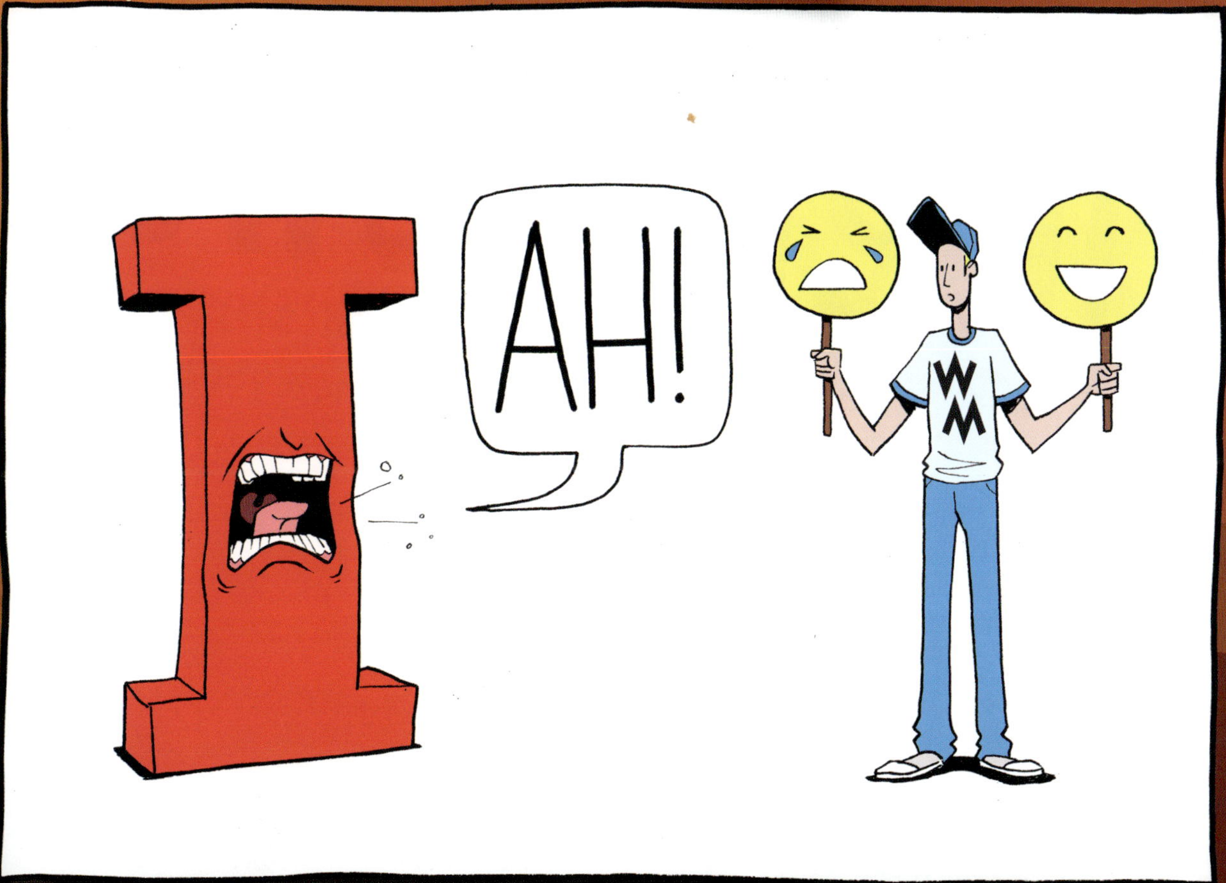

Yahweh

Jeremiah • 586–570 BC • Hebrew • Prophecy, Narrative

JEREMIAH • JUDAH

Sin • Punishment • Faithfulness

Judgment • Fear • Listen • Idols

JEREMIAH

Yirmiyahu: Yahweh establishes

"Call to me and I will answer you, and will tell you great and hidden things that you have not known."
Jeremiah 33:3

Jesus is the weeping prophet who loves His people so much.

Bible Reading

Jeremiah 31

Take it To Heart

"Call to me and I will answer you, and will tell you great and hidden things that you have not known"
Jeremiah 33:3

Key Word

Rotten Sash

Yahweh

Jeremiah • 586 BC • Hebrew • Poem

JEREMIAH • PEOPLE OF JERUSALEM

Destruction • Desertion • Mercy • Hope

LAMENTATIONS

Ekah: Oh-

The steadfast love of the LORD never ceases; his mercies never come to an end; they are new every morning; great is your faithfulness.

Lamentations 3:22–23

Jesus is my portion.

Key Word

Tears

Bible Reading

Lamentations 3

Take it To Heart

The steadfast love of the Lord never ceases; his mercies never come to an end; they are new every morning; great is your faithfulness.

Lamentations 3:22–23

Jeremiah Speaks

I didn't apply for the job of prophet. In fact, I tried to talk God out of choosing me, saying, "I do not know how to speak." Like Moses, I didn't relish my assignment to go and preach a very unpopular message. Indeed, I would be mocked, beaten, and imprisoned for telling the truth about the coming judgment. Government officials conspired to murder me, yet I would survive five kings of Judah as a solitary figure standing against a stubbornly pagan culture. That's why some call me "the weeping prophet." You may call me Jeremiah.

I was first called to prophesy during the reign of Josiah, the good king who rediscovered the book of God's law and set about ridding the kingdom of idols and idolatry. But the kings before and after Josiah encouraged worship of false gods, making the downfall of Judah inevitable. Yet the people ignored my warnings and frequent calls for repentance. They hated my message of doom and gloom and despised the messenger.

How would you feel if God gave you a message to share but no one listened to you and no one cared? What if you were ridiculed and jailed for delivering God's message? You might feel hurt, lonely, discouraged, maybe even angry that you weren't making a difference. This is what it was like for me. My anguish is fairly evident in my writings. Yet I refused to quit preaching, even when I was thrown into a pit and left to die.

Today, God has given you a message to share, one that is unpopular with a society that seems determined to defy God and celebrate sin. Many people will not listen, but the Day of the Lord is coming. So what will you do?

Apostasy

In Matthew 13, Jesus tells a parable about a farmer that went out to plant some seed. As the farmer tossed the seed here and there, some of the seed was eaten by birds, some was choked by thorns, and some fell on good soil, took root, and grew into healthy plants that produced much fruit. But some seed fell among rocks where the soil was shallow. This seed sprouted quickly and the plants looked healthy, but they soon withered and died because they didn't have deep roots.

In this parable, the seed represents the good news of the gospel. The seed that falls on rocky soil represents those who hear the word and receive it with joy but never develop good roots—they believe for a while but then fall away from the faith. These are people who once claimed to be Christians. They may have joined a church and attended regularly. They may have joined the worship team or even taught Sunday school. But their belief withered away, and they left the church. When a person decides he or she doesn't believe the gospel anymore, it is called apostasy.

There is nothing more sad than when someone knows the truth but chooses to reject it. Some Christians believe that such people have lost their faith. Others think they never had real faith in the first place but only acted like they did. Whatever the case, our faith is something we need to actively work on in order for it to stay healthy, like exercising our bodies and eating right to stay fit.

MOURNING

Every person mourns differently when a loved one dies. On the night of the Passover, "there was a great cry in Egypt, for there was not a house where someone was not dead" (Exodus 12:30). In many cultures, a ritualistic death wail—a sharp, shrill, ear-piercing shriek—informed the community when a beloved person died. Relatives and friends might continue the death wail from the time of death until the person was buried, usually the same day. Sometimes, professional mourners were hired to wail for the dead.

In biblical times, another sign of mourning was the wearing of sackcloth. Sackcloth was a coarse, black cloth made from goat hair that was uncomfortable to wear. Sometimes, the mourner would wear sackcloth and sit in ashes or pour ashes on his head to show deep sorrow.

Back then, the burial of the dead took place very quickly, often the same day. In some cultures, it was customary for the grieving family and friends to fast (go without food or drink) until the time of the burial. Following the funeral, they would be offered bread and wine as refreshment.

Wealthy families usually buried their dead in caves or tombs carved out of a hillside, and a large stone was used to seal the tomb. Poorer people were buried in graves in the earth. Only prophets and priests were buried inside the city limits; all others were buried outside of town.

Do you recognize any similar customs today? Many people still dress in black for a funeral. After the funeral, family and friends often gather at a reception to share food, fellowship, and memories of the person who has died.

Can you think of something you can say or do to comfort a person who has lost a loved one?

Prayer

Dear Heavenly Father,

Your love never ceases. You comfort me when I am sad or hurt. You have good plans for me, a bright future. When I am faced with a choice to follow You or do what the world is doing, help me to choose Your way. Help me not to stray from the path of righteousness; I don't want to fall away. Keep me on the straight and narrow path that leads to eternal life and happiness. Lord, I'm sad that so many people choose not to follow You. It makes me want to mourn loudly. Don't give up on me, and don't give up on them.

In Jesus' name, I pray. Amen.

PSALM AND PROVERB TO READ:
Psalm 74, Proverbs 25:21–22

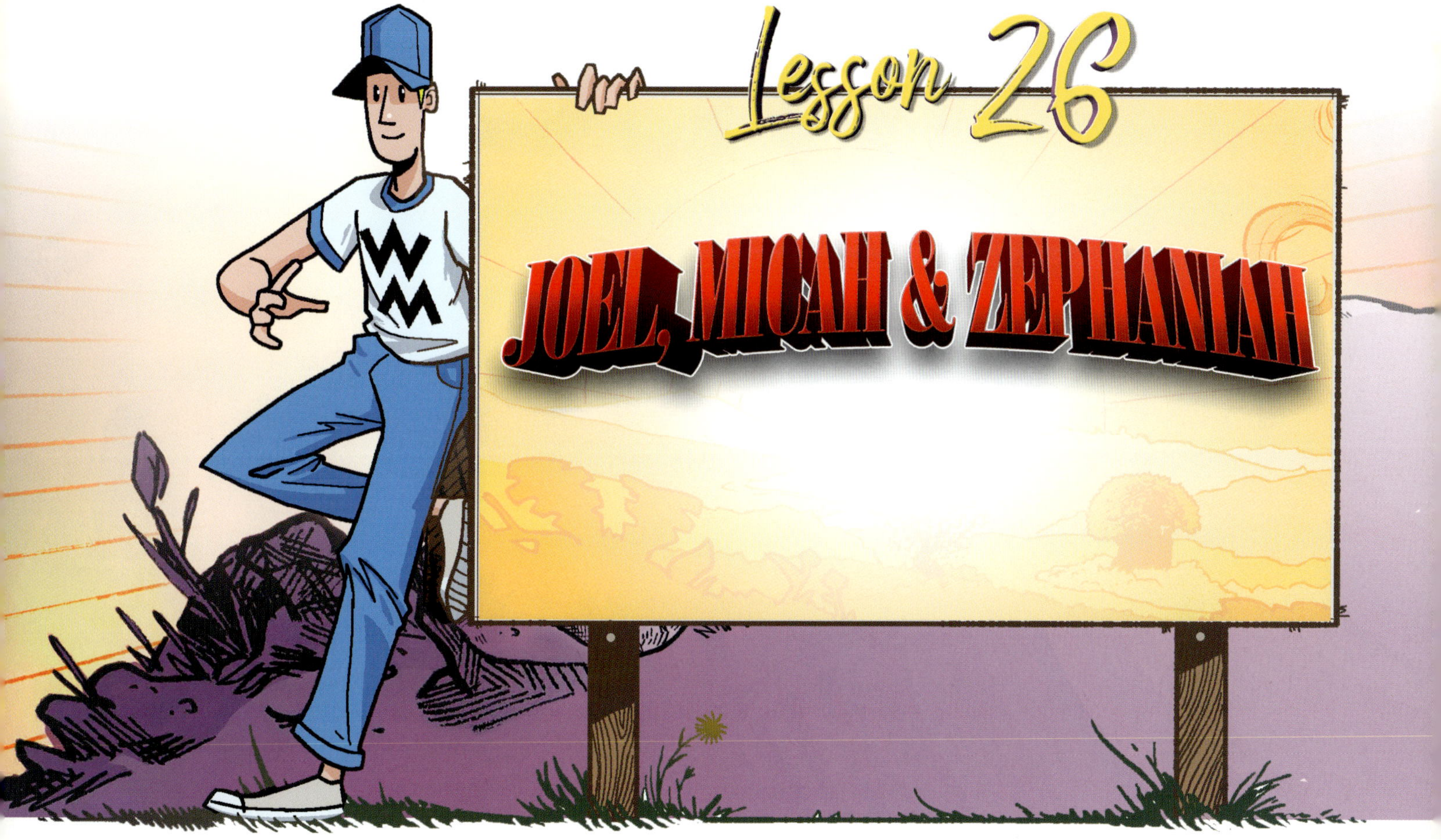
Lesson 26
JOEL, MICAH & ZEPHANIAH

Yahweh

Joel • ~830 BC • Hebrew • Prophecy

JOEL • JUDAH

Punishment • Forgiveness • Promise of the Holy Spirit

JOEL

Yechezqel:
God strengthens

"Yet even now," declares the LORD, "return to me with all your heart. . . ." Return to the LORD your God, for he is gracious and merciful, slow to anger, and abounding in steadfast love.

Joel 2:12–13

Jesus redeems the years the locusts have eaten.

Bible Reading

Joel 2

Take it To Heart

"Yet even now," declares the LORD, "return to me with all your heart. . . ." Return to the LORD your God, for he is gracious and merciful, slow to anger, and abounding in steadfast love.

Joel 2:12–13

Key Word

Locust

Yahweh

Micah • 735–700 BC • Hebrew • Poetic, Prophecy

People of Samaria and Jerusalem

Sin • Judgment • God's Love • Deliverance

MICAH

Mikah: who is like God?

He has told you, O man, what is good; and what does the LORD require of you but to do justice, and to love kindness, and to walk humbly with your God?
Micah 6:8

Jesus is the One born in Bethlehem.

Key Word

Day in Court

Take it To Heart

He has told you, O man, what is good; and what does the LORD require of you but to do justice, and to love kindness, and to walk humbly with your God?
Micah 6:8

Bible Reading

Micah 6–7

Yahweh

Zephaniah • 640–621 BC • Hebrew • Prophecy

Zephaniah • Judah

Sin • Judgment • Punishment

Complacency • Hope • Remnant

ZEPHANIAH

Tsephan-yan: Yahweh has hidden

Seek the Lord all you humble of the land,
who do his just commands; seek righteousness;
seek humility; perhaps you may be hidden
on the day of the anger of the Lord.
Zephaniah 2:3

Jesus is mighty to save.

Take it To Heart

Seek the Lord all you humble of the land, who do his just commands; seek righteousness; seek humility; perhaps you may be hidden on the day of the anger of the Lord.
Zephaniah 2:3

Key Word

Day of the Lord

Bible Reading

Zephaniah 3

Isaiah Speaks

My name is Isaiah, son of Amoz. I was married and a father of two. That pretty well sums up all the personal background known about me today. I am better known as an orator, a catalyst, and a blazing torch of truth in a land of darkness.

I spent my life preaching, writing, and counseling monarchs. My faith in God and my love for His people are evident on every page of my book. My mission, however, was demanding and costly. Hardship awaited me around every corner. Danger followed my every move. Disappointment watered my pillow with tears.

The opening verses of my book speak of a God who is brokenhearted: "Children have I reared and brought up, but they have rebelled against me. The ox knows its owner, and the donkey its master's crib, but Israel does not know, my people do not understand." Yes, Israel was a sinful nation loaded with guilt, its children given to corruption (Isaiah 1:2–4).

My portrait of the nation is one of darkness and decay. Hopelessness abounded. Lawlessness was rampant. True worship was nonexistent. Integrity had vanished from the courts, the market, and the temple. Oppression, cruelty, and immorality reigned.

Judgment was coming, but so was salvation! I was honored to tell of the Messiah's virgin birth (Isaiah 7:14), His ministry (Isaiah 61:1–2), His sacrificial death (Isaiah 52:13–53:12), and His second coming (Isaiah 60:2–3). I even foretold the preaching of John the Baptist (Isaiah 40:3–5).

redeem

The word *redeem* means much more than buying something or using a coupon, although that's often how we use it in our culture. In the Bible, the concept of redemption is something more specific and far more powerful. When someone is purchased so that he or she is freed from captivity or oppression, that person has been redeemed.

The Bible teaches that we sin because we are sinners, which means that we are born sinful and are slaves to our sin nature. Our sinfulness and all the individual sins we commit are wrongs that require punishment. Because God is holy, righteous, and just, He requires payment, for sins. When that payment is made, the hold that sin has over us is broken and we are saved. The problem is that you and I can never pay back the debt we owe to God for the sins we've committed. The punishment is eternal.

The word *gospel* means "good news." The good news is literally that God sent His one Son, Jesus, to do for us what we could never do for ourselves. Jesus paid the debt that we could never pay by dying in our place. Though He Himself was sinless and did not deserve death, Jesus took on the penalty we owe, and He purchased us with His blood. In other words, He redeemed us at the cost of His death.

Redemption is similar to paying a ransom. But because we are slaves to sin, it's our own nature that held us hostage. That is why we can't pay for our own redemption. Instead the "ransom" is paid to God, whose moral law we have violated. It is God who requires payment, even though He is not holding anyone hostage. Through Jesus, He pays Himself to redeem us.

FAMINE

You've probably said something like "I'm starving, let's eat!" This was likely an exaggeration. When you feel hungry, most of the time you know it won't be very long until your next meal. In a famine, however, there's not enough food to go around, and most people have no idea where their next meal is coming from or when.

A famine is an extreme shortage of food in a geographic region. A lack of food leads to malnutrition and starvation, for without food, the body cannot take in enough calories to stay healthy and grow. Eventually, the body will die.

Sometimes a drought—an extended period with little or no rainfall—causes crops to die and thus creates a widespread food shortage. Drought was the most common cause of famine in the Bible. But in fact, any extreme change in the weather over time can lead to famine conditions. For example, a long period of heavy rain can cause flooding and destroy crops. War, inflation, and unjust government policies can also lead to famine.

Famine is always devastating. A three-year famine from 1958 to 1961, the Great Chinese Famine, is the worst in modern times. At least 15 million people died in the Great Chinese Famine, though some estimates go as high as 43 million. The Indian Famine lasted six years between 1896 and 1902, killing an estimated 19 million people.

Sadly, famine is still with us. The African continent has been hardest hit in recent years. Somalia, Nigeria, Sudan, Ethiopia, and several countries in western Africa have experienced famine in this century as the result of war and drought.

Dear Heavenly Father,

Sometimes I get discouraged by all the sin, hatred, hunger, disease, wars, and evil that exist in the world today. I know such things have been around since before Noah, but it hurts to see so many people determined to disobey You. So I want to thank You for giving me real hope. Because of You, I am redeemed. Because of You, I can face tomorrow. Because of You, I can shout to the world Jesus lives and His way is a better way. Let Your will be done, Lord, on earth as it is in heaven!

In Jesus' name, I pray. Amen.

PSALM AND PROVERB TO READ:
Psalm 116, Proverbs 26:28

Lesson 27
JONAH, NAHUM & OBADIAH

Yahweh

Jonah • 775–760 BC • Hebrew • Autobiographical

JONAH • SHIP CAPTAIN AND CREW • NINEVITES

Listening • Disobedience • Consequences

Prayer • Repentance • Mercy • Anger

JONAH

Yonah: dove

When God saw what they did, how they turned from their evil way, God relented of the disaster that he had said he would do to them, and he did not do it.

Jonah 3:10

Jesus was three days in the belly of the earth.

Bible Reading

Jonah 1–4

Take it To Heart

When God saw what they did, how they turned from their evil way, God relented of the disaster that he had said he would do to them, and he did not do it.
Jonah 3:10

Key Word

Fish

Yahweh

Nahum • 663–612 BC • Hebrew • Prophecy

Nahum • Ninevites

Sin • Judgment

NAHUM

Nachman: comforter

The Lord is good, a stronghold in the day of trouble;
he knows those who take refuge in him.
Nahum 1:7

Jesus avenges His people and brings justice.

Bible Reading

Nahum 1

Key Word

Flood

Take it To Heart

The LORD is good, a stronghold in the day of trouble; he knows those who take refuge in him.

Nahum 1:7

Yahweh

Obadiah • ~845 BC • Hebrew • Poetic, Prophecy

EDOMITES

Pride • Judgment

OBADIAH

Obhadya: God's servant

But do not gloat over the day of your brother in the day of his misfortune; do not rejoice over the people of Judah in the day of their ruin; do not boast in the day of distress.

Obadiah 1:12

Jesus is our brother and our keeper.

Bible Reading

Obadiah 1

Take it To Heart

But do not gloat over the day of your brother in the day of his misfortune; do not rejoice over the people of Judah in the day of their ruin; do not boast in the day of distress.

Obadiah 1:12

Key Word

Brother's Keeper

Jonah Speaks

My story is a high seas drama about a prophet on the run from God. Some dismiss my book as a whale of a tale. Others say my story is living proof that you can't keep a good man down. Regardless, I was an actual prophet of God. Jesus even spoke of my preaching in His own ministry (Matthew 12:38–41). Ship ahoy! Jonah here!

My assignment from the Lord was to go to the city of Nineveh and preach to its people. Nineveh was the capital of the vicious, barbaric Assyrians. They would leave behind pyramids of human skulls as evidence of a conquest. They had abused Israel repeatedly, and just the thought of preaching to them gave me a serious case of acid reflux.

So instead of obeying God's command, I caught the first boat heading in the opposite direction. But the Lord was not to be denied. First, He sent a great storm that threatened to capsize the ship. When I admitted that my presence had put them all in danger, the sailors took my advice and tossed me overboard. Immediately, the storm subsided. I thought I was doomed, but the Lord sent a great fish to swallow me, and I survived in the belly of the fish for three days and three nights.

Three days of dog-paddling in gastric juices, seaweed, and undigested fish convinced me to reconsider my position on Nineveh. I cried out to the Lord, and the Lord answered. The fish spat me out on dry land, and I promptly went to Nineveh and preached the Lord's message. And wouldn't you know it, the people repented! They fasted and called out to God, and God forgave these enemies of Israel.

You'd think a prophet of God would be happy when a sinner repents, but I was *really* chapped. Angry with God, I shouted, "You knew this would happen! That's why I ran the other direction. I didn't want to preach to these barbarians, because I know you are a merciful and compassionate God, slow to anger and abounding in steadfast love, and you are eager to turn back from destroying people if they repent."

You see, my story isn't about a disgruntled prophet or a big fish. My story is about God. It's about a God who doesn't want anybody to perish, whether they reside in Nineveh or Moscow or Hollywood or Cape Town or your town! When God calls, answer. When He sends you, go. And when He forgives, rejoice!

The Problem of Evil

When we look around us at all the suffering in this world, especially suffering that is caused by man's inhumanity to man, we can't help but wonder why God allows evil to exist in the first place. In fact, some people say that the very presence of evil in the world proves that God does not exist, or at least couldn't be loving.

Their argument goes something like this: *If God is all-knowing, then He knows when evil is about to happen. If God is all-powerful, then He can prevent that evil from happening. If God is perfectly good, then He will choose to stop evil from happening. Therefore, an all-knowing, all-powerful, and perfectly good God cannot exist at the same time there is evil in the world.*

The answer to the problem of evil lies in mankind's ability to make free choices. The greatest good we can do is to love, and the greatest love we can have is for God. But for our love to be authentic and real, we must be free to choose to *not* love. If we choose to reject God, that is evil (and there are countless ways that evil will express itself). So for the greatest good to be a possibility, the possibility of evil must also exist. If God were to stop evil before it happens, then our love would not be love since we really had no choice in the matter. That would be forced obedience, and that's not genuine love.

Sometimes bad things are allowed to happen for a greater good to occur. When parents allow their kids to suffer a consequence for their actions, they are allowing a bad thing to happen so that their children will learn to do good, which is a better thing. God may allow evil for the same reason. After all, if there were no evil in the world, we could never know God's forgiveness, His righteousness, His holiness, and the profound depth of His love.

HEART HEALTH

Which organ in your body is the most important? Most doctors would say it's the heart. Your heart is certainly vital to your health. With every beat, your heart sends blood throughout your body, providing your body with the oxygen and nutrients it needs. If you live to be eighty years old, your heart will beat roughly three billion times!

What keeps your heart healthy? Diet and exercise play a very big part. A heart-healthy diet includes raw fruits and vegetables, fish, lean meats, and foods made from whole grains. Your body also needs sixty minutes of physical exercise a day on average. The choices you make involving food and activity will affect your heart's health both now and in the future.

But your physical heart was not what Solomon was referring to when he wrote, "Keep your heart with all vigilance, for from it flow the springs of life" (Proverbs 4:23). He was talking about a person's spiritual heart. Keeping your spiritual heart healthy is at least as important as caring for your physical heart. Interestingly, the health of your spiritual heart also depends on diet and exercise.

Reading God's Word is food for your spiritual heart. The Bible helps you to learn and understand His instructions for your life, keeps you on the path of righteousness, protects you from false teaching, fills you with joy, and prepares you to do good.

Exercises for your spiritual heart include prayer and biblical meditation. Prayer can include confessing your sins, asking for God's help, thanking Him, praising Him, or just talking with Him about your day. Biblical meditation means thinking about godly things, especially verses from the Bible.

Which of these things do you need to do more often to take better care of your physical heart and your spiritual heart?

Dear Heavenly Father,

I pray You will keep me far from evil in this world. Give me strength and wisdom to make good choices and flee from temptations. Fill my mind with godly thoughts about things that are true and right.

Give me compassion for people who don't yet know You and even those who have rejected You. They are made in Your image too. I pray that my words and actions will be a good example that points them to You. Keep my heart pure and healthy and help me to follow You all the days of my life.

In Jesus' name, I pray. Amen.

PSALM AND PROVERB TO READ:
Psalm 136, Proverbs 27:17

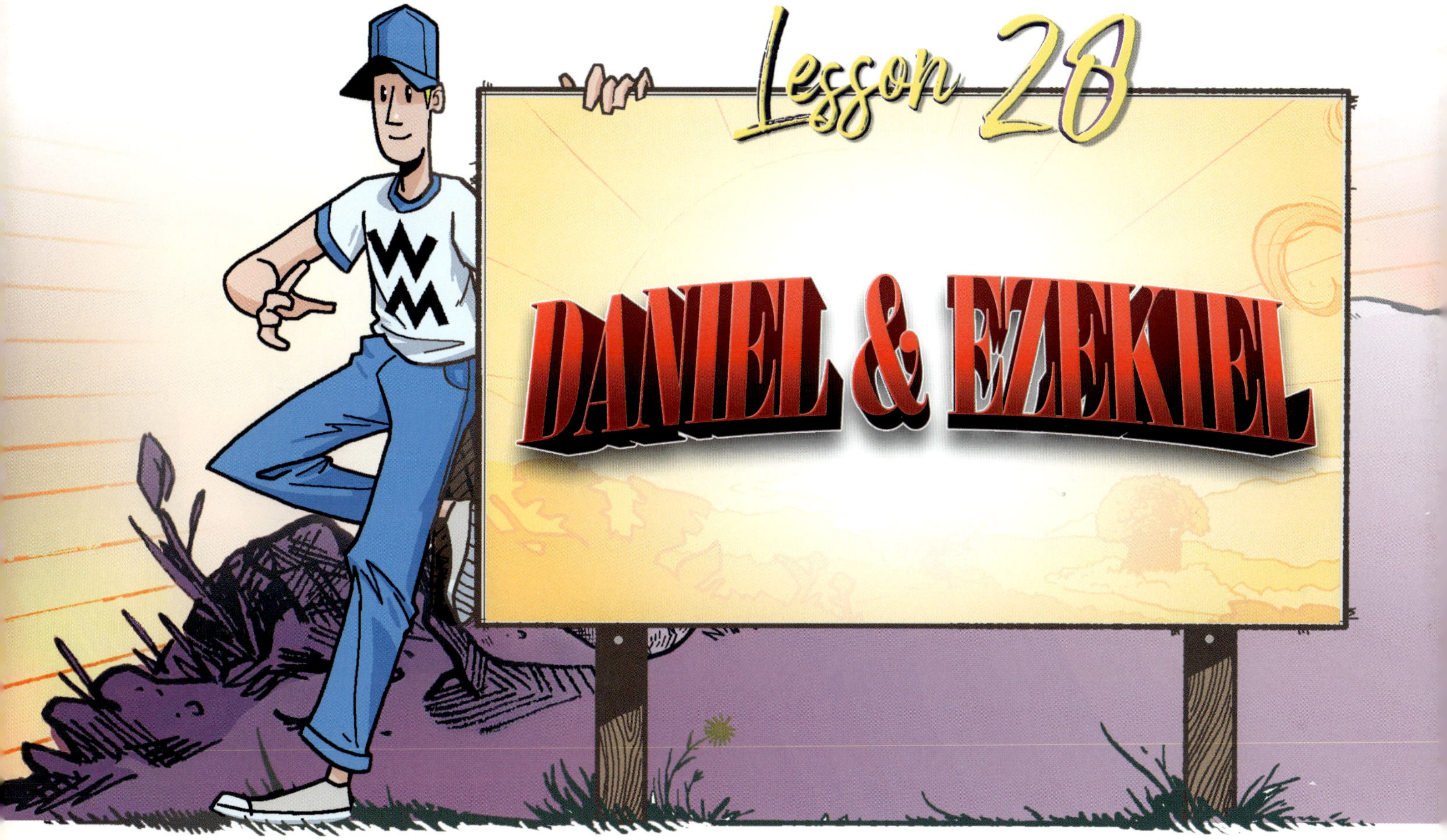
Lesson 28
DANIEL & EZEKIEL

Yahweh

Daniel • ~530 BC • Hebrew • Narrative, Prophecy

DANIEL • NEBUCHADNEZZER • BELSHAZZAR • DARIUS

Captivity • Resolve • Dreams • Friends • Prayer

DANIEL

Daniyyel: God is my judge

[Daniel] told them to seek mercy from the God of heaven concerning this mystery, so that Daniel and his companions might not be destroyed with the rest of the wise men of Babylon. Then the mystery was revealed to Daniel in a vision of the night. Then Daniel blessed the God of heaven.

Daniel 2:18–19

Jesus is the fourth person in the fiery furnace.

Bible Reading

Daniel 1–4

Key Word

Dreams

Take it To Heart

[Daniel] told them to seek mercy from the God of heaven concerning this mystery, so that Daniel and his companions might not be destroyed with the rest of the wise men of Babylon. Then the mystery was revealed to Daniel in a vision of the night. Then Daniel blessed the God of heaven.

Daniel 2:18–19

Yahweh

Ezekiel • ~570 BC • Hebrew • Narrative, Prophecy

Ezekiel • Judah • Nebuchadnezzer

Heart • Judgment • Blessing

Personal and National Responsibility

EZEKIEL

Yechzqel: stengthened by God

"I will give you a new heart, and a new spirit I will put within you. And I will remove the heart of stone from your flesh and give you a heart of flesh."
Ezekiel 36:26

Jesus is the breath of life in the valley of dry bones.

Key Word

Dry Bones

Take it To Heart

"I will give you a new heart, and a new spirit I will put within you. And I will remove the heart of stone from your flesh and give you a heart of flesh."
Ezekiel 36:26

Bible Reading

Ezekiel 37

Daniel Speaks

The summons was clear. Hananiah, Mishael, and Azariah were to report to the king immediately. A few years had passed since they were taken from the kingdom of Judah and brought to Babylon along with me, their friend Daniel. King Nebuchadnezzar changed our names. I was to be called Belteshazzar. My friends were given the names Shadrach, Meshach, and Abednego. We were enrolled in the royal academy and, later, put to work in the king's court after we excelled in school.

That's not to say our path was easy. For one thing, we insisted on following Jewish dietary laws; we refused to be defiled by the food and drink served at the king's table. God honored our commitment by causing us to flourish in the king's service. But now my friends faced a far more dangerous test of their faith.

The interrogation was quick and to the point. The king asked, "Is it true, O Shadrach, Meshach, and Abednego, that you do not serve my gods or worship the golden image that I have set up?" They would not and could not. Their answer enraged the king, and he had them thrown into a fiery furnace heated to seven times its usual temperature.

This is a familiar story from my book. Many have delighted in the courage of these young men to defy the pagan monarch. Theirs was not a fuzzy faith. They knew the God in whom they believed and why.

At any age, we are susceptible to Satan's intimidation tactics when our faith is shallow, untried, and untested. A fragile faith is an easy target for peers and professors who don't believe in God. But on the other hand, Satan trembles when we take a firm, unwavering, faithful stand. It's one thing to claim you have faith, but it's another to step into the furnace for your convictions.

Are you willing to actually die for your faith? My friends were. Is God's truth so sacred for you that you would never deny them, even under threat of death? Do you believe so strongly that you would rather walk through fire than bow down to the false gods of this world? When your faith is challenged, think of my three friends, be courageous, and stand firm.

Prophecy and the End Times

A prophecy is a message from God. A prophet is a kind of spokesman who is called by God to deliver His messages. We often think of a prophet as someone who predicts the future. In the Bible, many of God's messages had nothing to do with revealing the future, although sometimes a prediction that came true during the prophet's lifetime was used to prove that the person speaking was a prophet.

Sometimes, the events foretold by a prophet were so distant in the future that the message was probably not understood even by the prophet. And many of these prophecies were filled with symbolism, making them strange and even more difficult to understand. This type of prophecy is how the end times are spoken of in Scripture. The question of what happens before and after Jesus returns has fascinated believers for two thousand years. Most of the prophecies describing the end times were made by Old Testament prophets like Daniel, Isaiah, and Ezekiel. The New Testament book of Revelation uses much of their imagery while adding more detail to what the earlier prophets saw and wrote about.

Although God is revealing something specific in these prophecies and has a reason for doing so, it doesn't mean we always understand the images. After all, what does a lion with eagle's wings and the mind of a man mean? How about a leopard with four wings and four heads? Believers have come up with many interpretations of these prophecies. In fact, every generation since Jesus ascended to heaven has thought it could see the prophecies being fulfilled in their lifetimes.

The many different interpretations of these images gives us a clue for how to treat the end times prophecies. We shouldn't allow ourselves to be distracted by the details, as we will probably recognize what the symbols mean only after they are fulfilled, not before. The important thing to know is that in the spiritual war depicted by these prophecies, God ultimately wins.

DREAMS

The Bible contains many examples of God speaking to people in dreams. But prophetic dreams are different from the kinds of dreams we have most nights. Prophetic dreams are visions that happened to occur during sleep. Sometimes God speaks directly in the dreams, and sometimes He uses symbols that have to be interpreted.

Most of the time in Scripture, the person receiving the dream was a prophet, though not every time. For example, both Joseph and Daniel were asked to interpret dreams given by God to kings who were not believers. God used such dreams to give His prophets an opportunity to prove they spoke for God and should be listened to.

Daniel himself had prophetic dreams that he could not interpret on his own. The images were confusing and even disturbing. But as part of the dream, God sent an angel to explain to Daniel what he was being shown.

We may not understand why God chooses to reveal Himself in different ways to different people, but we can be certain that it is never random or meaningless.

Dear Heavenly Father,

Help me each day to be aware of Your presence and work in my life. I don't want to be like a dead man or a collection of old bones. I want to be fully alive and enjoy falling more in love with You each day. You give me hope for today, tomorrow, and eternity.

Although I would like to understand all the prophecies Your servants made about the end of the world, I trust that all of time is under Your Sovereign control. May Your will be done. I look forward to falling on my knees and worshiping You with all the nations of the world. Until then, may the words of my mouth and the meditations of my heart be pleasing to You.

In Jesus' name, I pray. Amen.

PSALM AND PROVERB TO READ:
Psalm 13, Proverbs 28:6

Lesson 29
EZRA & ESTHER

Yahweh

Ezra • ~450 BC • Hebrew • Narrative

ZERUBBABEL • JOSHUA, HIGH PRIEST • EZRA

Opportunity • Altar • Temple • God's Provision

Opposition • Prayer • Sin • Confession • Repentance

EZRA

Azaryahu: God's Help

For Ezra had set his heart to study the Law of the LORD, and to do it and to teach his statutes and rules in Israel.

Ezra 7:10

Jesus is like the leaders who return and rebuild our lives.

Bible Reading
Ezra 6

Key Word
Temple/
People

Take it To Heart
For Ezra had set his heart to study the Law of the Lord, and to do it and to teach his statutes and rules in Israel.
Ezra 7:10

Implied

Unidentified Jew • 450–330 BC • Hebrew • Narrative

XERXES • VASHTI • MORDECAI • ESTER • HAMAN

Family • Beauty • Submission • Authority

Loyalty • Boldness • Power • Arrogance • Challenge

Preparation • Courage • Discernment • Celebration

ESTHER

Hadassah: myrtle tree

"For if you keep silent at this time, relief and deliverance will rise for the Jews from another place, but you and your father's house will perish. And who knows whether you have not come to the kingdom for such a time as this?"
Esther 4:14

Jesus is for such a time as this.

Key Word

Queen of Persia

Bible Reading

Esther 8

Take it To Heart

"For if you keep silent at this time, relief and deliverance will rise for the Jews from another place, but you and your father's house will perish. And who knows whether you have not come to the kingdom for such a time as this?"

Esther 4:14

Esther Speaks

After my parents died, I had no idea what God had in store for my life. I was most thankful that a family member took me in and raised me as his own daughter. My name is Esther, and this is my story.

I was chosen by the king for my beauty, but I like to think I was much more than a pretty face. God blessed me with other qualities such as discernment and courage. He used me as a force for justice at a time when my people were being threatened with extinction. I dared to stand before the king and speak for my people while others remained silent. I became a voice for those who had no voice.

Mordecai was my cousin; he was also my guardian, advisor, and mentor. He raised me as his own daughter and prepared me for the difficult times to come. When I faltered, Mordecai encouraged me. When I was doubtful, he instilled hope. When he heard of the plot to assassinate the king, he informed me and I warned the king. When danger came, Mordecai reminded me that my appointment as queen was no accident. I had been raised up by God for such a time as this.

My story also has a villain. His name was Haman, and his heart was full of hatred for the Jews and Mordecai, in particular. When the king appointed him to a prominent position of authority, Haman immediately set into motion a plot to eradicate my people. His seething animosity for the Jews led him to erect a gallows seventy feet high for hanging every one of us, starting with Mordecai.

These events led to a lavish banquet, followed by a sleepless night for the king (probably from the Persian pizza). This was followed by another banquet and a hanging. Who was hanged? To find out more, open your Bible and read the book that bears my name.

We all need a Mordecai in our lives. Do you have a mentor or trusted adviser? If not, find someone who is qualified and willing to mentor you for God's service. It made all the difference for me.

god's sovereignty

One of the most important things God wants us to know about Himself is that He is sovereign. This means that God rules over everything that exists. There is nothing outside of His control. There are no accidents, no such thing as coincidence. No matter how big or how small, everything happens because God makes it happen or allows it to happen.

This is a big reason we pray to God. Whatever it is we ask or have trouble with, we know that God is in control of it. If God weren't in complete control of all that happens, we wouldn't have any reason to pray to Him because we could never know if He was able to answer our prayers. Sometimes, it can be hard to understand how God is in control of things, and He doesn't always make things turn out the way we hoped. But that doesn't mean God is not working things out according to His plan.

In fact, God's rule over this world is so powerful that He is in control even though we make choices on our own. God's sovereignty does not mean that we are like robots who can't make our own decisions or act contrary to our programming. It means that whatever we decide is still under God's control. God can even use people's evil choices to make good things happen.

Think about this: The most evil thing that ever happened was the crucifixion of Jesus. And yet, because of God's sovereignty, the crucifixion is actually the greatest thing that ever happened. What people mean for evil, God can use for good (Genesis 50:20).

XERXES

King Xerxes I, also known as Ahasuerus, ruled 127 provinces of Persia from 485 to 465 BC. His kingdom stretched from India to Ethiopia. Xerxes' father, Darius I, is mentioned in the biblical books of Haggai, Zechariah, Ezra, and Nehemiah.

According to the Greek historian Herodotus, Xerxes unsuccessfully tried to conquer Greece with a formidable army numbering more than two million men and four thousand ships. After he captured and burned the city of Athens, Xerxes returned home and left a portion of his army to complete the conquest of Greece. However, a year later, an alliance of Greeks from Sparta, Athens, Corinth and other city-states defeated the Persians at the decisive Battle of Plataea.

After King Xerxes returned home, he concentrated on building larger monuments than his father built. He taxed the people to raise the money needed to build the monuments. It was during this period that he chose Esther to be his queen.

When Esther learned that the Jews were targeted for genocide by the king's viceroy, Esther revealed her Jewish heritage to Xerxes and begged him to save her people. Xerxes granted her wish.

The story of Esther is today read aloud during the Jewish festival of Purim.

Prayer

Dear Heavenly Father,

I believe You made me for a purpose. I pray that I will listen carefully and be faithful to my calling. I know that You are working and intervening to make Your glory known in this world, and I want to be a part of that effort. Help me to not become discouraged when obstacles seem to block the way. Thank You for people You have put in my life to help me grow into the person You want me to be. If You need me to be a leader, then let me do this boldly and with confidence in You. I put my life in Your hands, where I am sure to be safe and sound.

In Jesus' name, I pray. Amen.

PSALM AND PROVERB TO READ:
Psalm 148, Proverbs 29:18, 23

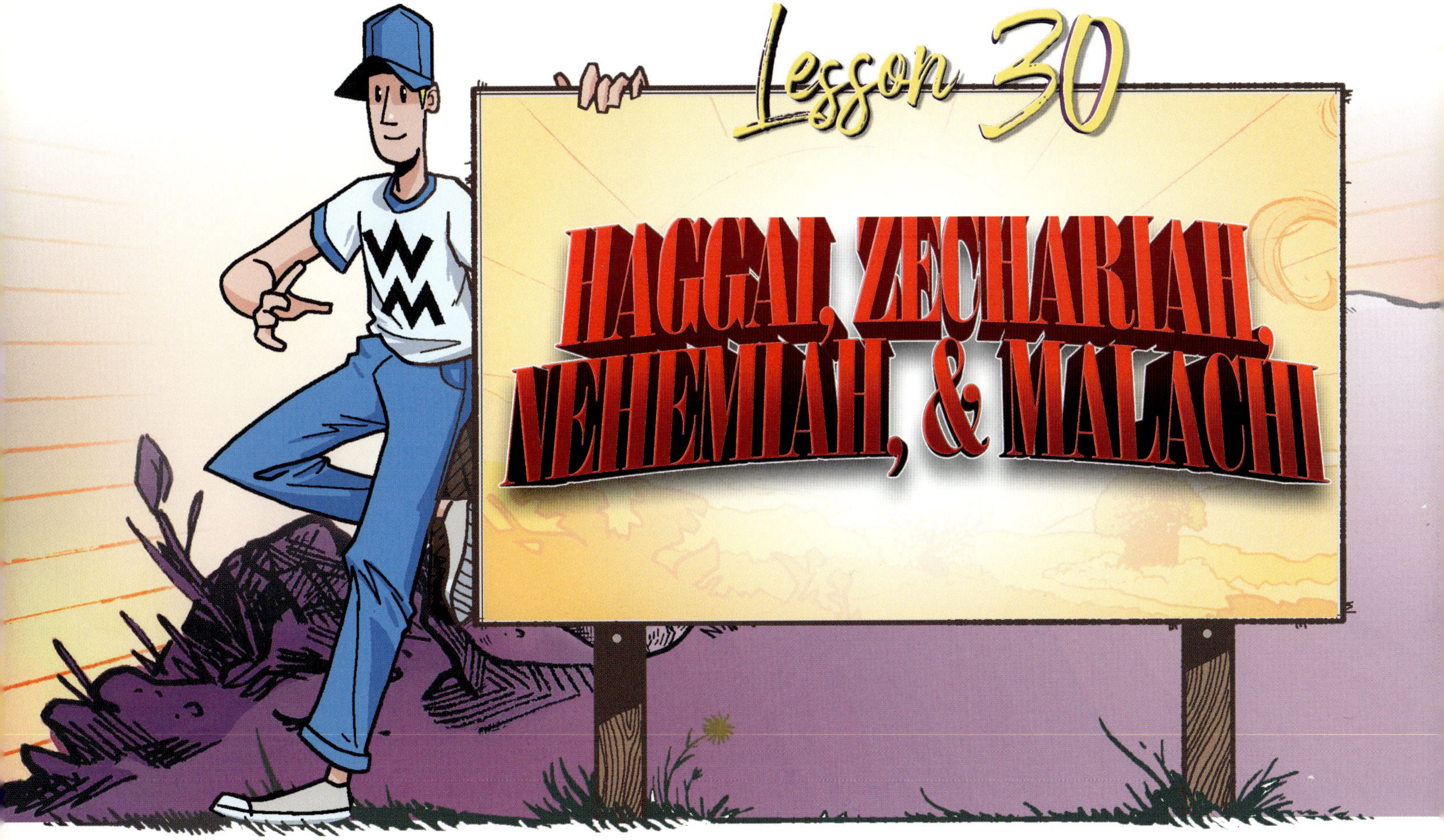

Lesson 30
HAGGAI, ZECHARIAH, NEHEMIAH, & MALACHI

Yahweh

Haggai • ~520 BC • Hebrew • Narrative, Prophecy

HAGGAI • ZERUBBABEL • JOSHUA

Discouragement • Resignation • Encouragement • Temple

HAGGAI

Haggaih: festive

Go up to the hills and bring wood and build the house, that I may take pleasure in it and that I may be glorified, says the LORD.

Haggai 1:8

Jesus is the restorer of our heritage.

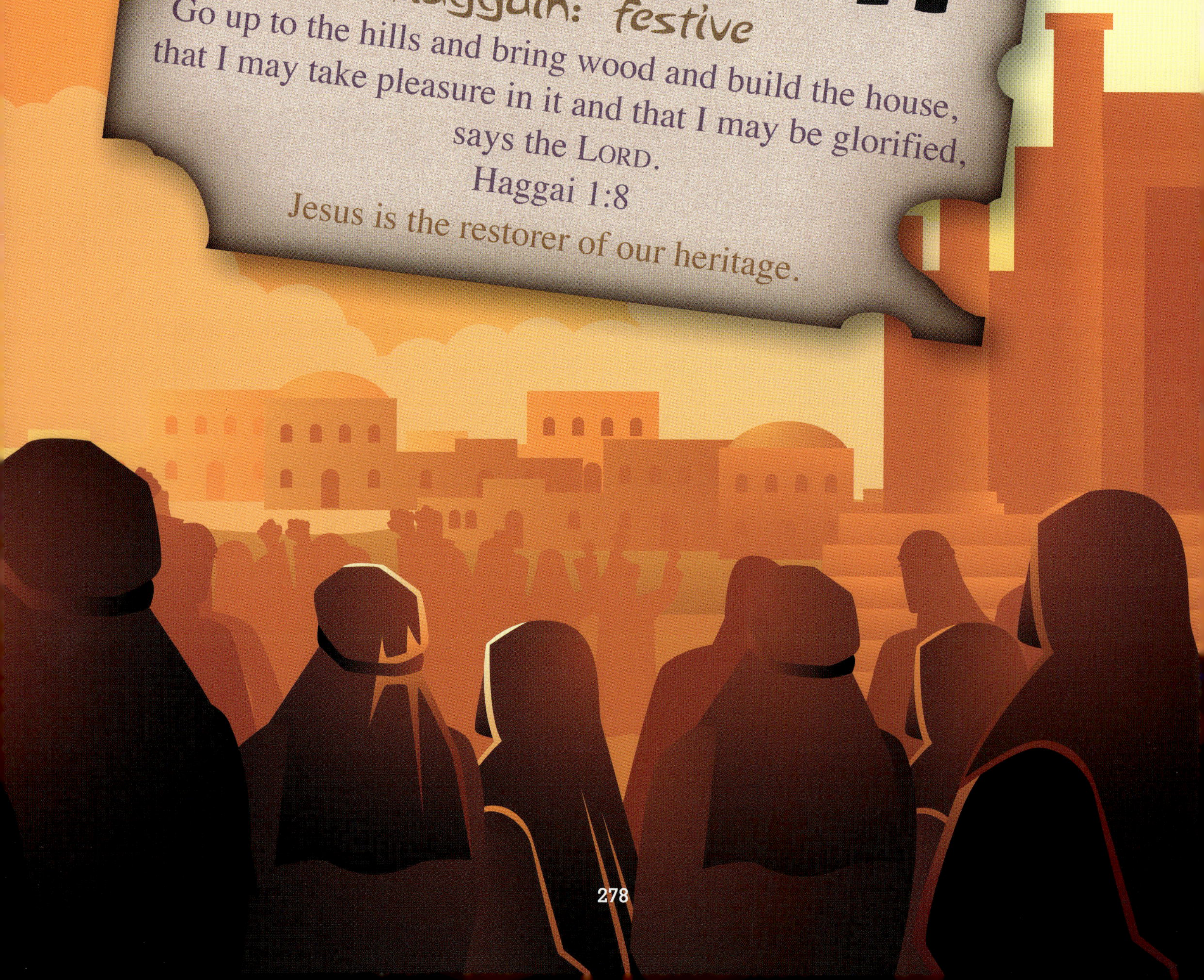

Key Word

Temple

Take it To Heart

Go up to the hills and bring wood and build the house, that I may take pleasure in it and that I may be glorified, says the LORD.
Haggai 1:8

Bible Reading

Haggai 2

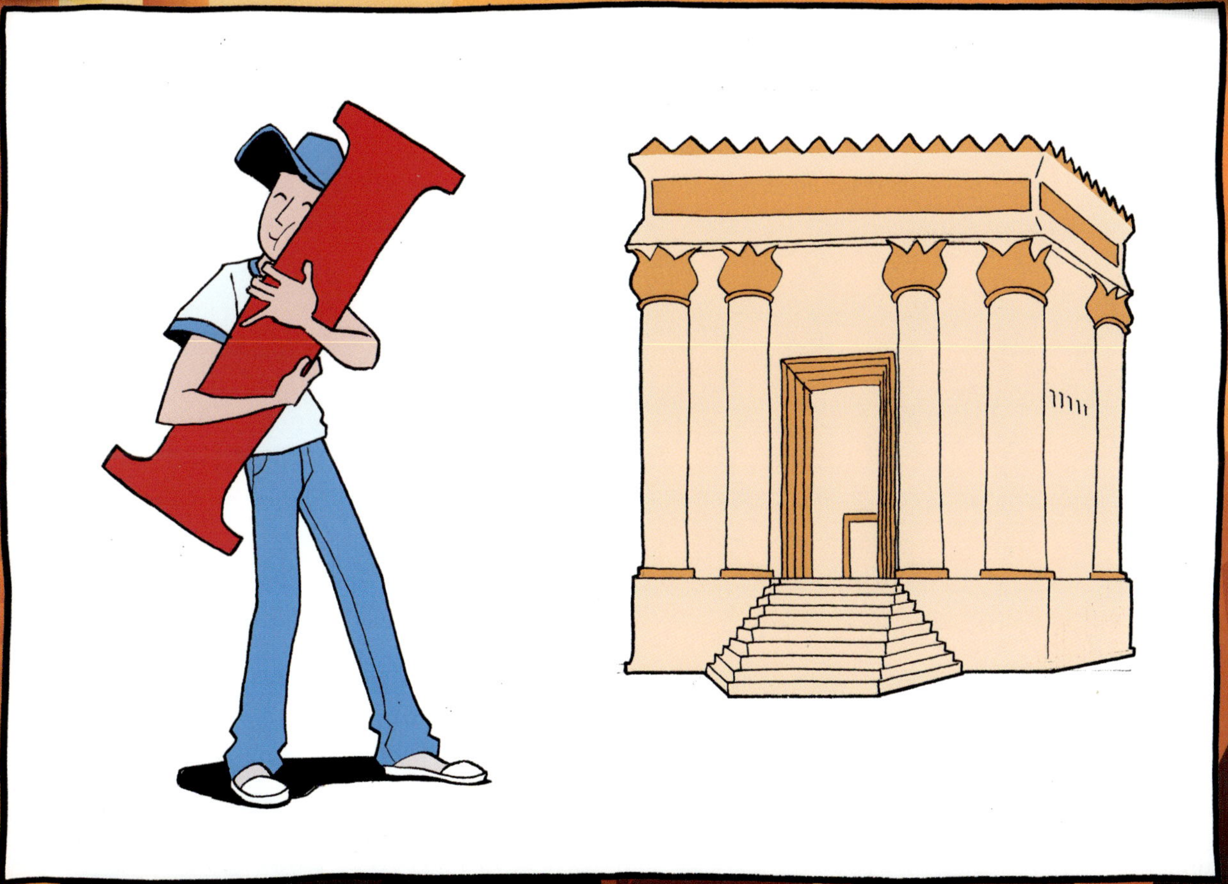

Yahweh

Zechariah • 520–470 BC • Hebrew • Narrative, Prophecy

EZEKIEL • JUDAH • NEBUCHADNEZZER

Repent • Visions • Messages • Messiah

ZECHARIAH

Zekar-yah: Yahweh has remembered

Rejoice greatly, O daughter of Zion! Shout aloud, O daughter of Jerusalem! Behold, your king is coming to you; righteous and having salvation is he, humble and mounted on a donkey.
Zechariah 9:9

Jesus is the righteous branch.

Take it To Heart

Rejoice greatly, O daughter of Zion! Shout aloud, O daughter of Jerusalem! Behold, your king is coming to you; righteous and having salvation is he, humble and mounted on a donkey, on a colt, the foal of a donkey.

Zechariah 9:9

Key Word

Messiah

Bible Reading

Zechariah 14

Yahweh

Nehemiah • ~425 BC • Hebrew • Narrative

NEHEMIAH • ARTAXERXES • EZRA • SANBALLAT • TOBIAH

Wall • Prayer • Vision • Sovereignty • Leadership

Opposition • Families • Preparedness • Restoration

NEHEMIAH

Nehemya: Comfort of the Lord

So the wall was finished . . . in fifty-two days. And when all our enemies heard of it, all the nations around us were afraid . . . for they perceived that this work had been accomplished with the help of our God.

Nehemiah 6:15–16

The joy of the Lord is my strength.

Key Word
Walls

Bible Reading
Nehemiah 9

Take it To Heart

So the wall was finished . . . in fifty-two days. And when all our enemies heard of it, all the nations around us were afraid . . . for they perceived that this work had been accomplished with the help of our God
Nehemiah 6:15–16

Yahweh

Malachi • ~435 BC • Hebrew • Oracle, Prophecy

Malachi • Priests • Jews

Heart • Questions • Covenant

MALACHI

Malakhi: My messenger

"And he will turn the hearts of fathers to their children and the hearts of children to their fathers, lest I come and strike the land with a decree of utter destruction."

Malachi 4:6

Jesus is the Son of righteousness who rises with healing in His wings.

Bible Reading

Malachi 3

Key Word

Hearts of Stone

Take it To Heart

"And he will turn the hearts of fathers to their children and the hearts of children to their fathers, lest I come and strike the land with a decree of utter destruction."

Malachi 4:6

Nehemiah Speaks

From Nehemiah's Journal:

21 Cheshvan 3314 (November 10, 446 BC), Susa: My brother Hanani, along with other kinsmen and friends, arrived late from Jerusalem. Our embrace lingered upon arrival. The tears were many. Their weary faces told me that the journey of a thousand miles had taken its toll. They spoke briefly of bandits and warring parties encountered on the journey. I provided them a room, poured them wine, and served them food from the king's table. Then they rested, with assurances that we would talk in the morning.

22 Cheshvan: I arose early after a restless night. In my dreams I saw the Judean hills, the walls of my city, and the temple of my God. The dream seemed to go on forever, and I hoped it would. I long to worship at the temple in the City of David. My brother did not rise till the sun was high. The news from Jerusalem was not good. As I listened, I wept and trembled. Although the temple has been restored for many years now, all attempts to rebuild the walls of Jerusalem have failed, leaving the City of David vulnerable to further attacks. My people sit in the rubble. The music of Zion is silent. The altars are empty. There are no walls. No gates. No song. No hope! My people are lost.

23 Cheshvan: My heart is breaking. I am overwhelmed with sadness. *O, God, take me home. Release me and let me soar on eagle's wings back to the Holy City. I long to restore your worship, revive your people, and rebuild your city. Send me back to your land of promise and the music from Zion will be heard again across the Judean Hills. Even now I can hear the song of redemption!*

11 Nisan: Four long months have I wept and prayed for Jerusalem since learning of its condition. Today the Lord remembered me. As I served at Artaxerxes' table, God moved the king to send me to Jerusalem to rebuild its walls and restore the hopes and dreams of my people. *Think upon me, my God, for good, according to all that I shall do for your people. Be glorified in this work!*

Jerusalem

Jerusalem is one of the oldest cities in the world. In 1000 BC, King David captured the city and established it as his stronghold and the capital of Israel. He brought the tabernacle and the ark of the covenant to Jerusalem and planned to build a temple where God would dwell forever among His people. Solomon built the temple based on his father's plans, and it became the center of religious life for the Jews.

Ceremonies were held in the temple daily, but some ceremonies were so important that the people of God came from all over to worship there. During the feasts of Passover, Pentecost, and Tabernacles, the population of Jerusalem would grow to several times its normal size.

Over the centuries, Jerusalem has been destroyed and rebuilt twice, and the city has changed hands many times through conquest and war. During the Middle Ages, a series of wars known as the Crusades were fought for the specific purpose of capturing and controlling Jerusalem. This history of turmoil and upheaval is largely due to the city's cultural and historical significance to the peoples of three major world religions—Judaism, Islam, and Christianity. Since Jews, Muslims, and Christians make up about two-thirds of the world's religious believers, Jerusalem is sacred to the majority of people in the modern world.

Jews consider Jerusalem to be a holy place because it is where God came to dwell with them. In fact, most Jews will not walk on the Temple Mount, the place where the temple once stood, so as not to accidently step on the place where the Holy of Holies once was. Instead, they worship at the nearby Western Wall, sometimes called the "Wailing Wall" due to the practice of Jews weeping there over the destruction of the first and second temples.

The city and the Temple Mount are also considered sacred by Muslims, who believe Muhammad visited heaven from there as part of an event they call the Night Journey. For more than 1,300 years, there have been Muslim shrines in Jerusalem.

Of course, Jerusalem is also profoundly important to Christians as the place where Jesus Christ worshiped, preached, and was crucified and resurrected.

ANCIENT CITY WALLS

Stop and look at a wall in your home. Estimate the width and height of the wall. What materials do you think were used to construct that wall? Do you think it would stand up to an attack by an invading army? Throughout human history, people have built walls to protect themselves and their loved ones. People need to feel safe, and so they build walls.

Historically, walls have been made from materials that were easily accessible nearby, such as mud, grass, straw, and wood. Adobe, or "mudbrick," is among the earliest building materials and is still in use. In dry climates, adobe structures have proved to be extremely durable and are some of the oldest existing buildings in the world.

In ancient days, larger walls were erected to control borders and protect entire cities and nations from invading armies. Jerusalem is known for its walls. Other ancient cities known for their walls include York, England; Harar, Ethiopia; Taroudant, Morocco; Itchan Kala, Uzbekistan; and Avila, Spain. The Great Wall of China is one of mankind's greatest architectural achievements. Including all of its branches, the Great Wall measures more than 13,000 miles in total length.

The walled city of Jericho was built on a hill. At the base of the hill, a retaining wall was built about twelve to fifteen feet in height. Atop that wall was a mudbrick wall six feet thick and between twenty and twenty-six feet high. Then at the crest of the hill, another forty-six-foot mudbrick wall was constructed. Can you imagine the thunderous noise and flying dust as the enormous walls came a-tumblin' down?

Now try to picture how much work went into constructing a wall like the one around ancient Jerusalem. Yet the book of Nehemiah tells us that families worked together, day and night, with a trowel in one hand and a sword in the other. Miraculously, the great wall was rebuilt in only fifty-two days! With God, truly all things are possible.

Dear Heavenly Father,

When I read about the Israelites returning to rebuild the temple and the city wall in Jerusalem, I am reminded how much You love me. Help me to love You with all my heart, with all my soul, with all my strength, and with all my mind. Hide Your Word in my heart so that I won't sin against You. Help me to remember that even when I think You are silent, You are working Your will in my life and in all the world. Use me to bring glory to Yourself, and may I live in Your house and praise You in Your courts forever.

In Jesus' name, I pray. Amen.

PSALM AND PROVERB TO READ:
Psalm 119, Proverbs 30:5 and 31:10

OLD TESTAMENT Books

Quick Reference to the 39 books

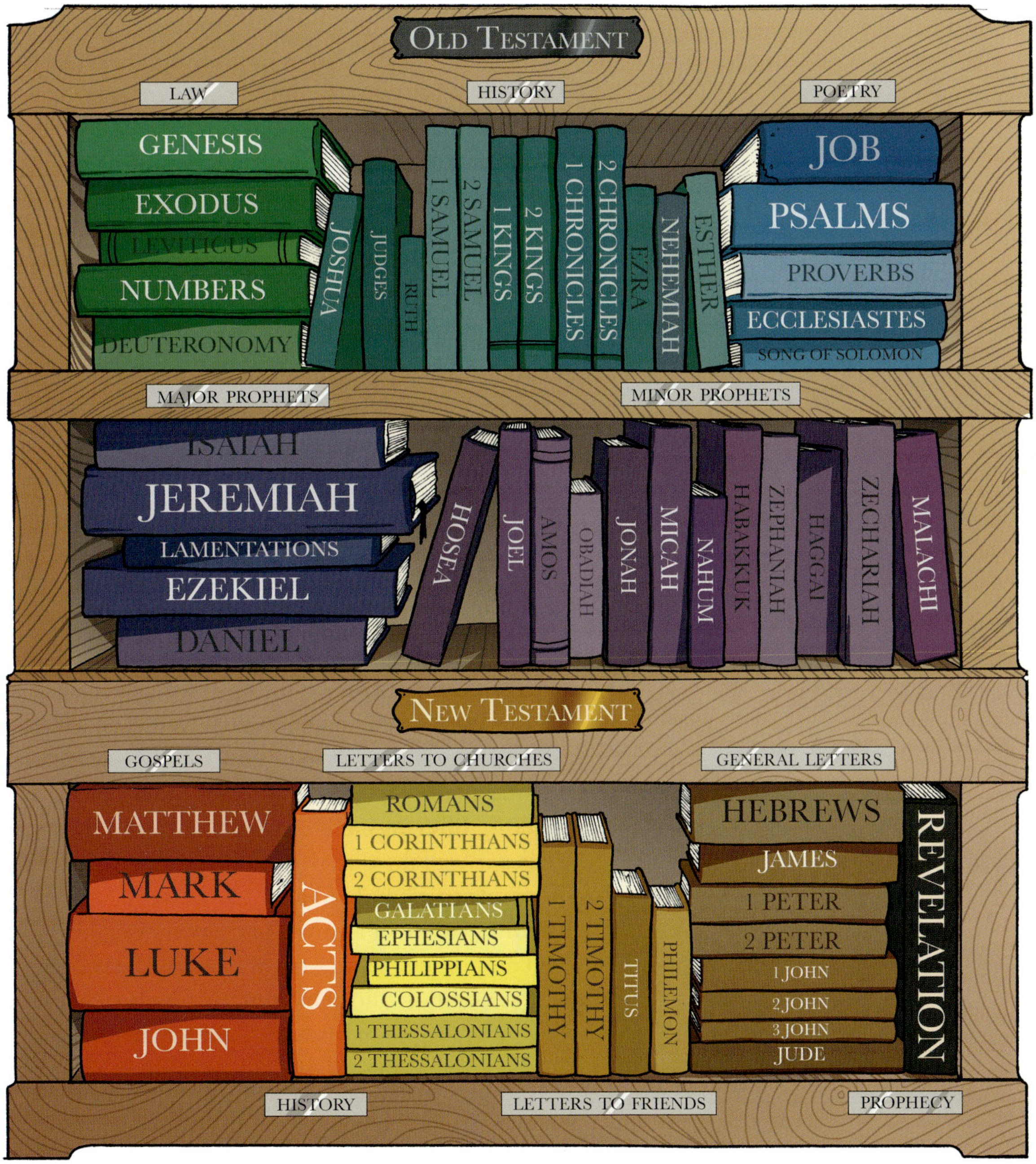

Genesis

Beginnings

Whenever you look at this picture, you'll see the big N in the middle of the word Genesis, reminding you that Genesis is the book of **beginnings** ("Big N-ings"). In fact, the word genesis is Greek for "beginning" or "origin." The heavens and the earth, night and day, man and woman, sin and redemption—it all starts here. Genesis introduces the key events and people He used to shape the beginnings of both sacred and secular history. Chapters 1–11 trace four key events—creation, fall, flood, and the establishing of nations—while chapters 12–50 tell the story of four key people—Abraham, Isaac, Jacob, and Joseph. It's the story of the one true God, whose word creates a world, whose sovereign choice of the nation Israel will ultimately bless the entire world, and whose watchful care determines the destiny of humanity.

Exodus

Exit

The children of Israel left Egypt in the exodus. In this picture, they walk right through the **EXIT** sign. The name Exodus comes from two Greek words meaning "the way out" or "exit." At the end of Genesis, the Jews were a "chosen few" living in the favor of the Pharaoh of Egypt. But after Joseph died, a new king came to the throne who felt no obligation to Joseph's descendants. As a result, Israel became a nation of slaves in a land not their own. Exodus is the story of their deliverance. In chapters 1–18, God calls Moses to declare judgment upon Pharaoh, take Israel through the "exit" from Egypt, and lead their long journey to the Promised Land. In chapters 19–40, God begins to teach His people how to live a holy life.

Leviticus

Offerings and Feasts

While the priest balances on his right foot in the picture, our friend Wyatt kneels and gives his "left-foot-a-kiss." Sounds like "Leviticus," doesn't it? The Levites and priests also balanced two key leadership roles in the nation of Israel: collecting **offerings** and conducting **feasts**. The book of Leviticus answers the question, "How can a sinful people worship and serve a holy God?" The book focuses on the five offerings (some of animals and others of grain, some required and others voluntary) and seven feasts (national times of celebration and remembrance) that God established for His people to observe. Leviticus also outlines regulations concerning priests and worship in the tabernacle, pointing to God's provision for the covering of sin: the blood atonement.

Numbers
Wanders

In this picture you see some numbers looking lost in the desert wilderness and reminding us of our key word: **wanders**. The book of Numbers begins and ends with an official count of the people of Israel. But the real story of the book is the wanderings of God's people in the wilderness. Twelve spies were sent to check out the Promised Land. Because of the negative report of ten of the spies, the fearful people chose to rebel against God despite His assurances of victory. And so, rather than enjoy the land of milk and honey, the Israelites spent nearly forty years wandering in the wilderness. Throughout Numbers, the faithfulness of God is contrasted with the fickle loyalty of His people. And even though God had to judge their disobedience, He faithfully led them through the agonizing detour they had created for themselves.

Deuteronomy
Second Law

Imagine a contest in which a set of stone tablets sings a duet. The set of tablets with "**Second Law**" written on them is running over our friend Wyatt. So you can remember the book of Deuteronomy if you think of this picture of a "Duet-Run-On-Me." Deuteronomy is about the second time God gave the law through Moses, so the key word is second law. The book of Deuteronomy reviews the forty-year period of the nation's walk with God and previews their new life soon to begin in Canaan. Taking the form of a series of sermons, the book addresses the new generation emerging from the wilderness march. Moses reminds them of the central importance of obedience and stresses holiness as a way of life.

Joshua
Conquers

What did Joshua do? He conquered the land, so the key word for the book of Joshua is **conquers**. Here, "General Joshua" leads the nation of Israel in a conquest of the land of Canaan. The book that bears Joshua's name is a tale of war and peace. Through three military campaigns involving more than thirty enemy armies, God's people learn a valuable lesson under Joshua's capable leadership: Victory comes through faith in God and obedience to His Word rather than by military might or numerical superiority. In the final chapters of the book, peace reigns as the people of God divide up their new homeland and settle there.

Judges

Cycles

This picture will remind you that the key word for the book of Judges is **cycles**. How many cycles were there? Seven. After the conquest of Canaan, Israel plunges into a 350-year period of national deterioration. A monotonous and deadly cycle develops: The people fall into sin; God disciplines them using foreign oppression; the people cry out in repentance; God raises up a deliverer; peace is restored. This five-step cycle—sin, servitude, supplication, salvation, silence—is repeated a total of seven times in Judges. But God, ever faithful to His covenant people, extends His grace again and again by sending judges, leaders like Deborah, Gideon, and Samson. And yet the book's sad epitaph reads, "In those days . . . everyone did what was right in his own eyes" (21:25).

Ruth

Love Story

See the book on top of the house? It's a romance book, but it's also the roof of the house. So this is the book of "Roof," or Ruth. Set in the time of the Judges in Israel, a time of human rebellion and divine judgment, the book of Ruth is a **love story** of devotion and redemption. A young widow who leaves her family and her native land of Moab to help the mother-in-law she loves, Ruth gleans in the fields belonging to a relative, Boaz, who grows to love her. Because of Ruth's faithfulness in a time of national unfaithfulness, God rewards her with a new husband, a son, and a privileged position in the lineage of Christ—she is the great-grandmother of David. By marrying the widow and redeeming the family's property, Boaz is a picture of Christ as the kinsman-redeemer.

1 Samuel

Saul

That's a "sand mule" on the beach to help you remember the book of 1 Samuel, which tells of Israel's first king, Saul. (He's holding a saw to help you remember his name.) After the chaotic period of the Judges, God's people are clamoring for a king. The book of 1 Samuel tells the story of the transition of leadership from Israel's last judge (Samuel) to its first king (**Saul**). But the book also tells of the early years of Israel's greatest king (David). Because Saul has no heart for God (see the "broken heart" symbol on Saul's crown), he is rejected by God. Young David is anointed to take Saul's place but has to flee to the wilderness to escape Saul's jealous pursuit. At last, Saul and his sons die in battle on Mount Gilboa, setting the stage for the book of 2 Samuel and the golden age of King David.

2 Samuel

David

Now there are two "sand mules" on the beach because this is the book of 2 Samuel. In the picture is a king—**David**—with a harp and a whole heart for God (see the crown). The life story of King David, whom God called "a man after My own heart" (Acts 13:22), unfolds in this book. After Saul's death, David rules first over Judah and then over a united Israel for a total of forty years, becoming Israel's greatest king. David's political and military victories bring Israel to a place of world prominence. But the secret sins of his personal life ultimately cause his downfall. A lustful look at beautiful Bathsheba leads to adultery and murder and then to insurrection, civil war, and unrest.

1 Kings

Solomon

This is King **Solomon**. He has a half-heart on his crown and a full moneybag. The book of 1 Kings tells of the end of David's reign and the ascension of his son Solomon for the throne. Solomon's reign is characterized by great accomplishments and worldwide fame. But while the brilliant and successful Solomon fulfills his father's dream of building a temple in Jerusalem, he fails to build his own life on the faith it signifies. As a result, his many pagan wives turn his heart away from God (chapters 1–11). The reign of half-hearted Solomon leads to a split of the kingdom, which you can remember by the splitting moneybag. His death marks the end of a unified nation of twelve tribes and introduces the period of the Divided Kingdom (chapters 12–22), with Israel in the north and Judah in the south.

2 Kings

Exile

There are two kings in the picture, signifying the book of 2 Kings. They are on an island with a pair of palm trees forming a big X, making it an "X-isle." The book of 2 Kings recounts the **exile** of the nations of Israel and Judah. As the glory of the once-united kingdom erodes, both Israel and Judah pursue a collision course with captivity. In spite of the efforts of Elisha and other prophets, the division ultimately ends in double deportation. Corrupt Israel is captured and dispersed by the Assyrians, and a century later, the people of Judah are carried away by Babylon. God's patience is long and His pleading persistent, but His love can also be tough. As a result, the Divided Kingdom of 1 Kings becomes the Dissolved Kingdom of 2 Kings.

1 Chronicles
Editorial on David

This newsboy is selling the Daily Chronicle, a newspaper with an **editorial on David**. That's King David on the front page. And since there's just one Chronicle, the picture represents the book of 1 Chronicles. The Bible's two books of Chronicles are divine "editorials"—priestly recollections and interpretations of the historical facts surrounding the life of God's people from the reign of David to the Babylonian exile. The book of 1 Chronicles tells of the righteous reign of King David. Chapters 1–9 catalog David's ancestry from Adam on. Chapters 10–29 focus on the details of David's administration. The book emphasizes the proper worship of the one true God—the kind of worship that David's life mostly exemplified.

2 Chronicles
Editorial on Judah

In this picture, Wyatt is holding two Chronicles, this time featuring an editorial on Judah. The book of 2 Chronicles spans Judah's history from its highest peak to its lowest ebb—from Solomon's reign to the Babylonian exile. First comes the building of the magnificent temple in Jerusalem. In the years after Solomon dies, the spiritual, moral, and military fortunes of the nation rise and fall with the quality of leadership on the throne. The few righteous rulers cannot stop the nation's downward slide, and God's judgment ultimately falls upon Judah, bringing invasion, defeat, captivity.

Ezra
Temple/People

Here's a big letter S leading a cheer, "Ra!" Put it together and you have "S-Ra!" That's Ezra. You also see the people cheering because the temple has been rebuilt. So Ezra's key word is **temple/people**. The Jews, who were held captive in Babylon for seventy years, are finally allowed to return to Jerusalem. The book of Ezra begins with a decree by the Persian king and the homecoming of the first returnees under Zerubbabel. Once the temple is rebuilt, a second group returns, led by Ezra the priest, this time to rebuild the spiritual vitality of the people. Between those two homecomings—when the temple and the people are "rebuilt"—is a fifty-eight-year interlude, during which the book of Esther takes place.

Nehemiah

Walls

In this picture, Wyatt reminds us of "Knee-High-Miah," or Nehemiah. You can tell because the wall he's building is knee-high to him. And the key word for the book of Nehemiah is **walls**. Though the Jews have rebuilt the temple and turned from their pagan ways, Jerusalem's walls still lay in ruin. But God finds a wall-builder in Persia. Nehemiah, cupbearer to the Persian king, will lead the third expedition of God's people back to their homeland and rebuild the city's walls. Like Zerubbabel and Ezra, Nehemiah faces fierce opposition to his reconstruction efforts. Even so, the project is completed in just fifty-two days. A public reading of God's Word then triggers a significant (though short-lived) revival within the rebuilt walls.

Esther

Queen of Persia

The queen has a letter S in her hand. What is she doing with the S? Stir. Put them together and you have the queen's name: "S-Stir," or Esther. Her Persian rug and Persian cat remind us of the key phrase of the book of Esther: **Queen of Persia**. Although Zerubbabel, Ezra, and Nehemiah led some 50,000 Jews back to Judah, the vast majority of Jews were reluctant to leave their adopted home in Persia. Esther's story takes place against this backdrop, between the returns led by Zerubbabel and Ezra. Even as Esther is chosen to replace the banished queen, her countrymen are threatened by an evil plot. As God sovereignly works behind the scenes, Esther's faithful and courageous action saves God's people from destruction and provides the occasion for an annual celebration still observed by Jews today—the Feast of Purim.

Job

Sovereignty

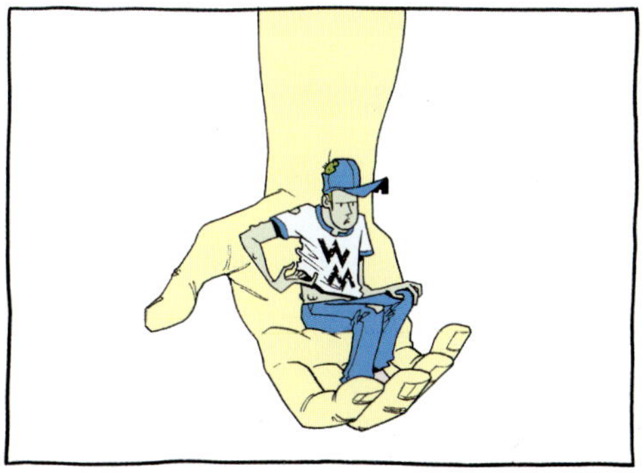

The miserable man in this picture is Job, but he is in God's hand. Since God is in control of all of life, we give the book of Job a key word that tells us God reigns: **Sovereignty**. This book examines one of life's most perplexing questions. It introduces a pious man of God named Job, who lived perhaps 4,000 years ago. In a sudden series of catastrophes brought on by Satan with God's sovereign permission, Job loses his family, fame, fortune, and health. For thirty-five chapters he searches his soul and debates with his best friends to find a reason for his misfortune. After exhausting the conventional wisdom of his four counselors, Job is confronted by God Himself, and his demanding "Why?" melts into humble worship when he realizes he is in the hands of a loving, sovereign God.

Psalms
Worship

One of the palm trees is singing, and the other one is praying, signifying **worship**. So this picture represents the book of Psalms. Written by at least seven authors, of which David is the most notable, the book of Psalms spans 1,000 years of Israel's rich history—from the time of Moses to the return from exile in Babylon. The word Psalm comes from a Greek word meaning "a song sung to the accompaniment of a plucked instrument." Used as the temple hymnbook, the Psalms express the diversity of human emotion—praise to God, fear of enemies, and an overriding confidence in God's goodness, majesty, and power.

Proverbs
Widsom

On the chalkboard in this picture is an example of a proverb. That's to remind us that the name of this book of the Bible is Proverbs. The wise old owl in the picture depicts the key word of this book: **wisdom**. Proverbs is a collection of 900 short, concise statements of wisdom (literally, "skill for living"). Using comparison, contrast, and metaphorical language, the author sets forth God's principles for wise and godly living—inspired precepts dealing with pride and humility, wisdom and foolishness, justice and vengeance, laziness and work, poverty and wealth, friends and neighbors, love and lust, anger and strife, masters and servants, life and death. While it takes only a few seconds to read a proverb, you can easily spend a lifetime working out the implications of that proverb in your daily walk with God.

Ecclesiastes
Vanity

The key word for Ecclesiastes is **vanity**, which amounts to emptiness. The book's author says, "Vanity, vanity, all is vanity." Or as another Bible translation puts it, "Meaningless, meaningless, all is meaningless." The point is that life without God is empty. So that's what we've pictured here—emptiness! The author of Ecclesiastes (traditionally thought to be Solomon) has enjoyed power, wealth, and access to all of life's pleasures. After experiencing a full measure of life "under the sun," he declares it all to be unsatisfying. He has discovered that only as he lives "above the sun," with an eye toward God, does life become meaningful and fulfilling. The bottom line of the book: Ultimate satisfaction comes not from the good things of life but from the Giver of life, the One we are to fear, honor, and obey.

Song of Solomon

Love in Marriage

This picture portrays King Solomon (with his half-hearted crown). What's he doing? Singing a solo. So this book is the "Song of Solo-man," or Song of Solomon. The scene is a wedding, and King Solomon is holding a ring in his hand. This reminds us of the key phrase of the book, **love in marriage**. Full of oriental imagery, the Song of Solomon recounts Solomon's marriage to a country maiden. While it extols the bliss of married love and the deep devotion of spouses to one another, it also speaks of the heartaches and challenges of marriage. In addition to recording a part of Solomon's life, the book's lovely lyrics also give us an intimate glimpse of God's fervent love for His people.

Isaiah

Groan/Glory

This image depicts an "I," and it's saying "Ah." "I say 'ah.'" Isaiah! Our friend Wyatt holds two masks—one groaning with sadness and the other exulting in God's glory. The key concept of Isaiah is **groan/glory** because the book starts with a groan and ends with glory. In the first thirty-nine chapters (the number of books in the Old Testament), the prophet Isaiah stresses righteousness, holiness, and the justice of God, announcing His terrible judgment upon a world stained with sin (1:18). Surely there is cause to groan under God's chastening hand. But the final twenty-seven chapters (also the number of books in the New Testament) reveal God's glory, as Isaiah announces the good news of God's compassion and undeserved favor: He will send a Savior to bear a cross, one who is also a Sovereign to wear a crown.

Jeremiah

Rotten Sash

In the picture we see a jury, and our friend appears before the court as "Jury-miah," or Jeremiah. He is holding a **rotten sash** as evidence against Judah. Jeremiah, one of Judah's greatest prophets, challenged his nation's greatest errors. Apostasy, idolatry, perverted worship, moral decay—for these and other sins, the nation has come under God's judgment. God graphically depicts the moral rottenness of Judah when He commands Jeremiah to bury a sash in the mud and then later dig it up. The sash is disgusting and ruined, just like the nation. Judah's response, however, is not repentance but rejection, and the prophet is opposed, isolated, and imprisoned. Throughout forty years of faithful duty, Jeremiah witnesses the fulfillment of many of his prophecies, including God's final judgment on Judah: downfall and exile.

Lamentations

Tears

Does the lamb remind you of a particular book of the Bible? How about "Lamb-entations"? The lamb is crying, for the book's key word is **tears**. For many years, Jeremiah, known as the "weeping prophet," has warned the people of Judah of their impending doom if they do not repent. When his prophecies are fulfilled and Jerusalem is destroyed by the Babylonians, Jeremiah writes the book of Lamentations, a funeral dirge for the city. Written in five poems, this sad book is full of defeat, slaughter, and ruination—the horrors he foretold for so long only to be ignored. However, Jeremiah sees ultimate reason and hope beyond the ruins of his city. His God is sovereign, and He is gracious. In His mercy, Jerusalem will one day be restored. Indeed, "Great is [God's] faithfulness" (3:23).

Ezekiel

Dry Bones

This friendly skeleton will help you remember the book of "E-Z-kiel," or Ezekiel. He's drying himself off with a towel to tell us that the key word is **dry bones**. The prophet Ezekiel was exiled to Babylon several years before the actual downfall of Jerusalem. He prophesied among the Jewish exiles there during the last days of Judah's decline and downfall. The first part of his prophecy stresses the sure completion of God's judgment against Judah, culminating in the destruction of the holy city. But then Ezekiel's tone changes to one of hope and consolation. He prophesies that God will one day restore His nation. The "dry bones" that had been scattered in the valley—symbolizing the spiritually dead and physically scattered nation of Israel—will be brought together and returned to life.

Daniel

Dreams

Wyatt is sleeping in the lions' den. The key word for Daniel is **dreams**, because nearly every chapter deals with a dream or interpretation of a dream. Exiled to Babylon as a youth, Daniel serves in the courts of Babylon and Persia during the seventy-year captivity. Used by God as His spokesman to both Gentiles and Jews, Daniel demonstrates God's power through his prophecies and a life of godly obedience. The adventures of Daniel and his friends in the palace, the fiery furnace, and the lions' den show that God has not forgotten His chosen people. And through Daniel, God provides dreams—and interpretations of dreams—designed to convince Jew and Gentile alike that wisdom and power belong to Him alone. His message is clear: God is in control, not only of the present, but of the future.

Hosea

Harlot

The garden hose pictures the book of Hosea, and the key word is **harlot**. This word summarizes the story of Hosea. Instructed by God to marry the harlot Gomer, Hosea finds mirrored in his home life an accurate portrait of the unfaithfulness of God's people—both the bride of Hosea and the people of God play the harlot and run after other lovers. With this striking parallel from his marriage, Hosea carries God's powerful message to the streets: The wickedness of Israel will call down upon itself swift tragedy and certain calamity. But unconditional love keeps seeking even when it is spurned. In Hosea's case, that means buying back his wife from the slave market; for Israel, it means purifying punishment followed by restoration to the Land of Promise.

Joel

Locusts

The shimmering dish of Jell-o will remind you that this picture represents the book of Joel. Locusts are trying to eat the Jell-o, and that's because the key word for Joel is **locusts**. The prophet Joel uses a recent calamity in the nation of Judah to teach his hearers a prophetic lesson. The locusts have come, and suddenly every green thing is gone. Joel uses this national disaster to sound a dire warning of a far worse catastrophe: An army from the north will attack and wreak a devastation more complete than that of the locusts. The only hope of escape in the day of the Lord is to repent. If His people will repent, then instead of devastating judgment, God will send unparalleled blessing. He will judge the nations that hurt His people and bring peace to Zion.

Amos

Plum Line

Wyatt is pictured riding a moose, so the prophet would be "A-moose," or Amos. The key word for the book of Amos is **plumb line**. Times are good in Israel. The nation is basking in prosperity, peace, strength, and security. Then along comes Amos. At God's direction, the prophet holds up the carpenter's plumb line to measure the nation against God's perfect standard—and finds only crookedness. Amos breaks through the people's facade of respectability to expose the rotten core of immorality, injustice, and shallow piety. The people have grown soft and lax in luxurious living, so Amos declares God's terrible warning, issuing His last call to repentance. But once again, the people fail to respond, and Amos announces God's coming discipline.

Obadiah
Brother's Keeper

What kind of bed is this? It's an O-bed, reminding us of the book of Obadiah. There are also two brothers, and one is holding a key to remind you that the key phrase of Obadiah is **brother's keeper**. The nations of Edom and Judah should have existed in harmony as neighbors. After all, they were from the same family—Edom was descended from Esau, and Judah from Jacob. But the feuding between their ancestors has led to enmity between the two nations. In a moment of urgent need, with Israel's enemies knocking at the gates of Jerusalem, the Edomites rush in to help . . . the enemy! So God sends His prophet Obadiah to predict Edom's extinction for being unwilling to serve as their brother's keeper. In contrast, He promises that His people will ultimately destroy their enemies and live in peace.

Jonah
Fish

You can tell at a glance this picture represents the book of Jonah, and indeed the key word for Jonah is **fish**. Jonah despises the brutal Assyrian people, so when God tells him to go to the capital city of Nineveh to warn them of their impending destruction, Jonah sets sail in the opposite direction! God sends a storm to bring him back, and at his own request Jonah is tossed overboard. A huge fish swallows God's prophet and, three days later, deposits him on dry land. Now Jonah goes straight to Nineveh and preaches repentance to the people. And when the people repent, God mercifully withholds His punishment. Though the preaching is successful, the preacher comes away angry and discouraged. So God takes the resentful Jonah to a scorching hill and there teaches him firsthand of His compassion upon sinful people.

Micah
Day in Court

In the picture is a microphone, also known as a "mike," which reminds us of the prophet Micah. The sun represents the day, and this day is in court. So Micah's key phrase is **day in court**. Micah delivers God's message of judgment to a corrupt and immoral Judah. The prophet aims his rebukes at false prophets, priests, and princes—those who use their God-given authority to cheat the poor and abuse the powerless. Sin has infiltrated every segment of society, so God gives Judah her day in court with Micah as the prosecutor. And the verdict is guilty. Throughout Micah's quarter-century of ministry, three themes ring clear: 1) Sin will not go unpunished; 2) judgment will be swift and soon; and 3) once the discipline is completed, God will restore His people to their covenant land.

Nahum

Flood

The key word for the book of Nahum is **flood**. In the picture, floodwaters are destroying the city walls, which form the word *Nahum*. It has been more than a century since Nineveh repented under the preaching of Jonah, and yet Nineveh has degenerated until it is now as wicked a city as it has ever been. But the people fear no judgment. After all, her walls are wide and high. But God speaks through Nahum of her destruction—not a warning of doom that can be averted but a description of her certain death. God's prophecy comes true to the letter as the Tigris River floods, washing away part of the city's walls. The Babylonian army then sweeps through Nineveh like violent floodwaters. Nineveh's "grave" is so effectively dug that the city will lay undiscovered for 2,500 years!

Habakkuk

Watchtower

Here's Wyatt carrying a huge backpack. What kind of backpack? It's a "HA-backpack" to remind you that the book's name is Habakkuk. Wyatt is also standing on a **watchtower**, the key word for this book. Like Job, the prophet Habakkuk honestly raises the perplexing question of why a just God is silent and why the cries of the faithful seem to go unheard. Habakkuk sits in his watchtower, awaiting God's answer. In reply, God declares to His prophet a timeless principle of trust in His sovereignty. The wicked will be dealt with—in God's own way and in His own time. He will even use the vile Babylonian nation as His divine instrument of justice. When Habakkuk reacts with dismay and shock, God patiently instructs His messenger, until at last the prophet is able to respond with praise and trust.

Zephaniah

Day of the Lord

Wyatt is fanning the letter Z, representing "Z-Fan-iah," or Zephaniah. The sun represents the day, and this is the **Day of the Lord**. During Judah's history, reform came from time to time. Zephaniah's forceful prophecy may have been a factor in the reform seen during Josiah's reign—a "revival" that produced outward change but could not remove the inward heart of corruption which characterized the nation's leaders. So Zephaniah proclaims the impending Day of the Lord. This day signifies the final judgment of God on the Earth and an eventual time of blessing and peace. Judah will indeed be punished, but beyond that cloud, brightness blazes. God will purify His people and restore their fortunes. He will rejoice over them with shouts of joy. He will make them great and remain in their midst forever.

Haggai
Temple

Wyatt is hugging a big letter I, so this must represent the book of "Hug-I," or Haggai. And he's on his way to the **temple**, which is the key word for the book. Having just returned from exile in Babylon, the people are confronted by a heartbreaking sight: The Persians have destroyed their city, including the glorious structure that was once Solomon's temple. Work begins on a new temple and progresses until opposition arises. For some sixteen years, the Jews ignore the unfinished temple to pursue personal prosperity. Onto the scene steps Haggai, an aged, straight-talking prophet of God, who admonishes the people to finish what they have started. He calls the builders to renewed courage, renewed holiness, and renewed faith in God.

Zechariah
Messiah

Here's another Z, but this one is crying. Thus we have "Z-cry-ah," or Zechariah. The theme of this book is the **Messiah**, whose coming the prophet foretells. In 536 BC, the temple rebuilding had begun amid great excitement. But the early enthusiasm has waned, and sixteen years later, the only movement in the unfinished building is the stirring of the wind. Enter Zechariah, commissioned by God to join the prophet Haggai in motivating the workers to finish what they started. But where Haggai is the exhorter, Zechariah is the encourager. His message is one of promise: This will be no ordinary building but will house Messiah Himself! All must rise to the task, for the King is coming (9:9)! But this future blessing—including both the first and second comings of Christ—depends on the people's present obedience.

Malachi
Hearts of Stone

And finally, here is Wyatt with a mallet, beating on a heart of stone. The mallet reminds us of the prophet "Mal-let-chi," or Malachi, and the key phrase of his book is **hearts of stone**. God has restored His people to their land, but they soon lapsed into the very sins that had led to their years of captivity. So God sends Malachi to remind His people that, although He loves them dearly, they have not returned His love. The priests have dishonored Him and led His people astray, while the Jewish men have married pagan women. They can never hope to prosper because they all have hearts of stone and persist in their sins. Malachi gives them a final warning of the purifying Day of the Lord. After this follows 400 years of silence in the biblical record—until the light of the New Testament dawns.